W9-CUS-148

HOW WILL YOUR HORSE RUN TODAY?

Unlocking the Secret of the "Form Cycle"

William L. Scott

Foreword by James Quinn

Published by: Amicus Press
4201 Underwood Road
Baltimore, Maryland 21218

Distributed by: Liberty Publishing Co., Inc.
50 Scott Adam Road
Cockeysville, Maryland 21030

Copyright ©1984, 1986, by William L. Scott

ISBN 0-89709-147-7

All rights reserved. No part of this work may be reproduced or
transmitted in any form or by any means, electronic or
mechanical, including photocopying and recording, or by any
information storage or retrieval system, except as may be
expressly permitted by the 1976 Copyright Act or in writing
from the publisher.

Requests for permission should be addressed in writing to
4201 Underwood Road, Baltimore, Maryland   21218.

Library of Congress Cataloging in Publication Data

Scott, William L.
How Will Your Horse Run Today?

1. Horse race betting—United States. 2. Scott, William L.
3. Horse players—United States.

I. Title

Printed in the United States of America

All past performances and charts in this book are reprinted
by special permission from *Daily Racing Form, Inc.*
Copyright ©1981-2. Reproduction prohibited.

Cover photographs by Bob Coglianese
The New York Racing Association

Table of Contents

To my beloved sons and daughter
Who have taught me so much.

FOREWORD

THE BOOK YOU ARE ABOUT TO READ is surely the most important yet delivered on the riddle of thoroughbred form. It unravels that tricky riddle at last, revealing to handicappers of all persuasions the most precise, effective operational definitions of positive and negative form so far identified by valid, uncompromising research.

Author William L. Scott is an empiricist. He depends on carefully structured observation and experience to conduct a painstakingly continuous logical inquiry into the most difficult questions of handicapping. In his previous book, *Investing at the Racetrack*, Scott asked whether a speed-class rating method (ability times) might be elaborated so completely and specifically that strict adherence to its rules would beat the game with unflagging reliability. He succeeded, but the method ran counter to the individual taste and temperament of many regular handicappers.

Now Scott has asked that always critical question of, How Will Your Horse Run Today, and he has proceeded to find answers that are not only suitable to individual differences, but will be fully engaging and rewarding for practically all of us.

This study concentrates on a 433-race sample at four eastern tracks in 1981, embraces various applications of first findings at several tracks across two years, and climaxes with a 500-race replication of the original results at numerous racetracks nationally throughout 1982. After presenting his findings, with illustrations of each point, Scott demonstrates their application on a card chosen randomly at Golden Gate Fields in San Francisco.

In a brief but careful two-week application of the book's guidelines, I used Scott's form rules for five days at Keystone, and for another five days at Hollywood Park. They worked impressively, resulting not only in a few generous winners I otherwise might have missed, but also in the reliable elimination of many false favorites characterized in the past performances by what Scott has called "form defects." Handicappers can be assured that favorites with "form defects" are very likely to lose.

Historically, the American horseplayer has confronted two enduring, fundamental problems with the form factor.

First, operational definitions of good and bad form have been either unavailable or so broadly stated they did not permit the separation of contenders based on variations of form.

Second, recent statistical studies designed to define "good" form more specifically have regularly collapsed on the profit criterion. Horses having acceptable form won more races than probability estimates would expect, but those horses also returned sizeable losses when bet to win. The probability studies proved mainly that the public bets too much money on "good" form horses. They go off as underlays, and often are favored to win.

What has been needed by students of *Daily Racing Form* past performances are not so much statistical studies which examine a priori definitions of positive and negative form, but rather carefully calculated empirical studies which ask new key questions about form, i.e., How Will Your Horse Run Today? There was also the need to try to isolate the numerous and particular variations of form within the well-known parameters of recent action. William L. Scott has contributed precisely that kind of research, precisely those kinds of results.

In *How Will Your Horse Run Today?*, handicappers will find positive, neutral and negative form indicators which might readily be applied as extensions or supplements of whatever rating methods or analytical approaches are now engaged. Few of us can afford not to be persuaded of a central theme in the book, that there are certain fundamental defects of form which can reliably eliminate horses from further consideration as contenders.

As Scott's research has shown, many favorites in apparently sharp form in fact suffer form defects. These can be summarily dismissed, without eliminating many winners. That happy practice opens many races to other solid handicapping selections, and at juicier prices.

Form being the global, complicated factor that it is, handicappers will vary individually in their preferences for the book's various findings. My own, for example, are two. Scott has taught me how to rate a horse's last useable running line in a way that has improved my game. The technique has become a slice of my regular routine.

And the book has opened my eyes widely as to how to evaluate the prospects today of last race winners. Which of the many are solid bets to repeat? Scott will tell you in no uncertain terms which are very likely to lose. As last race winners attract lots of action, it is nice to know which will probably take the money down to defeat.

Scott also spells out the strict conditions under which last out winners are likely to repeat today. During my trial run at Hollywood Park I encountered an overnite claiming sprint for three-year-olds entered at $32,000 in which no fewer than six of the 12 entrants had won their previous start. Of the six, only one horse satisfied Scott's repeat win conditions. It won drawing out at 14-1, paying $31.80.

In its most complicated section, the book reveals an arithmetical technique for identifying declining and improving horses. And in perhaps its most provocative section, it presents new and exciting guidelines for evaluating stretch performance. We have been missing the point here all along. And throughout his discourse on form Scott relates that fundamental factor to matters of class, distance, and footing. Especially interesting to many will be the interplays between class and form. Comprehensive handicappers will be pleased that the several qualifications of and exceptions to the form guidelines honor the other fundamental factors of handicapping.

How might handicappers best use the form factors they discover here? Method players, those having well-defined approaches to the past performances already, might apply Scott's fundamental form defects at step one, to eliminate the non-contenders. Eventually they might involve any "plus" factor in their rating processes.

Novices, those without systematic methods, and devotees of what is included here can use these form rules alone to get the job done reasonably well.

Scott's exposition in this book reflects the same logical progression of thought and judgment that so impressively marks his original research. Empirical study is easily subverted by sloppiness or by taking shortcuts to the facts. These traps are fallen into regularly by practitioners and authors alike in this unbelievable field. But your author here is absolutely our leading practitioner of this fine research art. In guiding these events toward their natural completion, towards the end of the book Scott elaborates four methods of play which have been demonstrably effective in sustaining profits. Three concentrate on favorites and second choices which fit the form rules admirably well, and thus win more frequently than favorites as a group.

Considerably more appetizing to the tastes and sensibilities of the great majority of recreational handicappers will be method four, which Scott concedes is greatly preferred and strongly advocated by his youngest handicapping son. The method entails handicapping each horse on the card, as with fundamental handicapping, and considering for play only those horses with no form defects that are not outclassed. The method gets both winners and prices, thus the youngest son prefers it to the more conservative tendencies of his father, the researcher.

Me too.

JAMES QUINN
Los Angeles

PREFACE

EVERY HORSEPLAYER who uses past performances to handicap a race—attempting in advance to predict the probable outcome—tries in some manner to deal with current form. "This horse looks pretty good," or "this one does not figure at all." This book is designed for every player, to help deal with every race, to provide a powerful guide toward the probabilities that confront you in selecting winning horses.

My previous book on playing the thoroughbreds, *Investing at the Racetrack* (Simon & Schuster, 1982), was primarily concerned with a method of play that rated horses for speed and class according to artificially constructed figures which were called "ability times." But current form impacts on any rating method, so it cannot be ignored. Thus, in providing a selection method in that book, I set forth rules for current form. These rules were extremely sound and are as workable today as they were when *Investing at the Racetrack* was written.

Because my own inquiring spirit never allows me to believe that any method of play in this complex and fascinating contest of predicting the outcome of a horse race before the race is run cannot be improved upon, I set about to re-analyze *Investing at the Racetrack* after it was written. The major question that I continued to ask was, if my ability point ratings were so good, why did horses with the highest points sometimes lose? Obviously, an answer for every situation would not be possible, but what I was looking for was a set of sound probabilities that would point out likely losers and turn me toward a different selection that would win enough times to strongly upgrade the whole process.

Study, analyze, reflect. Where was any one clue that would make a substantial contribution to the process? Going back over the past performances set forth in the Big Week at Belmont, I began to detect certain form deficiencies that hung over the horses that lost. The winners were relatively free from these defects. Armed with this realization, research began in earnest. The methods and the findings are set forth in this book.

Every horseplayer who looks at past performances must have some method of rating a racehorse. This book, by its concentration on current form, allows every individual to combine their own selection method with the new form ratings set forth herein, some of which are highly original.

My own constructed ability times continue to prove to be a most effective rating method. I have even revised them very slightly, and for the many thousands who have bought *Investing at the Racetrack* and have responded so favorably to it, I have added in an appendix the revised energy adjustments for use in my own rating of contenders. Obviously, though, the new findings on form in this book supersede, for me, everything else on the subject. When these form insights are combined with ability time ratings developed in *Investing at the Racetrack*, the horseplayer will have a most effective weapon to use in the battle to select winning horses.

For those unfamiliar with the ability time concept, I am sorry that the theory and practice cannot be put into *How Will Your Horse Run Today*? First of all, ability times being a separate subject, they are beyond the scope of this book. Secondly, it would be largely repetitive of what has been written.

My last remark is that nothing in this book is in any way inconsistent with what was set forth in my earlier book. There are only improvements. So good luck and good handicapping!

WILLIAM L. SCOTT

ACKNOWLEDGEMENTS

No book could be produced without the help of others. Those "others" who have helped so much and given so much, and to whom such grateful appreciation is due are: Jim Cianelli, Pam Christie, Lucinda Finley, Scott Finley, William Finley, Lew Horowitz, James Quinn, Lisa Steinberg and Mary Sue Sweeney.

W.L.S.

1 What This Book is About

THE TITLE OF THIS BOOK, "How Will Your Horse Run Today?" deals with that ever present question that arises every time you look at a race. Everything set forth here is shaped toward helping you answer this most important inquiry. Your horse may have outstanding breeding, class, recognized ability, all the speed you would want, and yet when the finish line is reached, some other animal may be there ahead of him. Why?

Every race presents a challenge, a mystery before your eyes. Conflicts and cross-currents and puzzles abound—yes, in every race you play. But, if you can look at the past performances of the horses entered and from the mass of information before you select the winner, oh, imagine how bountiful both your pockets and your joy would be.

Suppose, for example, that you were only one of the crowd at Hollywood Park in Los Angeles, up Century Boulevard from the airport, amidst the palm trees and grass and the exciting surroundings of the racing world on June 18, a typical Friday with a good solid card. The eighth race, feature on the program, showed these conditions in your *Daily Racing Form*.

8th Hollywood

7 FURLONGS. (1.19²/₅) CLASSIFIED ALLOWANCE. Purse $32,000. 4—year—olds and upward, which have not won $17,700 in 1981–82. Weight, 121 lbs. Non-winners of $14,000 twice since December 25, 1981 allowed 3 lbs.; of $14,000 twice since September 1, 1981, 5 lbs.; of $17,600 since December 25, 1981, 7 lbs. (Claiming and starter races not considered.)

Six horses originally were entered in this competitive, classified $32,000 allowance race, but one was scratched, leaving a field of five. Now that should not be too difficult, should it? Any good handicapper ought to come up with a winner in such a small field, right? Perhaps you like the favorite, Walter Osborne. The crowd certainly does, as the odds on the tote board go down to 4-5 at post time. Will he be your winner today?

This Irish-bred was shipped over from England by R. E. Sangster, the famous British soccer pool magnate. In his very first outing at Hollywood Park, Walter Osborne ran a strong race to beat the American horses by a nose. In 31 lifetime starts, he has run in the money 18 times, and his reputation gained on the British tracks made him so well backed in his California debut that he went off only slightly higher than 3-1, with the outstanding jockey Laffit Pincay, Jr. riding him to victory.

But how will Walter Osborne run today? Did his victory in his last race take just enough out of him that he might not do as well

*Walter Osborne			Ch. h. 5, by Welsh Pageant—Island Princess, by Raise a Native		
			Br.—Fort Union Stud Farm Ltd (Ire)	1982 1 1 0 0	$16,500
Own.—Sangster R E		114	Tr.—Winick Randy	1981 11 3 1 2	$27,199
			Lifetime 31 9 5 4 $73,152	Turf 30 8 5 4	$56,652
3Jun82-7Hol	6¼f :22 :44¹ 1:153ft	3¼ 117	3½ 1hd 1hd 1no Pincay L Jr⁶	75000 92 WalterOsborne,FlyingChick,StndPt	8
21Sep81◊3Edinburgh(Scot) 5f	1:01²gd *3-2 129	ᵍ⑦ 1½ Lucas T	Tote All Ag Spnt Walter Osborne, Artipiar, Dafyd		7
10Sep81◊2Doncaster(Eng) a5½f	1:08²gd 13 131	⑦ 21 Lucas T	Portland H Touch Boy, Pencil Point, Kiss		21
18Aug81◊7York(Eng) 5f	1:00²gd *2¾ 129	⑦ 7 Lucas T	Harewd H Crofthll,Tobermoryboy,BlueSingh		10
28Jly81◊3Goodwood(Eng) 6f	1:11³gd 25 133	⑦ 20 LucasT	Tote Stwds Cp H Crews Hill,Ferryman,SparklingBoy		30
10Jly81◊4York(Eng) 5f	1:00³gd 4½ 140	⑦ 1no Lucas T	Rvaulx H WalterOsborne,Kimlw,Westcombe		11
26Jun81◊3Newcastle(Eng) 5f	1:01 gd *5 137	⑦ 8 LucasT	Gosfrth Pk Cp H Ferriby Hall, Sanu, Sandon Buoy		15
26May81◊3Redcar(Eng) 5f	:58³gd 6 142	⑦ 32¼ Lucas T	Nrthrn Spnt H RssnWntr,MssRdmrshll,WltrOsbrn		13
12May81◊2York(Eng) 5f	1:02³gd *2½ 125	⑦ 13 LucasT	Dvd Dxn Spnt H WalterOsborne,Escovitch,Balvima		13
Jun 11 Hol ⑦ 5f fm 1:90⁴ h (d)	●May 28 Hol 6f ft 1:114 h	May 23 Hol 4f ft :49⁴ h			

today? Or, was his first outing on June 3 just a warmup for better things to come? Will Walter from Ireland do it again? There is a lot of money out there that says he will – 4-5 is indeed a powerfully short price.

In the fifth chapter of this book, where we discuss the third of four major form factors that dominate this work, we will review fully the question of how well a horse in Walter Osborne's position might run today. We have conducted extensive research and analysis on last race winners. You will find important figures on how they fare, and under what conditions they are likely to repeat their victories. But even more important, what factors, or absence of factors, might drag them down to defeat.

But here, it is vital for the handicapper to know. If a 4-5 favorite is going down the drain, the price on the winner, whichever horse it may be, could be pretty tasty. But what if Walter wins? That short price is not too promising, but 4-5 shots usually do well. Could the crowd be wrong? Do you have the courage to bet against such a strong favorite?

Obviously, most of these questions cannot be answered without looking at the rest of the field. You blink when you see that the second choice in the wagering, J.D. Quill, is at 7-2 on the board, a horse out of the east that has not run since back in December of 1981 in Maryland. What is a horse out of action for so long doing in this race anyway?

J. D. Quill

Own.—T 9 0 Ranch

B. c. 4, by Noholme II—Nuquill, by Noble Union
Br.—Davis Mr–Mrs J (Mich)
114 Tr.—Fanning Jerry

										1981 17 5 3 2		$77,755
										1980 2 1 0 0		$4,800
			Lifetime	19 6 3 2	$82,555					Turf 1 0 0 0		

19Dec81-7Lrl   1   :454 1:10 1:353ft   3½ 112   43½ 33   33½ 35½ Grove P3   Aw18000 89 Buck's Chief, Prete Khale, J.D.Quill 9
21Nov81-8Lrl   1⅟₁₆⑦:462 1:11 1:43 fm   26 114   42½ 64   56 58½ Miller D AJr2 Japan H 79 ThrtyEghtPcs,St.Brndn,ClsscGoG 12
7Nov81-4Lrl   6f   :222 :461 1:113ft   7½ 114   76½ 54   33 42 † Miller D A Jr2 HcpO 83 ‡Mr.Baggins,LordlyLove,Bolductive 8
    † 7Nov81—Disqualified and placed seventh
31Oct81-8Key   7f   :222 :443 1:221ft   7½ 115   62½ 66½ 67 59   D'AgstoJG3 Quaker H 87 LinesofPowr,Pikotzo,ChtingArthur 7
30Oct81-8Key   6f   :223 :462 1:112ft   2½ 118   64 62   31½ 2nk Barrera C5 Flintlock H 85 Lordly Love, J. D. Quill, Sicilian Jet 7
15Sep81-8Bow   7f   :223 :454 1:232ft *9-5 1105 22½ 22   11½ 11½ Miller D AJr4 Aw15000 88 J. D. Quill, Ten Bore, St. Brendan 5
24Aug81-8Del   6f   :214 :45 1:101ft   6 1125   44 43½ 2hd 11¾ Miller D AJr1 Aw12000 90 J.D.Quill,LordlyLove,Whistler'sTrgt 6
4Aug81-7Del   1⅟₁₆:462 1:101 1:421ft   6½ 115   3nk 52   612 623 Whited D E3 Aw15000 74 St.Brendan,MsterTommy,SilentBsis 6
15Jly81-8Pim   6f   :232 :463 1:111ft *7-5 113   31½ 31½ 31 1no PassmoreWJ2 Aw17000 90 J.D.Quill,CapricornBbe,WithCution 6
14Jun81-9HP   6½f :223 :47 1:203sy   *1-2 128   66 53½ 78 88½ GrcJR10 ⑤Lansing PH 68 MistyVelvet,OleBobCts,BrznBndit 10
    Jan 17 Hol 3f ft :353 h   ● Jun 10 Hol 6f ft 1:111 h   Jun 4 Hol 6f ft 1:113 h   May 29 Hol 6f ft 1:123 h

Can a horse that has not raced in six months win an allowance race like this one against quality horses? He shows four workouts, all nicely spaced, but is that sufficient to get him ready for today's test? He has run in the past in modest allowance races on the Maryland circuit and in some minor stakes at Keystone. But whatever you think about J.D. Quill, the big question on this horse remains, how will he run today after such a long layoff?

In my previous book on handicapping, *Investing at the Racetrack* (Simon & Schuster), I rated the form of any horse that had not run in 28 days as an unknown factor. But I also said that a stakes caliber horse could qualify off four recent workouts. But you may have some doubt whether J.D. Quill is a genuine stakes horse or not. Maybe the four workout rule was not sound. Has continued research shown that it still holds up?

In the third chapter of this book, which is on recent action, there is new research on the effect of workouts. It provides findings on what kind of workouts are most effective, and within what time frame they should be held. The research reveals that one type of workout is truly potent, so much so that I even call it "fabulous." Will J.D. Quill fit the findings that are set forth in the third chapter? Or should we throw him out altogether as too risky because of the long layoff? If you like J.D. Quill how will your horse run today?

If you think the layoff was too long, take a look at the next choice. Answer to Music is at 4-1 on the board. As you see, the odds begin to rise, as they must in a field where there is a 4-5 favorite. This is how he looks.

Answer to Music — B. c. 4, by Northern Answer—Lady Rhythm, by Mister Jive

Answer to Music		**Br.—Schmidt H C (Fla)**	1982 9 0 3 2			$31,125
Own.—Henderson S F	**114**	**Tr.—Taliaferro Charles L**	1981 2 1 1 0			$19,500
		Lifetime 14 4 4 2 $83,675	Turf 1 0 1 0			$6,400

6Jun82-6Hol	1	$:45^{4}$	$1:09^{3}$	$1:35^{3}$ft	29	115	1^{hd}	2^{hd}	5^{3}	5^{6}¼	Black K^{4}	Aw40000	82	Egg Toss, Pompeii Court, Wickerr	6
8May82-9Fno	6f	$:21^{3}$	$:44^{1}$	$1:09^{1}$ft	*4-5	115	1½	1^{hd}	2½	2^{1}½	Yanez R^{3}	Bulldog	92	AmnBrothr,AnswrtoMusic,WrHous	6
30Apr82-8Hol	7f	$:21^{3}$	$:44^{1}$	$1:21^{2}$ft	4½	114	1^{hd}	2^{hd}	5^{2}	7^{7}¼	Black K^{2}	Aw32000	83	NavarinoII,MisterWilder,Guarantee	7
9Apr82-8SA	6f	$:21^{4}$	$:44^{2}$	$1:08^{2}$ft	*3	114	2^{hd}	2^{hd}	2½	2no	AsmussenCB^{4}	Aw32000	96	MdKey,AnswertoMusic,AmnBrothr	7
26Mar82-5SA	a6½f Ⓣ	$:21^{3}$	:44	$1:14^{1}$fm	9½	114	1^{2}½	2^{hd}	2½	2^{1}	AsmussenCB^{9}	Aw32000	87	GftdDncr,AnswrtoMusc,SRullhRn	12
21Feb82-10TuP	6f	$:21^{2}$	$:43^{3}$	$1:09^{1}$ft	40	114	6^{5}½	8^{9}½	5^{9}½	5^{7}¼	RamirezO^{1}	Phx Gd Cp	84	Imperial Lass, Mad Key, Bold Ego	9
13Feb82-7SA	6½f	:22	:45	$1:15^{2}$ft	6¾	114	1^{1}	1^{1}	1½	3½	AsmussenCB^{2}	Aw32000	92	KngrooCort,Arstocrtcl,AnswrtoMsc	6
31Jan82-7SA	6f	$:21^{3}$	$:44^{2}$	$1:08^{4}$ft	3¾	114	2^{hd}	2½	3^{3}	4^{6}½	AsmussenCB^{1}	Aw35000	87	Mr.PrmMnstr,Emprr'sKy,FlngChck	6
20Jan82-5SA	7f	$:21^{4}$	:45	$1:24^{4}$sy	9-5	114	3^{nk}	3½	4^{2}¼	3¾	AsmussenCB^{5}	Aw32000	75	Gristle,QuntumLep,AnswertoMusic	5
3Jly81-5Hol	6f	:22	$:44^{4}$	$1:09^{2}$ft	2½	113	1^{hd}	2^{hd}	1^{hd}	1^{hd}	Lipham T^{6}	Aw26000	90	AnswertoMusic,DiscoLrk,Stelinctiv	7

Jun 15 Hol 3f ft $:35^{3}$ h   Jun 4 Hol 4f ft $:48^{1}$ h   May 30 Hol 3f ft $:36^{2}$ h   May 25 Hol 4f ft $:48^{1}$ h

Maybe you think he does not look "too good." But in this field, even at 4-1, there is a plenty of big California money riding on his nose. He ran 12 days ago and worked three days before this race. What is the effect of a return to the races in 12 days with a three furlong workout? The chapter on recent action will talk about that, too.

Maybe you think the running line of Answer to Music's last race is a little bothersome. This horse shows strong early speed, and sometimes he fades, but on the other hand, sometimes he does not. His last race was at one mile and today he is shortening up to seven furlongs. Will the shorter distance bring him back to winning form?

How should you evaluate that last race running line? One of the most important parts of this book deals with what is called the second form factor, "the last useable running line." This section of the book evaluates positions at the various calls of the last race and shows, through careful research, how a horse is likely to perform off its running line. Does the loss of ground in the stretch evident in his last race mean anything for today? That, too, is taken up in precise detail, as you will find when you come to the fourth form factor, "stretch performance." There are certain kinds of stretch losses that nearly doom a horse to failure in his next race and there are other kinds that can be disregarded. Where does Answer to Music fit into this scheme?

What about another entrant in this field, Stand Pat? This old gelding ran against Walter Osborne in his last race and was gaining nicely from the stretch call to the finish, as you can see. But you can also see that Stand Pat has not won in the last 24 starts. But what kind of form does he show in his past performances?

```
Stand Pat *                        Dk. b. or br. g. 7, by Run of Luck—Good Thought, by On-and-On
                                   Br.—Rowan L (Cal)                        1982  5  0  0  1    $10,175
Own.—Ferguson Mrs J K         114  Tr.—Richardson Thomas F                  1981 19  0  2  5    $57,650
                              Lifetime   81  8 15 10  $219,800              Turf 13  0  1  0     $7,450
 3Jun82-7Hol  6½f :22  :441 1:153ft  19 116  64¼ 55  45¼ 32   Guerra W A7     75000 90 WalterOsborne,FlyingChick,StndPt 8
 9May82-7Hol  6f  :222 :444 1:083ft  8½ 114  53¾ 55  46  44½  ValenzuelPA2 Aw32000 89 Gray Dandy, Motivity, Shady Fox  6
17Apr82-5SA  a6½f ⓣ:212 :44 1:132fm  20 115  57  78¼ 89  66¾  Black K9       Aw32000 85 Captain Nick,LaughingBoy,Isopach 9
 9Apr82-8SA   6f  :214 :442 1:082ft   5 117  67¼ 55¾ 44  43¾  Pincay L Jr1   Aw32000 92 MdKey,AnswertoMusic,AmnBrothr    7
13Mar82-7SA   6f  :221 :452 1:103gd  13 114  78¼ 76¾ 57½ 52¾  Pedroza MC7    Aw35000 82 Belfort, Mad Key, A Run         10
11Nov81-9Hol  6f  :212 :444 1:083ft  16 114  79  63¾ 62½ 33   HnsnRD3 Sprnt Chmp 91 Smokite, I'm Smokin, Stand Pat    8
     11Nov81—Run in two divisions, 8th & 9th races.
 1Nov81-5SA   6f  :213 :434 1:084ft  32 114  99¾ 911 87¼ 3nk  Hansen R D2    Aw40000 94 Mr.PrimMinistr,I'mSmokin,StndPt  9
21Oct81-7SA   6f  :22  :444 1:091ft  16 115  68½ 69½ 58½ 44½  McHrgueDG4     Aw34000 87 TonUp,DoubleDiscount,Sham'sFool 7
 8Oct81-5SA   6f  :212 :442 1:094ft  9¾ 115  89  86¾ 76  32¼  McHargue D G5   50000 87 Mister Wilder, HardtoLee,StandPat 8
 9Aug81-7Dmr  6f  :221 :444 1:094ft  14 117  97¾ 811 46½ 23¼  McHrgueDG8     Aw25000 86 Benny Bob, Stand Pat, Cuchillo  11
    May 31 SA 4f ft :481 h       May 27 SA 5f ft 1:013 h       May 20 SA 5f ft 1:013 h       May 6 SA 4f ft :49 h
```

Before you start to discount this horse because of his failure to win in the last two years, take a peek at his lifetime record, where you see earnings of $219,800, more than any other horse in the race. But such evaluation factors deal with the broader spectrum of total handicapping, and in this book, we want to concentrate on recent form to try to understand how a horse will run today, regardless of his past record, and regardless of how he looks otherwise.

Stand Pat was not very close to the lead in his last race at any time until late in the stretch. What does this last race running line thus tell us? Is the stretch gain something that will make him move up today? Is he a greater threat to Walter Osborne? Now take a look at the ten races shown for Stand Pat, with an eye on the first call after the start of each race. This horse lacks early speed, as shown by the fact that he is always running far back in his field at the first call. Is this lack of early speed fatal in today's seven furlong race? How would it affect the horse if this were a six furlong race?

These questions, as they affect how the horse will run today, will be treated fully as you move into this book. You should be able to place a fairly reliable form rating on Stand Pat after you see what our research shows.

Thus far, we have looked at four of the five entries. We might as well view the one long shot, Gristle, who is 10-1 on the board. Would you agree that he does not look that bad?

Gristle *

Own.—Mill House **116**

B. h. 7, by Never Bend—Top Round, by Round Table
Br.—Mill House (Ky)
Tr.—Barrera Lazaro S
Lifetime 42 8 3 8 $178,313

1982	7	1	1	0	$24,275
1981	4	0	0	0	$4,350
Turf	15	2	0	5	$27,303

31May82-10Fno	1⅛	:46 $1{:}11^{2}$ $1{:}48^{4}$ft	2¾	121	53¾	3^{nk}	1½	2^{nk}	Cruz J B^{2}	Valley H	93	Stingingly, Gristle, Norbet	7
20May82-8Hol	1	Ⓣ:46^{4} $1{:}10^{1}$ $1{:}33^{3}$fm	26	118	53½	54	54½	68½	ValenzuelPA[1]	Aw35000	92	Piperhill, Faiz, Quantum Leap	8
18Apr82-7SA	1	$:45^{3}$ 1:10 $1{:}34^{3}$ft	40	114	55½	42½	32	55½	Guerra W A[3]	Aw40000	90	Rock Softly, Sir Dancer, Tell Again	8
4Apr82-7SA	1	$:45^{2}$ $1{:}09^{4}$ $1{:}34^{4}$ft	15	116	57½	44	55¾	68¾	McCarronCJ[1]	Aw35000	86	Maxistar, Son of a Dodo, A Run	7
28Feb82-6SA	$1\frac{1}{16}$	:47 $1{:}10^{4}$ $1{:}41^{2}$ft	19	114	64¾	54¾	56¾	54¾	Hawley S[2]	Aw40000	89	Egg Toss, Rock Softly, Western	6
30Jan82-5SA	1⅛	Ⓣ:46^{4} $1{:}11^{3}$ $1{:}49^{3}$gd	9¼	114	8^{12}	86½	66¼	5^{10}	Guerra W A[2]	Aw35000	69	Monico, Pettrax, Lord Trendy	10
20Jan82-5SA	7f	$:21^{4}$:45 $1{:}24^{4}$sy	11	114	59¼	58½	2^{hd}	1^{nk}	Guerra W A[2]	Aw32000	76	Gristle,QuntumLep,AnswertoMusic	5
12Nov81-8Hol	$1\frac{1}{16}$	$:46^{2}$ 1:11 $1{:}42^{2}$ft	52	115	65¼	54½	5^{10}	5^{18}	Rivera M A[2]	Aw32000	65	Jimsel, Rumbo, Double Discourt	6
6Feb81-7SA	$1\frac{1}{16}$	$:46^{3}$ $1{:}10^{2}$ $1{:}41^{1}$ft	6¼	115	56	56	58	5^{12}	McCarronCJ[5]	Aw37000	83	Fingal, Three Bits, CrestoftheWave	5
24Jan81-8SA	$1\frac{1}{16}$	$:46^{4}$ $1{:}10^{4}$ $1{:}41^{1}$ft	57	112	43	43½	45½	6^{11}	LovatoFJr[5]	Sn Psql H	84	Flying Paster, King Go Go,Fiestero	6

May 27 Hol Ⓣ 5f fm $1{:}02^{2}$ h (d) May 18 Hol 5f ft $1{:}00^{2}$ h May 12 Hol 4f ft :48 h

Before you dismiss him too quickly, notice that he is trained by Laz Barrera, and any horse handled by this wily veteran cannot ever be dismissed out of hand. But what does his form show? That last race at Fresno in a minor stakes race was pretty nifty, as Gristle was narrowly defeated at a mile and an eighth. You should also note that in January at Santa Anita he won a seven furlong allowance race with the same $32,000 purse that is offered today.

Your long shot favoring brethren should like this horse. Maybe he can surprise the others. But how do we rate him off that last race at Fresno, which is a minor track compared to Hollywood Park? Was his performance in his last race affected by the level of competition he faced? Does the $32,000 allowance race today offer better horses than those in a stakes race at Fresno? Does Gristle have enough class in his past to make up for any supposed rise in competitive levels today? Those questions, too, will be discussed in later chapters of this book.

Maybe the eighth at Hollywood is not so easy after all. Or maybe all the others are so laden with form defects that Walter Osborne ought to do what the mass of money in the crowd is so sure will happen. If you can design how each of these horses will run today based on what you see in their past performances, you are indeed a strong student of current form.

This book deals with every question raised so far, based on more than the seasons of experience that go to make a good handicapper. Too often, initial perceptions may get imbedded in stone unless they are continually subjected to the sort of detailed research that went into this book. Let us run through a brief listing of some of the book's major points and what you can expect it to show.

Major Features in This Book

● IDENTIFYING AND ANALYZING THE FORM CYCLE OF HORSES. We do this as a first step, and for one major reason: it helps you apply the form factors that are described in this book. A form cycle is not always related to a time span. Events and circumstances can control a horse's form, such as a recent claim, or a shift in surfaces. We will identify each circumstance that denotes a new form cycle. In the end identifying form cycles will always be directed to weighing the form factors detailed herein.

● DEVELOPING RATINGS FOR FORM. Without using a single number we can rate horses on form. Using the four form factors that are discussed in this book, we have developed three major ratings: positive, or plus "+"; neutral, or non-applicable, which we label "N"; and negative, or minus, for which we give a zero "O". The zero, as you will see, generally means a form defect that will disqualify a horse as a serious contender today. Would any of the horses in the eighth at Hollywood on June 18, 1982, have a disqualifying O form defect? If so, could they overcome it?

● A RESEARCH DEMONSTRATION ON RECENT ACTION seeks to show what time span between races is most effective and what is a serious defect. It integrates workouts into recent action in a way you surely have not seen before. As we have previously said, this part of the book will apply directly to J.D. Quill in the race we just observed. By the way, who won that race?

● LAST RACE RUNNING LINES have been treated by handicappers as long as there has been a *Daily Racing Form* (or *Morning Telegraph*, for that matter). Is there anything new that we can learn from them? While considerable progress was made in evaluating running lines in *Investing at the Racetrack*, the analyses set forth here are vastly improved and add new elements that have never been considered before.

● HORSES THAT WON THEIR LAST RACE are found on every racing card. Many of them are favorites and are often bet heavily, just as Walter Osborne was in the eighth at Hollywood. How will they run today? How did Walter Osborne run? Last race winners, as we intimated some pages ago, are studied in great detail in this book, with new findings and new guidelines that should be of great assistance to you.

● IMPROVEMENT OR DECLINE WITHIN FORM CYCLE is presented with some new analyses. This is probably one of the most difficult assessments to make in the handicapping game. A wrong diagnosis can be a disaster. Yet, if a horse is truly on the decline, he is a wretched prospect in today's race. The animal that is looking upward, showing real signs of improvement, is likely to do well in his next race. These old truths are subject to a probing re-scrutiny that is designed to leave you with a better feeling of confidence in how you deal with this problem.

● A CERTAIN KIND OF STRETCH BEHAVIOR IN A HORSE'S LAST RACE is demonstrated to be such a serious form defect that horses that show it can be eliminated from most races with a great degree of certainty. This is one of the most important of the new findings in this book. On the other hand, those circumstances where a horse is likely to be an exception to the rule are also shown, which again allows you to separate the good prospects from the bad.

● A MAJOR DISQUALIFYING FORM DEFECT IN SPRINT RACES is revealed that is as near a certainty as anything you will ever find in horse racing is demonstrated. In sprint races only, a horse lacking early speed is destined to lose when certain standards are satisfied. You will be shown where to draw the line and what exactly is required to meet these definitive standards.

• AND FINALLY, WE WILL OUTLINE METHODS OF PLAY based upon the discoveries in this book that lead to steady, consistent profits over any reasonable period. One example deals with favorites only, showing regular profits based upon a frequency of play that is sufficient to keep the player reasonably engaged.

The Research That Developed the Findings in This Book

While every good student of handicapping learns something almost every time they go to the track, and over a period of years acquires enough hard and painful experience to alert them to many of the pitfalls of this game, one can never be too sure of implanted beliefs until they are put to some kind of comprehensive test. In my own career work, I have long been involved in careful, documented research in two professions, the law and writing. This is not laboratory or test tube research, but documentary studies. In handicapping racehorses, the student has readily at hand the most complete and comprehensive collection of data of almost any enterprise: *Daily Racing Form.*

In this age of computerized wonders, perhaps the skilled system analyst can find new guides to predictability. My own experience (and insufficient knowledge in the science of computers) has required me to do it the hard way—analysis of one race after another—one by one, with tabulation of the results. When a sufficient mass of data is assembled, then one can evaluate what is at hand, and what can be learned from the data.

After I had developed the points that I wanted to study, I gathered a collection of back issues of *Daily Racing Forms* that permitted simultaneous study of four eastern tracks for a concentrated number of days. If any method of play is deemed to be workable, it ought to show sound results over any reasonably short period of time, and if it fails, then it should be discarded. What works at one track may not work at another, so I wanted a minimum of four. What works in one week may not work in another, so I wanted to compress what could be learned into a consecutive time frame.

The first comprehensive study, which will be referred to often in this book, began with race son Tuesday, September 29, 1981, and continued through October 13, 1981. The four tracks under study were Belmont Park in New York, Meadowlands in northern New Jersey, Keystone Racetrack (now called Philadelphia Park), and Bowie Race Course (now closed) in Maryland.

The total study involved 433 races: 13 racing cards at Meadowlands, 12 at Keystone, and 11 each at Belmont and Bowie, for a total of 47 racing cards. This produced every kind of race likely to be encountered, from maiden claimers to graded stakes, from sprints to marathon distances, from grass to mud.

Experienced researchers in any field know that quite often preconceived ideas prove faulty when subjected to careful scrutiny. They also know that thoughtful study of a subject will often lead to new learnings and to new concepts that were not apparent before. Both these phenomena happened time and time again as I worked away at the 433 races. In fact, when new lines of inquiry opened up, I was forced to go back over the whole spectrum of races again and again. The *Daily Racing Forms* I used were turned so many dozens of times that they became tattered, with holes in the folds, and appeared to be almost falling apart before I finished, but I was determined to work off this information base to support the results that would come out of what I was learning.

When the foundation findings were completed, there was still more work to be done. Even as I continued my research week after week, I was going to the track, usually on Saturdays, to test what I was finding. An accumulation of *Racing Forms* in 1982 provided fertile ground for validating what the earlier studies revealed. Not only did I tabulate results from a variety of eastern tracks, from Calder to Saratoga, but I picked up *Daily Racing Forms* from the west coast to integrate as many races from that section of the country as well.

The tabulations from the 1981 studies, which are set forth so frequently in this book, are not intended as the last scientific word. The sample itself is too small, standing alone, to withstand the scrutiny of the mathematical researcher. But indeed, something more is added, **and** this now embraces literally thousands of races—good old O & E: Observation and Experience. It was Observation and Experience in the first place that led me into the hypotheses. A theory founded on O & E has to be tested—the 1981 studies were the first successful round of validation.

When theories based on Observation and Experience begin to come apart at the seams, as they often do, the gaping holes ordinarily turn up early in the process. Usually, it takes less than a hundred races for something you think may be pretty good to start falling apart. These studies did not make my theories disintegrate, of course, but far more was needed before I could rest assured.

The wide ranging 1982 research follow-ups became an important annex. They actually produced better results than the concentrated 1981 tests, perhaps because so many of the racing cards came from Saturday's events, when the caliber of horses is somewhat higher than on weekdays. Thus, the 1982 studies, blended with a generous mixture of O & E, when added on to what I had so laboriously tabulated earlier, were sufficient proof for me.

But that is not all. Even as the book was being written, the testing went on and on, right down to submission to the printer. The results continued in the same steady flow, further supporting the findings. There was no longer any doubt about the overall computations and the probabilities they produced.

The key word is "probabilities."

Playing With Probabilities

Every one of us has learned that there is no "sure thing" in horse racing. Even a Secretariat could lose, and did. In this book, there is a concentration both on the positive and the negative. When positive factors, no matter how strong the probability, indicate success and negatives tell us the opposite, sometimes the results still do surprise us. A horse with powerful positive form factors may run up the track. A horse with negatives hanging all over him may emerge from the pack and take it all. These are the times that make every student of this incredible game shake his head in wonderment and ask, what more can be done?

But we can be consoled by the confident knowledge that sound form probabilities, if they are indeed sound, will work far more often than not. They are an indicator of success, not an infallible guide. They lead you to sound ratings, not definite certainties. They are as vitally important to sound handicapping as are the factors of speed and class.

Thus, this book is intended to be the most incisive analytical dissertation on current form thus far produced. It is not intended as the last word. It therefore deals only with form and form factors, leaving any handicapper free to apply their own method of rating to go with a consideration of form. It is not intended to be a treatise on total handicapping, but only on the vital, crucial, necessary ingredient of form, as directed toward probably the most important question you will have to face at the racetrack: How Will Your Horse Run Today?

Even after mastering the intricacies of current form, you are still left playing with probabilities, because form ratings, as has been repeated again and again, are not infallible. There are innumerable other rating factors that are beyond the range and scope of this book, because of the determined concentration on form itself. Besides the evaluations of current form, there may be many reasons why a horse might not run up to the rating that may be established.

As one prime example, astute handicappers today deal with what is popularly called "trip handicapping." In any consideration of the big question of how your horse will run today, an understanding of how he fared last out is critical. What kind of a trip did he have? Did he get knocked around out of the starting gate? Did he get boxed behind a wall of horses? Was he pinned in along the rail on a dull strip? Was he forced so wide that he lost valuable ground at a crucial part of the race? Did the jockey make a mistake at some key point in the race that cost the runner dearly?

The player who benefits the most from trip handicapping is the regular who can go to the track every day. Keen observation and a good memory can become invaluable. But the Saturday player who has to get his information from the *Racing Form* is forced to rely upon what they read there. The "trouble line" in the *Form* may often give you such terms as "blocked," or "steadied," or "poor start." I have studied the next races of horses that show the kind of trouble that could affect the trip they may have had and I have never been able to develop any sound standards from the comments in either the eastern edition of *Daily Racing Form*, or the old listings of "Horses in Trouble" prior to the 1983 insertions of trouble lines in all other editions.

On the other hand, I have watched many horses get late starts out of the gate, particularly in sprint races, and then rush up so quickly to make up lost ground that by the first call they may even be in the lead. Invariably, they burn themselves out and by the time the critical stretch call arrives, they are through for the day. But how will they run their next time out? Bad trip or not, I have been unable to blend this reality into an overall concept of form, because many kinds of bad trips are not evident from the running lines in *Daily Racing Form*. Perhaps it can be done—for I would be the last observer to downgrade the importance of a bad trip as a factor to be taken into account in the next race.

There is also the critical problem of track bias. Sometimes a track will show a dead rail and horses on the outside enjoy a major advantage. On other occasions, the inside of the strip may get firmly packed and early speedballs will go all the way without stopping. These kinds of situations can change almost overnight. I will never forget a few seasons ago when my youngest handicapping son came home for a Christmas vacation from college. The track bias against inside speed was so great that not only was it written about in the local newspapers, but every track watcher seemed to know about it. Horses on the rail were dead—the outside post positions brought home the money.

On his first afternoon at the track, he noticed that an inside horse with good early speed surprisingly went all the way in the first race. He watched two more races where inside speed seemed to do well. Was the track bias in the midst of a sudden change? He plunked down a $2 win bet on a long shot with early speed out of the number one hole in the next race, and supplemented it with $2 to show. This horse with poor form was never touched and the proceeds of a $66 win ticket filled my son's pockets.

Before the afternoon was over, he was putting down $50 on early speed on the inside and he went home with enough money to make his entire vacation period one of bounteous financial joy. He went with me the very next day and racked up another stunning pile of profits. After a couple more afternoons, the track subsided to a more normal strip and there appeared to be no bias at all. He was fortunate enough to strike at precisely the right time. Good handicapping figures, or good form ratings, may not have been helpful in this brief sustained period.

This book, perhaps regrettably, does not deal with either trip handicapping or track bias, both of which are valid components of consideration for How Will Your Horse Run Today? We return to our probabilities, based on what current form affected by levels of competition can tell us. If you are able to make adjustments for what you may know about a bad trip in the last race or a track irregularity, by all means do so. What is set forth here is meant to give you a solid foundation for *any* kind of handicapping.

Now that we have sifted through all of this, and before we get down to the specifics of the form factors with which we will deal, how about that eighth race at Hollywood Park that we have wondered about since this chapter began? The result chart tells us what happened:

EIGHTH RACE
Hollywood
JUNE 18, 1982

7 FURLONGS. (1.19⅘) CLASSIFIED ALLOWANCE. Purse $32,000. 4-year-olds and upward, which have not won $17,700 in 1981–82. Weight, 121 lbs. Non-winners of $14,000 twice since December 25, 1981 allowed 3 lbs.; of $14,000 twice since September 1, 1981, 5 lbs.; of $17,600 since December 25, 1981, 7 lbs. (Claiming and starter races not considered.)

Value of race $32,000, value to winner $17,600, second $6,400, third $4,800, fourth $2,400, fifth $800. Mutuel pool $176,985. Exacta Pool $215,827.

Last Raced	Horse	Eqt.	A.	Wt	PP	St	¼	½	Str	Fin	Jockey	Odds $1
19Dec81 ^{7}Lrl^{3}	J. D. Quill		4	114	4	3	3^{6}	$2\frac{1}{2}$	1^{hd}	$1^{2\frac{1}{2}}$	Olivares F	3.50
3Jun82 ^{7}Hol^{3}	Stand Pat	b	7	115	1	4	4^{hd}	5	5	2no	McHargue D G	5.60
6Jun82 ^{6}Hol^{5}	Answer to Music	b	4	114	5	1	1^{1}	$1\frac{1}{2}$	$2^{2\frac{1}{2}}$	3^{nk}	McCarron C J	4.10
3Jun82 ^{7}Hol^{1}	Walter Osborne		5	117	2	2	2^{hd}	3^{4}	3^{2}	4^{2}	Pincay L Jr	.80
31May82 ^{10}Fno^{2}	Gristle	b	7	116	3	5	5	$4^{1\frac{1}{2}}$	4^{1}	5	Guerra W A	10.70

OFF AT 5:33. Start good. Won driving. Time, :21⅗, :43⅗, 1:07⅘, 1:20⅗ Track fast.

$2 Mutuel Prices:				
	4–J. D. QUILL	9.00	5.00	3.80
	1–STAND PAT		5.20	3.20
	5–ANSWER TO MUSIC			2.80

$5 EXACTA 4–1 PAID $111.00

B. c, by Noholme II—Nuquill, by Noble Union. Trainer Fanning Jerry. Bred by Davis Mr–Mrs J (Mich).

J. D. QUILL, in contention from the outset, eased to the outside nearing the far turn, responded when set down in the stretch drive, got the lead in the upper stretch and drew clear in the final sixteenth. STAND PAT, outrun early, went to the middle of the track entering the stretch and closed strongly. ANSWER TO MUSIC outsprinted rivals for the early lead but hung in the final sixteenth. WALTER OSBORNE, in contention from the outset, was steadied momentarily at the far turn, remained in close contention but lacked the needed closing response.

That heavily bet 4-5 shot, Walter Osborne "lacked the needed closing response." He wound up out of the money, a sad disappointment to the thousands of players who backed him. But should it have been foreseen?

And the winner, J.D. Quill, pulled away in the stretch to a splendid victory, returning $9.00 to those who backed him. What caused him to run so well? Stand Pat, the perennial closer, was last at the stretch call, but went around the others to put a nose in front of Answer to Music for the place. Poor Gristle, our long shot, could not do it, and came in fifth and last, but only four and a half lengths from the front in a race run in splendid time.

This race was run just about as the form factors in this book will tell you it should have been. J.D. Quill's performance, as you will find, was no surprise at all. And neither was Walter Osborne.

With that, let us turn to how we can rate these horses on form, to see if we can tell in advance how our horse will run today.

2 How to Find a Form Cycle

THE TERM "FORM CYCLE" has been used frequently in handicapping literature. Most of us recognize it as some definite period of time in which a horse has been competing, sufficient to indicate how efficiently he is performing. But for our purposes here, we will endeavor to set forth some defined form cycles and use them for analyzing current form—always pressing toward an answer to the critical question, How Will Your Horse Run Today?

Generally for our purposes, a form cycle is that period of time between changes in circumstances that may affect a horse's performance. Do not worry about such a wordy definition—we are going to move immediately into a practical application of it that you will soon learn to recognize, and will be able to use as a method of looking at a horse's record.

Bear in mind that we are not talking as much about a span of time as an indicator, because good form can hold for a considerable time period over many changes in circumstances. Our concentration here will be on events. Time span is one kind of event that has its own separate importance. We will be looking for the kind of events that mark a change in a horse's handling or level of competition, as well as time span, and try to put them all together to help us with our central inquiry.

Identifying the Form Cycle

To help in identifying form cycles it is very useful to draw a line in a horse's past performances where a new form cycle begins. This can be done quickly after a glance, and your hand-drawn line will usually not be too ragged, since doing it between lines provides a guide to keep you on the "straight and narrow."

We have broken form cycles down into seven different circumstances which affect how a horse might run today.

1. THE LAYOFF, where we are dealing entirely with time, is, of course, the most common circumstance. A period of rest in which a horse is taken out of competition is an important changed circumstance, and when a horse returns to the track after a layoff, he will begin a new form cycle. What is a requisite layoff period? Twenty eight days, or four weeks, or almost a month, is the line selected. A horse that does not run in four weeks, or almost a month, is not bringing money into the barn. It goes without saying that he is out for what we old World War II lads used to call "R and R," which for us means, "rest and rehabilitation."

After the animal has been inactive for four weeks or more and comes back to the races, there is an understandable urge to push him toward recouping some of the cost of those prolonged feed and handling bills that kept going on during the four weeks of idleness. That is always a key ingredient in the new form cycle that the horse begins. How soon will he bring home a paycheck?

2. A MAIDEN VICTORY occurs after a horse wins the first race of his career. This may not be related to a time span at all, but deals entirely with entering a new level of competition. Horses that compete only against other maiden non-winners and then score a triumph, are ready immediately thereafter to launch into a new range of competition against other horses that have also won. They are no longer running against a crowd of misfits, some of whom may never win a race in their careers. They are competing against an entirely new level of opposition, and how they perform in this company will have a great deal to do with their future in racing. It thus becomes time to judge their form in their new competitive level. Accordingly, we draw a line above the maiden victory and start a whole new evaluation of the horse's performance in his new form cycle.

3. A CHANGE IN CLASS CONDITIONS, other than when a horse first leaves the maiden ranks, marks the beginning of a similar kind of new form cycle. He may be entering a new level of competition against winners, just as a victor out of a maiden field will be entering a new level of competition. As an example, a horse may

have run regularly for a claiming price of $20,000. His trainer, not satisfied with the lack of success there, may move the horse downward into a lower competitive bracket against horses valued at $14,000. We then would want to measure the horse's form anew against this lesser level of runners.

Of course, a definitive rise in class brings the same change in circumstances. If a horse has been winning or running well with a claiming tag of $10,000, his trainer may feel he is ready to take on $14,000 horses, and may raise the class level accordingly.

In drawing form cycle lines based upon changes in class, we want to avoid temporary experimentation, where a trainer may raise or lower a horse in value for a race to see how his animal performs. When a horse is on the decline, he may be entered at lower claiming prices in race after race, which may leave us without any definitive starting point for the evaluation of a new form cycle. Accordingly, we want a change in class that has enough stability to allow us to form a reasonable opinion.

We can do this by requiring at least two races in succession at a particular class level before we consider it a new form cycle. This keeps us away from up and down hopscotching, and gives us a sounder look all around. This can be shown in many of the illustrations you will see throughout this book.

In addition, when dealing with class-based form cycles, we must be careful to distinguish between true changes in the class level of competition and mere slight changes in claiming price. A quick look at the conditions of most claiming races will reveal that horses in a single race may run for a defined range of claiming price tags, with the reward of less weight assigned to horses whose owners are willing to risk losing them for a lower price. For example, a race may establish the claiming price as $25,000 to $20,000. Thus a horse whose record shows two successive races, one where he was entered to be claimed for $25,000, and the next where he ran for a tag of $22,000, most likely did not drop down in class from one race to the next.

As a rule of thumb, there should be a change in claiming price from one race to the next of 20% or more before marking a new form cycle for a change in class level.

4. DISTANCE SWITCHES, which involve stretching a horse out from sprints to routes, or shortening him from longer races down to a sprint, produce another change in the form cycle. Once again, to make sure we have a definitive cycle on our hands, we will require two races in a row before drawing our line. To illustrate, a trainer may have run his horse in a sprint, which is defined for these purposes as races of seven furlongs and shorter, and then concluded that the horse should be ready to run longer, and then entered him in distance events. Sometimes, a single sprint race or a distance race is used as a training device for a horse that is better suited to the opposite sort of race, and we want to avoid labelling such a prep race as a form cycle.

Only after a horse has run at the different kind of distance for two consecutive races will we start evaluating his form cycle from the first race of the new distance. It generally takes at least two races in a row for us to know whether the trainer is serious about the change in distance.

5. A CHANGE IN RUNNING SURFACE from grass to dirt, or from dirt to grass can mark the beginning of a new form cycle. A horse may be a poor performer on the dirt, have good grass breeding, and do very well on the new surface. After two consecutive runs on the grass, and if he continues, we are compelled to consider his grass form cycle and evaluate it, rather than relying on dirt form. Likewise, if a horse has been running on the grass and the trainer moves him to the dirt for two races, that is the signal for the beginning of a new form cycle.

One word of caution though. When evaluating changes in racing surface, it is important to consider whether a race on the main track was originally carded for grass, but had to be switched to dirt because of poor turf conditions. A trainer may have intended to run his horse on the grass, but the weather dictated otherwise. When a horse primarily has turf races in its past performances, dirt races with sloppy, muddy or good track condition sandwiched between the turf races are a good indicator of whether the dirt race was originally carded for grass. Better yet, keep a record of race days when weather conditions forced a shift from turf to dirt.

6. A MOVE FROM ONE RACING CIRCUIT TO ANOTHER can produce meaningful change in the handling of a horse. Here it becomes important for racing fans to know what is meant by a racing circuit. It is easy enough to read in the *Racing Form* the name of the track where the horse ran, and if a horse shows a race at Laurel and then one at Bowie, most players know that this is a part of the Maryland circuit and there is nothing unusual involved. New Yorkers know that Aqueduct, Belmont and Saratoga are the essential ovals of the New York circuit, and Southern California fans link Santa Anita, Hollywood Park, and even Del Mar into the same embrace.

But when a horse is shipped from one group of tracks or circuit to another, he will usually be running under different conditions and against a different brand of competition. Even though the change may have involved only a week or so in time, we think it is significant enough to start a new form cycle.

As an example, horses running in the spring in Florida are often shipped north to enter summer competition without missing a regular turn at the entry box. A horse coming north from Hialeah or Gulfstream Park may run at Monmouth, and regardless of the intervening time span, this change of scenery is enough to consider his efforts at Monmouth, for the most part, as beginning a new form cycle.

Most racing regulars soon learn the circuits. An excellent discussion on the location and level of every North American track is found in Ainslie's *Encyclopedia of Thoroughbred Handicapping* (William Morrow, 1978), which will benefit even the oldtimers in determining which tracks are part of a circuit.

7. FINALLY, A CHANGE IN OWNERSHIP OF THE HORSE is perhaps the most important change in circumstance that will launch a new form cycle. This usually comes in the claiming ranks. When a new owner acquires a horse, a different trainer takes over. He may, and usually will, do things somewhat differently, for better or worse, than did his predecessor. The horse is in a new stable and will be

under the standards of the new trainer. There is also a rather evident desire to have that horse win as soon as possible for his new owners—to try to earn back as much of the purchase price as possible in quick time.

Horses outside the claiming ranks may sometimes be sold at horse sales, or even privately. But this information will not be shown in the past performances. If you happen to know that an allowance or stakes horse has changed hands, you may start to define a new form cycle at the point where the new interests take over. Often there may be enough of a time span in between to allow you to use that as the proper measuring device. On the whole, though, when we are dealing with changes in ownership, it is usually the claiming horse that we are considering.

Separating Form Cycles

By identifying form cycles we are able to focus more sharply on what is happening to the horse. For example, separating out the form cycles will cause you to pay attention to the reality that a horse coming off a layoff, with a race or two, is surely being prepared to at least try hard for a victory, as will a horse after a claim has occurred. A trainer trying a new distance, or a new surface, may want to succeed very badly in the new conditions, even if only to demonstrate his wisdom in making the switch. On the other hand, he may have miscalculated badly, and this may be revealed in the form cycle.

Likewise, a horse that has just won its maiden race is almost always rising in class in his next effort, and a sound handicapper will always want to keep that in mind. Separating the form cycles also helps you see how a trainer may be experimenting with a horse in both class and distance, and show you that guesswork is no substitute for a sound racing plan.

The hand-drawn line in the past performances defining form cycles helps bring them full force into our handicapping consideration and aids in understanding the four major form factors we will discuss in this book. The beauty of, and reason for, this exercise is that you can do it with any horse in any race and quickly get a better idea of what the horse is doing in today's race, and most often, what it is likely to do, since the form cycle provides us with a quick insight into what the trainer's intentions may be. We cannot always know, of course, but you will surely soon agree, even after we run through only a few of these exercises, that this is not only relatively quick and easy, but will open up some visions that you may otherwise have overlooked.

We can begin by taking some horses from the second race at Golden Gate Fields on June 16. We started with the conditions of the race and the number one entry, High Caliber, who was the second coice in the better at 9-2.

2nd Golden Gate

$1\frac{1}{16}$ MILES. (1.40⅘) CLAIMING. Purse $9,000. Fillies. 3-year-olds. Weight, 120 lbs. Non-winners of two races at one mile or over since May 1 allowed 3 lbs.; one such race since then, 6 lbs. Claiming price $16,000; for each $1,000 to $14,000 allowed 1 lb. (Maiden, starter and claiming races for $12,500 or less not considered.)

High Caliber — Dk. b. or br. f. 3, by Dimaggio—Queen's Caliber, by King's Balcony
Own.—Friendly E — **114** — Br.—J P Talbert Estate (Cal) — 1982 7 0 0 1 $1,975
Tr.—Shoemaker Leonard $16,000 — 1981 3 1 0 0 $7,550
Lifetime 10 1 0 1 $9,525

27May82-3Hol	6f	:22	:45^{2}	1:10^{4}ft	2e	115	$6^{5\frac{3}{4}}$	6^{12}	6^{11}	6^{12}	Castaneda M^{7}	(F) 20000	71	Judrick, Fancitate, Carz	7
19May82-3Hol	6f	:22	:45^{2}	1:10^{3}ft	14e	115	$6^{9\frac{1}{2}}$	$6^{9\frac{3}{4}}$	6^{12}	6^{11}	Castaneda M^{1}	(F) 25000	73	Implentytuff,EweWin,GloriousGren	6
6May82-3Hol	6f	:22^{4}	:46^{2}	1:12 ft	16	115	$5^{4\frac{1}{2}}$	$6^{3\frac{1}{2}}$	$3^{3\frac{1}{2}}$	3^{5}	Castaneda M^{1}	(F) 20000	72	Win Bold, Ewe Win, High Caliber	6
9Apr82-1SA	6f	:22	:45^{2}	1:10^{3}ft	60	115	12^{15}	12^{17}	10^{13}	9^{14}	Guerra WA^{8}	(F)[S] 25000	71	ModestyBlaise,DuchessTina,Bjikin	12
4Mar82-9SA	1	:46^{4}	1:11^{2}	1:37 ft	15	115	$8^{6\frac{3}{4}}$	$8^{9\frac{1}{4}}$	9^{13}	8^{14}	Castaneda M^{7}	(F) 32000	70	Sh'sSplndid,P'titNN,Horizon'sDrm	10
24Feb82-2SA	6f	:21^{4}	:45	1:11^{3}ft	5½	117	7^{10}	7^{11}	7^{10}	$5^{5\frac{3}{4}}$	CastanedM^{7}	(F)[S] 25000	74	FleetMelinda,NaturllyGood,Sufrett	8
3Feb82-2SA	1	:47	1:12	1:38 ft	12e	115	$10^{9\frac{1}{2}}$	10^{10}	8^{11}	7^{9}	CastanedaM^{10}	(F) 50000	70	Tayana,BuoyantLss,BorrowedMid	10
16Dec81-4Hol	6f	:22^{3}	:46^{4}	1:13^{2}ft	5½	117	$5^{3\frac{1}{2}}$	5^{3}	$4^{3\frac{1}{2}}$	1^{nk}	Sibille R^{2}	(F)M25000	70	HighCaliber,Fancitate,LeahaNegra	12
22Oct81-3SA	1	:47	1:12	1:37^{2}ft	3	115	$6^{1\frac{3}{4}}$	$4^{6\frac{1}{2}}$	4^{12}	5^{19}	VlenzulPA^{5}	(F)Mc32000	63	AegenQuen,TriplMch,BorrowdMid	10
14Oct81-3SA	6f	:22^{1}	:45^{4}	1:11^{3}ft	6½	115	11^{11}	8^{11}	7^{9}	$4^{4\frac{3}{4}}$	McCrronCJ^{7}	(F)M32000	75	Belltrista,TripleMach,AegenQueen	12

May 15 Hol 4f ft :48^{1} h May 3 Hol 4f ft :48^{1} h

You should never try to handicap any race without paying particular attention to the conditions. In fact, it will be difficult in many situations to make proper form analyses without a full understanding of the conditions of the race. These conditions establish claiming prices in claiming races, the weight horses will carry, the competitive level in allowance races, and numerous other conditions in every type of race. Since the class level of competition is an essential element of any sound handicapping method and actually controls many of the form decisions we have to make, you must never overlook what each race provides. Here, of course, we have a typical claiming race, at a mile and a sixteenth, and as we comment on High Caliber, you must always keep the date of the race before you in mind—June 16, 1982.

You can start drawing lines either from the top or bottom of a horse's past performances. The bottom is the best place to start, since it compels you to do a complete form cycle breakdown for the horse. Most of the time, it is difficult to keep from starting at the top because of one's natural impatience to find out as quickly as you can how the horse might perform. But after your lines are drawn, you can concentrate on the current form cycle.

At the very top of High Caliber's record, we have drawn a line above her last race, signifying the break of a form cycle and the start of a new one. This one comes first from the fact that the filly is up from Hollywood Park, shipped northward to the Bay Area to run at Golden Gate. This is an entirely different circuit, since northern California and southern California are two distinct racing worlds. Southern California racing rates with New York as the best in the country with the largest purses, the highest attendance, the biggest handles and horses ordinarily superior in caliber to those that run at the Bay Meadows–Golden Gate–northern California fair circuit. In addition, the filly is dropping in class from $20,000 to a claiming price of $16,000, a 20% drop in price.

Thus, we see the owner and trainer, unable to win against the tough competition at Santa Anita and Hollywood Park, shipping this filly north possibly to look for an easier touch, and giving her a class drop of some substance. Accordingly, High Caliber is embarking upon a new form cycle in her race at Golden Gate after not having raced in 20 days and no published workouts showing.

The real question for the handicapper is whether her marked drop in class from the better ranks at Hollywood will be enough to overpower the lesser valued fillies at Golden Gate. In this case, the defects of poor recent form were too much to overcome, but even so, High Caliber did manage to finish second.

But continue to analyze the form cycles of this filly and you may readily see why her handlers wanted so badly to win. Drop down to the next line, the one between April 9 and March 4, 1982.

She had a layoff of 36 days between these two races which meant a new form cycle began on April 9. She ran four races in that form cycle, before shipping north, all at six furlongs and with sad results. Thus, today, we have new scenery and an effort at a new distance of a mile and a sixteenth. Plainly, the trainer is experimenting today, riding on hope.

The previous form cycle, between February 3 and March 4, 1982, coming after a 51-day vacation also produced virtually nothing. Then note on October 22, this filly was claimed for $32,000 at Santa Anita. The owner and trainer are willing to sell her today for $16,000 and pick up the winner's share of the purse of $9,000, if "hope" prevails, and eat their losses as well.

The favorite in the race was Cutesy, and in her handling, you will see another case of the "wobblies."

Cutesy

Dk. b. or br. f. 3, by Bold Tactics—Mickey's Marquessa, by Mickey McGuire
Br.—Frankel J (Tex)
Tr.—Greenman Walter

Own.—Traver & Traver   114 $16,000

1982 10 1 0 3 $13,615
1981 0 M 0 0
Lifetime 10 1 0 3 $13,615

4Jun82-4GG	6f :22³ :46 1:12³ft	*9-5 114	44	44	45½	34	Meza R Q³	Ⓕ 20000	72 Extenuating, Tronds Key, Cutesy	6
14May82-6GG	6f :22¹ :46 1:12⁴ft	5 114	43½	44	5⁴	3¹	Meza R Q⁶	Ⓕ 25000	74 ColdwaterCanyon,AnnSham,Cutesy	7
30Apr82-6GG	1¹⁄₁₆:47¹ 1:11⁴ 1:46¹ft	3½ 114	44	31½	43	44¾	Meza R Q⁶	Ⓕ 25000	67 Dream of Tina, Prepense, Excess	7
15Apr82-6GG	1¹⁄₁₆:47² 1:11³ 1:46 ft	4½ 112	46	55	46	42¾	Nicolo P⁵	Ⓕ 30000	70 Lillian Savage, Dini K., Prepense	6
2Apr82-6GG	6f :23 :46² 1:13 sy	7½ 114	3¹	3³	34½	31½	Meza R Q¹	Ⓕ 25000	72 ColdwterCnyon,SplendidMrk,Cutsy	6
24Mar82-6GG	1¹⁄₁₆:48¹ 1:13 1:46¹ft	10 113	1½	31½	46	46½	Meza R Q⁶	ⒻAw13000	65 Surely a Winner, Soft Silk, Din' K.	7
2Mar82-7GG	6f :22³ :46¹ 1:12³sl	6½ 114	53½	56½	77	65	Meza R Q⁴	Ⓕ 32000	71 Dream Gal, Splendid Mark, Dini K.	8
19Feb82-4GG	6f :23 :46⁴ 1:13¹gd	9½ 114	42½	55	57½	45½	Meza R Q³	ⒻAw11000	67 Cakebread, ForeignFunds,MadDeek	6
10Feb82-6GG	1 :48³ 1:14³ 1:40⁴ft	3½ 114	56	78½	61⁴	61⁵	Baze R A³	Ⓕ c25000	49 Prepens,Controllingintrst,MissGlry	7
7Jan82-4BM	1¹⁄₁₆:49 1:15³ 1:49¹gd	7½ 117	68½	22	1hd	1½	Nicolo P⁴	ⒻM25000	53 Cutesy, Swaps Came, Nina L. C.	7

A line has been drawn across the top to signify the beginning of a new form cycle with the race under consideration on June 16, although this one could be omitted at your discretion. The reason for drawing the line is that the June 16 race was at a mile and a sixteenth after two sprint races for Cutesy, and she was dropping in class again. Look down at the intermingled pattern of two sprints and two routes. The owners have not yet made up their minds as to whether Cutesy is best suited for sprinting or for distance running. And when you see that an owner and trainer cannot make up their minds as to where their horse best fits, you ought to make up your mind not to play. Note also there was a claim back on February 10, 1982, for $25,000, another investment that leaves the ownership somewhat short of the mark of recovery. You will ordinarily not see so many lines across a past performance, but this one is meant to demonstrate erratic distance shifts as well as class uncertainties.

It will not surprise you that this favorite finished back in the pack, some 12 lengths behind the winner. Even this cursory examination of Cutesy's form cycle, without serious analysis of the key factors we will discuss later, demonstrated the unlikelihood that she would win.

At this point, after looking at only two horses in an ordinary claiming race, you have seen six of the seven events occur which generally note the commencement of a new form cycle. You saw in High Caliber a change of racing circuit, a layoff, a maiden victory, and a claim. In Cutesy, in addition to seeing a claim, maiden victory, and a layoff, you also observed a distance switch, and a change in class.

It is unusual to look at the record of any horse without seeing some change of circumstance that indicates the beginning of a new form cycle. It will show up more frequently in older geldings, who are put to the fire as often as their legs will hold up.

You must also bear in mind that a change in circumstances may happen in the middle of a normal form cycle, as far as timing of races and consistency of performances are concerned. This compels us to draw a line to start a new form cycle for analysis purposes, but it also requires us to keep in mind the performance of the horse within the broader range. A good example is when a horse is claimed during a period when he is performing well, and then runs right back with no significant vacation. But the change in circumstance is enough to cause you to do some important reevaluation. You may want to call this an "overlapping" form cycle. Also, an up and down rise and drop in class may occur in the middle of a normal form cycle, but this short term change ought not alter your general view of the horse within the broader form cycle of its recent past performances.

Now that some of these elements have been repeated, we should take a look at the winning horse in the second race at Golden Gate on June 16, who was the fourth choice in the betting and returned a $15.20 mutuel for her victory.

Luciernago — B. f. 3, by Astray—Crimson Flame, by Stage Door Johnny
Own.—Granja Vista del Rio — 117 — Br.—Granja Vista del Rio (Cal) — 1982 6 1 0 2 $9,065
Tr.—Orr Ike — 1981 7 M 0 0 $2,325
Lifetime 13 1 0 2 $11,390

19May82-4GG	1 1/16	:48	1:13	1:47^{2}ft	6	114	3$^{3\frac{1}{2}}$	3$^{1\frac{1}{2}}$	3^1	1no	Lamance C^6	Ⓕ 16000	66	Luciernago, Rule the Sun, NinaL.C.	8
27Apr82-4GG	1 1/16	:47^4	1:12^1	1:45^{2}ft	4¼	112	7$^{8\frac{1}{2}}$	6^6	5^6	4$^{7\frac{3}{4}}$	SchvnevldtCP^5	ⒻMdn	68	Dr. Laura, Maradardi, Swaps Came	7
15Apr82-6GG	1 1/16	:47^2	1:11^3	1:46 ft	11	112	5$^{6\frac{1}{2}}$	4^5	5^6	5$^{4\frac{3}{4}}$	Lamance C^1	Ⓕ 30000	68	Lillian Savage, Dini K., Prepense	6
23Mar82-4GG	1 1/16	:48^1	1:13^1	1:46^{2}ft	5	114	7^{11}	6$^{8\frac{1}{4}}$	5^6	3$^{7\frac{1}{2}}$	Lamance C^2	Ⓕ 20000	63	SweetMrzipn,SupriseGift,Luciergo	7
10Mar82-4GG	1 1/16	:49^4	1:14^3	1:47 ft	10	114	3$^{1\frac{1}{2}}$	3^1	2^2	3$^{3\frac{1}{2}}$	Lamance C^3	Ⓕ 20000	64	Snowymist,SweetMrzipn,Luciernago	6
29Jan82-3SA	1 1/16	:46^4	1:12^1	1:46 ft	19	114	9^{17}	9^{17}	8^{20}	8^{18}	WinlndWM^6	ⒻM28000	53	RoyaCurie,MissOutdoors,FoxyToy	12
31Dec81-3SA	1	:49^1	1:16^2	1:44^{2}hy	9¼	111^5	9^{10}	7^{10}	5^{10}	5$^{9\frac{1}{4}}$	WinlndWM^3	ⒻM32000	38	FortyKrts,StreetLover,BemofHop	10
16Dec81-1Hol	1	:47^3	1:13^3	1:40^{4}ft	12	117	10^{10}	9^{11}	5^7	5^9	Sibille R^{10}	ⒻM32000	53	PorFavor,StrwberryStick,WrAhed	10
19Nov81-3Hol	1	:47^4	1:13^3	1:39 ft	15	111^5	7^9	3$^{\frac{1}{2}}$	3$^{2\frac{1}{2}}$	5$^{6\frac{1}{2}}$	WinlndWM^7	ⒻM32000	64	SrtogRoxi,DomnntL,StrwbrrySlck	10
22Oct81-3SA	1	:47	1:12	1:37^{2}ft	23	110^5	8$^{3\frac{3}{4}}$	7$^{7\frac{1}{4}}$	—	—	WinlndWM^2	ⒻM32000	—	AegenQuen,TriplMch,BorrowdMid	10

22Oct81—Fell

Jun 14 GG 5f ft 1:03^1 h — Jun 9 GG 4f ft :50^1 h — Jun 2 GG 5f ft 1:03^3 h — May 17 GG 4f ft :48^4 h

This one represents a bit of an unusual pattern, since she scored her first victory against winners, not against maidens. This speaks of some rather unusual confidence by the trainer, even though she was going from a maiden special weight race to a $16,000 claiming race which most would agree is a drop in class. Look down the past performances and note that between January 29 and March 10, 1982, there was a layoff where this young filly was shipped upstate from Santa Anita to Golden Gate, changing racing circuits. She ran against winners three times in a row in higher priced claiming races, with only modest success, and then ran in a maiden special weight race. The reason a line was drawn between the races of April 27 and May 19, 1982, was, as noted above, that a drop in class appeared to be occurring, sufficient to start a new form cycle.

While moving from a maiden special weight down to a $16,000 claimer might not always represent a drop in class, the fact that Luciernago had been running against $20,000 and $30,000 claimers indicates without question that the race of May 19 did involve a drop in class. She scored her first victory and has had a 28 day layoff between the last race at $16,000 and today's race at $16,000. The 28 day layoff requires us to start a new form cycle beginning with the race before us.

You will also note three intervening workouts since her last race, two at five furlongs, which you will hear much more about later in this book. While the three workouts indicate that Luciernago was not exactly on the shelf, it is somewhat puzzling why she was not entered for four weeks. The five furlong workout two days before the race definitely demonstrated fitness, and consequently, the victory on June 16 against a so-so field is far from surprising.

Let us do a few more form cycle exercises to be sure you are on the right track, although in the many examples that will be dealt with in this book, you will have ample opportunity to become familiar with form cycles. Take a grass race and integrate this factor into our form cycles. Look at the ninth race at Hollywood Park on June 17, where we can see the conditions of the race and the form of Janets Kindy, the second place finisher.

9th Hollywood

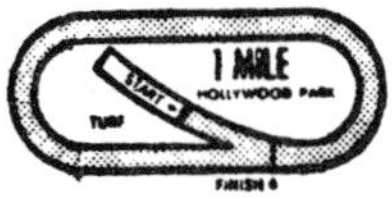

1 MILE. (TURF). (1.33⅗) CLAIMING. Purse $26,000. Fillies and mares. 4-year-olds and upward. Weight, 122 lbs. Non-winners of two races since April 18 allowed 3 lbs.; a race since then, 6 lbs. Claiming price $50,000; for each $2,500 to $45,000 allowed 2 lbs. (Races when entered for $40,000 or less not considered.)

Janets Kindy *
Own.—Bloom Jr & Vienna Jr — **112**
B. f. 4, by Bold Joey—Winaza, by Windsor Ruler
Br.—Dante T C (Cal)
Tr.—Vienna Darrell — $45,000
Lifetime 19 3 1 2 $56,450

1982	6	0	0	0		$4,675
1981	13	3	1	2		$51,775
Turf	2	0	0	0		$1,125

8Apr82-7SA	6½f :222	:451	1:153ft	29	115	78¼	77¾	77½	45	Sibille R7	ⒻAw22000	87	MirculousKte,SMyAgnt,IrishO'Brin	7
25Mar82-5SA	6½f :214	:443	1:151ft	12	116	712	714	59¼	58	DelhoussyeE5	Ⓕ 50000	86	Grndp'sPooky,MirculousKt,Ancmu	7
[illegible]Mar82-7SA	6f :22	:452	1:093ft	11	116	87	87¼	77¼	57¼	Olivares F3	Ⓕ c40000	83	HomeRunGl,SweetSket,RingofErin	8
28Feb82-5SA	1 1/16 :461	1:102	1:423ft	28	1095	69	812	813	812	Steiner J J3	ⒻAw25000	76	ScrletO'Wonder,Lur'sJet,Delightdly	8
12Feb82-4SA	1 1/16 :484	1:132	1:484gd	53	114	45	46	48	49	McHrgDG2	ⒻAw25000	48	CourtlyCannon,Mayan,GraniDuques	5
23Jan82-7SA	6½f :22	:451	1:164ft	12	114	79¼	75¾	51½	76¾	Olivares F7	ⒻAw22000	79	Parky'sFancy,Inisfada,OceanSunset	8
[illegible]Dec81-6SA	6f :212	:441	1:092ft	22	114	97¾	811	1010	88¾	McCrrnCJ5	ⒻAw22000	82	Raja'sSong,AmigaLG.,MissPeruvin	11
8Jly81-7Hol	1 1/16 Ⓣ:46	1:102	1:414fm	37	117	55	53	62½	65¾	Rivera MA6	ⒻAw24000	84	FrenchChrmer,Cndidly,TrickyF'nss	8
27Jun81-8Hol	1⅛ :472	1:122	1:50 ft	98	121	43	4¾	76¼	712	RiveraMA2	ⒻHol Oaks	67	PstForgetting,BHetomn,GlittrHittr	7
13Jun81-8GG	1 1/16 Ⓣ:471	1:12	1:44 fm	11	120	53½	52½	67	67½	LosthC4	ⒻHgh Estmt	74	Glitter Hitter, ‡HailLake,PlusU'tra	11

13Jun81—Placed fifth through disqualification

Jun 11 Hol 6f ft 1:134 h — Jun 5 Hol 5f ft 1:003 h — May 31 Hol 6f ft 1:134 h — May 26 Hol 5f ft 1:002 h

This high-priced claiming event carries a purse of $26,000, which is more than the value of some stakes races at many tracks. We start by drawing a line at the top of the past performances, since Janets Kindy has not run in 39 days, which means that her effort today will start a new form cycle. We see also the string of four workouts since her last race, a matter that will be discussed when we come to recent action as a form factor. But you can be sure that these five and six furlong sessions in the morning will make this filly a factor to be considered today.

The line between her races on March 25 and March 10 shows a claim at $40,000. This now helps you evaluate what went on after trainer Vienna took charge. He ran her in a sprint with a claiming price of $50,000, and then in an allowance race with a $22,500 purse, which is somewhat less than the claiming purse in today's race. There is also the shift to the turf today, despite having a poor grass record. But since this is the third race under the new ownership without a meaningful pay check (the fourth place finish on April 8 brought in a small amount, but hardly enough to make a dent in the $40,000 investment), you can be sure that the new ownership is looking for some money, if at all possible.

You see also some experimentation between distance races and sprints, but this was done by the previous owners before the claim.

You see other form cycle lines for a layoff between July and December and for a substantial drop in class between June 27, 1981 and July 8, from stakes races down to allowance competition. For Janets Kindy, there is no prolonged change from grass to dirt and vice versa to illustrate that sort of a new form cycle.

The dirt-to-grass form cycle shows up a little better in the past performances of Burst of Song, although these changes were accompanied by a maiden victory in one instance and a change of circuit in another.

Burst of Song — B. f. 4, by Cannonade—Gourmet Lark, by T V Lark

Own.—Waranch R — 112 — Br.—Bolas G A (Ky) — Tr.—Stute Warren — $45,000

1982	5	1	1	0		$8,745
1981	8	M	1	1		$7,830
Lifetime	17	1	2	1	$16,875	
Turf	9	0	1	1		$3,380

3Jun82-5Hol	1 1/16 Ⓣ:46^3 1:10^4 1:42^2 fm	45	114	6$^{9\frac{1}{2}}$ 8$^{8\frac{3}{4}}$ 7$^{4\frac{1}{2}}$ 6$^{4\frac{3}{4}}$	Ortega LE^6	ⒻAw22000	82	Latrone, Opalescence, Tree House	8
6May82-8Hol	1 1/16 Ⓣ:47 1:11^2 1:42^1 fm	30	114	3^1 1^{hd} 3$^{\frac{1}{2}}$ 5$^{7\frac{3}{4}}$	Ortega LE^3	ⒻAw22000	80	Creatively, Tree House, Latrone	10
29Apr82-8GG	1 Ⓣ:46^4 1:11^1 1:37 fm	4	114	6^5 6$^{6\frac{3}{4}}$ 5^{13} 6$^{9\frac{1}{2}}$	Munoz E^5	ⒻAw15000	73	Muffle, Pale Purple, Fast Tracie	8
7Apr82-4GG	6f :23^1 :47^2 1:13^4 ft	*3-5	119	1^{hd} 2^{hd} 1$^{\frac{1}{2}}$ 1$^{\frac{1}{2}}$	Munoz E^6	ⒻMdn	70	Burst of Song,OnYourLeft,Cruzella	6
2Apr82-5GG	6f :22^3 :45^4 1:12 sy	4	114	4$^{3\frac{1}{2}}$ 2^3 2^4 2^6	Munoz E^8	Mdn	73	Mnotti,BurstofSong,APrsntofSong	8
10Dec81-5Hol	1 1/8 Ⓣ:49^2 1:14 1:50^2 fm	39	114	2^1 3^{nk} 6$^{4\frac{1}{2}}$ 8$^{6\frac{3}{4}}$	CastnedM^1	ⒻAw19000	71	Balsam, Leading Dancer, Sajama	9
17Jly81-6Hol	1 1/16 Ⓣ:47^2 1:11^3 1:43^1 fm	3$\frac{3}{4}$	115	4^2 2^{hd} 2^{hd} 3$^{1\frac{3}{4}}$	McHargue DG^4	ⒻMdn	81	RealWisdom,Colacka,BurstofSong	10
1Jly81-3Hol	1 Ⓣ:47^4 1:12^2 1:36^2 fm	3$\frac{1}{2}$	116	2^2 2$^{\frac{1}{2}}$ 2^{hd} 2no	DelhoussyeE^4	Ⓕ 40000	87	CllMeGorgeous,BurstofSong,Mirge	7
19Jun81-6Hol	1 1/16 Ⓣ:46^1 1:11^1 1:42^4 fm	5$\frac{1}{2}$	115	7^{13} 8$^{8\frac{1}{2}}$ 6$^{3\frac{3}{4}}$ 5$^{6\frac{1}{2}}$	Gilligan L^2	ⒻMdn	79	Aggrndizement,Ambern,WingingIt	10

Laying out defined form cycles where turn racing is concerned is often somewhat difficult, since some horses quickly move back and forth between dirt and grass. A look at Delta Green, out of that same ninth race at Hollywood on June 17, shows how this works.

Delta Green — Gr. f. 4, by Orbit Ruler—Audrey of Greece, by Isle of Greece

Br.—Cofer R S (Cal) — 1982 6 2 0 1 $30,900

Own.—Friendly E — 119 — Tr.—Fulton John W — $50,000 — 1981 18 3 4 2 $62,975

Lifetime 25 6 4 3 $98,275 — Turf 11 2 1 0 $29,900

6May82-7Hol	7f	:221 :443 1:22 ft	*8-5	116	32	31½	42	1hd	McCarron CJ1	Ⓕ 50000	87	DeltGreen,Messround,GrdeningGirl	5
28Apr82-3Hol	1 1/16	:472 1:112 1:431ft	*6-5	116	1½	1hd	11	1¾	Diaz A L6	Ⓕ c40000	79	DeltaGreen,Messaround,Doon'sLdy	6
16Apr82-5SA	1⅛Ⓣ	:4541:1021:48 fm	5½	117	1hd	1hd	31½	610	Diaz A L6	ⒻAw30000	77	Pink Safir, Mayan, Maple Tree	7
3Apr82-7SA	1 1/16	:462 1:11 1:431ft	10	118	1hd	1½	2hd	31¼	Diaz A L7	ⒻAw30000	83	Delightedly,TournmentStr,DeltGren	7
5Mar82-5SA	1⅛Ⓣ	:4611:1021:473fm	9½	117	1½	41¼	66½	87¾	Hawley S3	ⒻAw30000	81	PrincessGyle,MpleTree,PrincessB	10
20Feb82-6SA	1	:444 1:092 1:342ft	10	118	23	33	58	617	GuerraWA2	ⒻAw30000	80	Cat Girl, LovelyRobbery,MapleTree	8
21Dec81-5Hol	1 Ⓣ	:4621:1031:354fm	6	112	11½	1hd	11	11¼	VlenzulPA6	ⒻAw22000	90	Delta Green, Damariscotta, Muffle	7
18Nov81-5SA	1 1/16	:453 1:101 1:421ft	9½	114	15	11½	21	22¼	VlenzulPA1	ⒻAw28000	87	Colacka, Delta Green, Retracking	8
28Oct81-9SA	1⅛Ⓣ	:4641:12 1:502fm	15	1115	1½	1½	3½	45	LmbertCT4	ⒻAw28000	70	BeeaScout,OrangeLeaf,MaudGonne	7
10Oct81-5SA	1⅛Ⓣ	:4611:1041:492fm	11	1115	12½	13	2½	53	Perez J L8	ⒻAw26000	77	Potter, Granja Deseo, Grasiosa	10

Jun 11 Hol 6f ft 1:15 h — Jun 6 Hol 4f ft :504 h — Apr 24 Hol 5f ft :594 h

The major point with this horse is to remind you that it is best to require two consecutive races under the same general conditions before we place a new form cycle label on the changed condition. Note how Delta Green was moved back and forth from turf to dirt throughout her recent past. If you drop down to the race of October 28, 1981, the second turf race in succession, you will see the next effort on the dirt, which, standing alone, does not signify a new form cycle. Then, after a layoff, she was back on the grass, then another layoff, and then back on the dirt, and back to the turf once more at Santa Anita on March 5, 1982. Things apparently were not going too well and we see once again a layoff of 29 days to April 3, 1982, and back on the dirt again. In each instance, we drew lines to mark new form cycles because of the layoffs, and not because of the single grass races interspersed with dirt races.

This constant switching from dirt to grass and back to dirt again in the allowance ranks produced very little, and after the turf race on April 16, Delta Green was put back on the dirt once more with a claiming price tag of $40,000. She picked up the prize money but a new owner moved into the claim box. Thus, we draw a line after her April 28 race to show a new form cycle. This reveals that the new owner made a quick recovery of that outlay on May 6 at seven furlongs, still on the dirt. But now, in today's race, after another layoff, we find Delta Green once more running on the grass.

What is going on here? Apparently there is some versatility with this filly, since she does show two victories on the grass. She went off as the third choice in the betting but finished far back in the pack, ninth in a field of ten.

This should be enough to demonstrate how we lay out form cycles, and since you will be seeing many of them hereafter, you will become quite familiar with form cycles and be able to establish them quickly.

How Better Horses and Better Tracks Affect Form Cycles

There is another significant factor that must be taken into account as we deal with form cycles. The quality of the horse and the quality of the racetrack involved—which in the end gets down to money—has an effect on form cycles that the careful handicapper cannot afford to ignore.

Quality of horses and racing run in tiers, all related to such essential ingredients as purse distribution and betting handle, the necessary fuel to propel the operation. At the top of the structure, we have the two outstanding major racing centers, New York and southern California.

Below this first rung comes a good, high class second level, sometimes not far behind at all. In this category are tracks such as Monmouth Park, Meadowlands, Oaklawn Park, Keeneland, Arlington, and Hialeah and Gulfstream in their major seasons.

It is difficult to draw a line at the next level, since it almost blends into the second tier, with tracks such as Ak-Sar-Ben, Churchill Downs, the three major Maryland ovals, Pimlico, Laurel, and Bowie; Keystone, Calder, Hawthorne, Bay Meadows, Golden Gate, Woodbine, Fairgrounds, Louisiana Downs, and Fort Erie and Suffolk Downs during their summer meets. We are not trying to get into a debate over the relative merit of tracks, but are merely trying to point out that certain class and purse levels are maintained, and that these class and purse levels have a great influence on how form cycles unfold.

Let us start with the significant change that always initiates a new form cycle, the layoff. Owners and trainers seem to give high valued stock more frequent layoffs, and thus launch them into more separate form cycles. At the very bottom of the class ladder at the cheaper tracks, where horses run in claiming races for as low as $1,500, any layoff is rare. The pressing need for cash to pay the bills requires an animal constantly to be cranked up for a race, unless the horse's physical problems are so severe that it must be taken out of competition. At these minor racing circuits it is common to see a horse run thirty or forty times in a year, while at Belmont and Hollywood Park, this is nearly unheard of.

This phenomenon runs up and down the price ladder. High valued horses get greater care, and when they have slight pains, they are permitted to take time off. At some of the cheaper tracks, it is not uncommon to see an entire field come on the track in which every horse is wearing front bandages. They have to stay in competition with the hope of winning some money.

Likewise, at lesser tracks, there is less experimentation with such variables as class, distance, and track surface. High priced horses that do not return early dividends may be dropped quickly down the class ladder, or moved to distance races or to the grass in an effort to find out if their better breeding will lead to a reversal of slow earnings. Lower valued horses, on the other hand, usually reach their class level much quicker and become established at that level. A horse running at $5,000 or $8,000 at Bowie or Keystone, by the time he is four years old, is not going very far up the class ladder, and there are not too many lower levels at which to place him. These cheaper horses also find their best distances earlier, possibly because they are run more often, and are not likely to be moved from sprints to distances and back and forth as much as better animals.

What all this means is that you will find fewer form cycles as you descend the class and quality ladder among horses and tracks. This makes the beginning of a new form cycle at a smaller track even more important, as you will learn. You may be confronted with a past performance history of ten races where not a single line will be drawn across your *Racing Form* because there are no defined cycles. All ten races may be one form cycle, and here the last race of the horse under study becomes critically important.

All these variables add to the complexity and even the fascination of this difficult game of handicapping. But where form is concerned, the first crucial step in evaluating any horse is to define and lay out the current form cycle. For example, at a major track, the fact that a horse's last ten races show no intervening layoffs of any kind indicate immediately that a rather sound, steady animal is out there on the track today, one likely to give a reasonably good performance near to the top of his ability. You need to know that.

Then, where we have defined form cycles, you will see how important it is to rate a horse within his current form cycle, and then relate that to how he has performed within other distinct form cycles. The examples we gave a few pages back of horses being switched back and forth in distance illustrates how looking at past form cycles gives you an idea of how the horse is being handled and what his trainer expects of him.

All in all, laying out specific form cycles, from ten past races all within one cycle to none within the new cycle just beginning, tells you something about the horse under consideration and should lead to a better insight into how your horse will run today.

3 The First Form Factor: Recent Action

ONE OF HANDICAPPING'S MOST ELEMENTARY REQUIREMENTS is to consider how recently a horse ran in competition. An animal without action in the last six months is usually disregarded quickly. A horse coming right back after a recent race is considered, and usually rightly so, as being in good form.

Always the question is, where does one draw the line? At what point do you start downgrading a horse's chances because he lacks recent action? How many days since his last race will he hold the form he showed in his previous effort? Almost every writer on the subject of handicapping has been compelled to at least try to come up with some line-drawing. In *Investing at the Racetrack* I treated any horse that had run in the past 28 days as a bona fide contender. Some say 30 days, which is not much different from the line of four weeks that I used. But is this good enough? Are there finer lines that will make your handicapping more effective, that will allow you to play a possible winner and slide away from a horse that may lose because of lack of recent action?

Every sports fan knows that human athletes, after they take time off from their performances, may not be in top trim their next time out. A baseball pitcher who misses a couple of turns on the mound may need a little extra work to regain his sharpness. The tennis star who misses a few tournaments, for whatever reason, must work extra hard to get back to the form that makes the difference between winning and losing. Horses get hurt and get tired and when they do, they have to be rested, and like their human counterparts, they usually need periods of work to regain their form.

But what about workouts between races? Can a trainer put his horse on the track in the morning and work him enough to make him competitive in his next start? Workouts are extremely difficult to gauge, because their reported times often do not tell us very much. The exercise rider may carry much greater weight than a horse would have to carry in a race, he may keep the horse wide, or the dogs—or inner rail—may be up, or there may be no real effort made to push the horse. For such reasons, the times of works, except very fast ones, are not of major significance.

Many research hours have gone into studying workouts as an element of recent action. We will start our guidelines on recent action with workouts, and see what we can do with them.

The "Fabulous" Five Furlong Workout

The one kind of workout that stands out in every study I have made is the five furlong work. Good horses in New York and California often go further to work six furlongs and sometimes seven (and even eight), but the five panel work is the common strong one at the better tracks. For our purposes, however, as a conditioner, we shall classify six furlong and seven furlong workouts along with five furlongs as a major element in getting a horse ready to run.

A fast five furlong workout is always something to consider. Based on my studies, any work of five furlongs or longer must be factored in when a handicapper deals with recent action.

In the comprehensive study of 433 races that you will read so much about in this book, I kept a careful distinction between Belmont and the other tracks. As tracks descend in class value, based upon the prices of horses and the size of purses, the five furlong workout shrinks in frequency along with the lower class levels. At a minor racetrack you may never see a five furlong workout reported in your *Racing Form's* past performances. At these ovals, even a plus workout may be rare. As our workout story unfolds, you will see more clearly how this comes about.

At Belmont and in Southern California, five furlong works abound in rather considerable numbers. Among the horses working that distance, there will be animals with miserable form who are out in the morning for a five-eighths turn, which will hardly convert them into contenders in their next effort. Therefore, to make any study of the five furlong workout meaningful in New York, I concentrated on the first two favorites in the 97 races at Belmont that were analyzed.

I first searched for horses that have run within 21 days and worked five furlongs (or six furlongs or seven furlongs) in the intervening period. I found 26 such horses among the first two favorites in the 11 racing days under survey. This amounts to 26 out of a total of 194 horses, or roughly about a 12% frequency. This low frequency among the favorites is not surprising because there will be many favored horses coming back in seven to ten days who may have sparkling form and have no occasion to show a five furlong workout, or any at all, for that matter. Among these 26 top favored horses, there were occasions when both the two leaders in betting action had the same five furlong preparation. But, taking these 26 horses, without any attempt to handicap them, or separate them in any manner, and playing them both when both qualified as five furlong workers, I recorded 11 winners. These 11 winners returned a total of $69.80 against the $52 that would have represented a $2 flat bet to win on every one of them. The purpose in telling you this is not to recommend a system in any manner, but is to show you the effectiveness of the five furlong workout for good horses who have run within 21 days and are strongly played at the windows.

On the down side of the five furlong workout study at Belmont, horses running back within 21 days that were in poor form and were not one of the first two betting choices did almost nothing in their next races, as the lengthy workout did very little to improve their lackluster form.

Thus, the first category of impressive five furlong works concerns the two top betting choices who have run within the past three weeks, where they do consistently well in their next race.

The second major area where five furlong workouts earn their rating of "fabulous" comes with horses that have not run within the past 21 days. Some of them have run in slightly less than four weeks, others have taken longer layoffs, and some have worked five furlongs as well as other distances as their trainers ready them for a return to competition.

Again, analyzing the first and second betting choices at Belmont, once more without any effort to handicap them in any manner—taking lower class horses running over their heads, horses with poor ability times, and the like—there were 32 coming within this category in the 11 days under study. There were ten winners among them, and the prices, even for the first two betting choices, moved up to better levels, showing two winners in the $11 range and another paying $10.20. If all 32 horses were bet to win, the $64 invested in $2 tickets brought home $82.40, again a good flat bet profit.

Now, looking again at the 194 horses making up first and second betting choices in the 97 races, we find 58 entries with five furlong workouts. They produced 21 winners with no other handicapping of any kind. The 58 plays would have required $116 at the windows, with the return bringing in $152.20. Hmm, not bad at all, you say!

But before you begin turning handsprings, I must tell you that the results at Belmont are somewhat different from those at the other tracks studied, for which there are very sound reasons.

When we total up all the Belmont five furlong workers who had not run in 21 days, regardless of their odds, and then lumped first time starters, horses that had been away for a year, hapless maidens, or any other old creature strong enough to run five furlongs, there were 130 horses to be found. In addition, there were another 74 non-favorites who had run in less than 21 days and worked five furlongs since their last race, but we must leave them aside for the moment. The longer vacationing horses turned in ten winners, some of them with bountiful prices, with a total payoff of $224, which would show a loss because of the $260 required to bet, but this is hardly disturbing when you consider the mass throw-in. If one applied even the most rudimentary handicapping methods, you could whittle the 130 horses down very quickly, such as throwing out first time starters with very slow works, of which there were many.

In summary, the five furlong workout at Belmont is quite common, and highly benefits the horses that are well enough considered to be among the first two betting choices. My less extensive California observations lead me to believe that the same pattern occurs on the Santa Anita-Hollywood Park circuit.

Now, if we step down the class ladder just slightly, we can see how horses with five furlong workouts fared at Meadowlands, where 130 races in 13 days were studied. Once again, we start with the first two betting choices. Since there were not too many that had raced within 21 days and worked five furlongs before running again, I looked at every single first and second betting choice, regardless of form and regardless of how long these horses had been away from the races.

There were but 37 in this category with five furlong workouts, a substantial falloff from the Belmont frequency, but 16 of them won, a nifty 43%. If $74 had been wagered, the return was a lusty $127.20, a rather substantial flat bet profit at a track where favorites were not faring well.

An interesting observation at this point was that at both Belmont and Meadowlands there were not many of these horses coming in second. They either won or were back in the pack. Place betting, which has always had a strong appeal as an insurance wager, would have done little in these circumstances.

Next, I looked into *all* Meadowlands horses that had not run in the past 21 days but had recently worked five furlongs, and found 87 in this group. There were another 49 horses that had run within 21 days who were not among the two betting favorites, and they were not considered, because, just as at Belmont, they rarely won. This is a very important point—do not forget it! A horse working after a poor race in a fresh time span simply does not appear to benefit very much from the five furlong workout—he is working off bad form and will likely repeat his weak effort.

The Meadowlands group of 87 who had not raced within 21 days, but had five furlong workouts, again included first time starters, horses coming from long layoffs, horses with miserable form (with the only requirement that they not have run within the past 21 days, which would give them some opportunity to allow rest and rehabilitation to negate their woeful form), and any and all that could meet this simple standard. There were 11 winners in this group, not bad at all when you consider that this is better than

12.6% of the whole gang.

The returns were stunning, largely because of two blockbuster prices. Off the $174 that would have been required to bet $2 on every one of them, the 11 winners returned $308.00. While several paid in the $20 range, if one eliminated the two monster returns ($82.20 and $68.80, although neither horse looked that bad), you would still have $157 for the $170 involved. The big returns always distort studies like this, and I am inherently suspicious of them, since some system sellers load up their "workouts" with one or two of this kind to show their "magic formula for riches." And, of course, you could go for months without stumbling onto such high paying winners again.

But when I went on to Keystone and Bowie, I could hardly discount the big prices, since they continued to come in. But now we are beginning to step down to a slightly lower level of track, since neither Keystone nor Bowie quite measures up to Meadowlands in horse value. Consequently, there were fewer five furlong works at these tracks, as we begin to see the descending level at work. Even when horses are of only slightly less value, which is enough, they cannot seem to work the demanding distance of five furlongs and longer the way good allowance and high priced claiming horses can be worked.

A close look at Bowie shows how this comes into play. In the 98 races (involving approximately 800 horses all told, figuring an average of eight entries per race), there were only 69 horses with recent five furlong workouts. At Belmont, in the exact same time frame, there were 269 horses working five furlongs or longer, almost three times as many. Considering the small number of horses in this category at Bowie, we did not divide the study into horses that had run within 21 days and those away longer.

The first two betting choices at Bowie provided only 22 entries with recent five furlong workouts in the 11 days under study. Seven won, returning $34.40, for a flat bet loss from the $44 that would have been required to play them all. At Keystone, almost the same picture emerged for the first two favorites. But at Bowie, when all 69 horses that had recently worked five furlongs or longer were lumped into one group, and every single one was played, without exception, no matter what, there were 11 winners, averaging one per racing card, or 16% of the whole—again, an excellent showing. When all horses were thrown in, the big prices rolled out, and the total return, favorites, longshots, and all, was $152.40 against the $138 that would have been required for the $2 bet. Once more, a flat bet profit. And at Keystone, there was also a slight flat bet profit when all horses were considered.

Now, you may see why I call the five furlong workout "fabulous." It opens up so many handicapping possibilities. I had been observing the effect of five furlong workouts for some time, but until I went through the hard chore of checking and tabulating these 433 races, I had no precise handle on what kind of bottom line might emerge.

If one eliminated the big group of Belmont horses that were not among the first two favorites and had run within 21 days, and took all the others at all tracks, a flat bet play on every remaining horse would have scored a healthy flat bet profit. But the beauty of this is that with some elementary handicapping, this can be improved upon readily. Here is where the long shot players can take heart, for in addition to the two big balloons at Meadowlands, there were two Bowie horses at better than $40, there was one $57 price at Belmont, and many others turned up in the $20 range.

But the real significance of these remarkable figures is that they give us a new insight into the value of the five furlong workout as an element of recent action.

From all this, I learned something that I had begun to suspect, but was never sure about until the hard work was done. A five furlong workout is indeed sufficient to prepare a horse for a race, within normal handicapping concepts. Taking the other side of the coin, I will no longer ever again throw out a horse that has not run in months, as long as he shows a recent five furlong workout, regardless of the time that is posted for it. The same concept applies, of course, to the six furlong workout, and even to the seven furlong effort, which does not occur nearly so often.

Now that we have accepted the five furlong workout as a bona fide element in considering recency as a form factor, there are still a number of considerations to deal with. In the use of our rating symbols, do we give it a + or an N, or even something less? In aiding our handicapping, we want to reserve a plus (+) in the recency factor for only those situations where it really counts as a strong positive sign. Consequently, since recency deals with time, we cannot give a + for a five furlong workout, except under the very special condition of an unusually fast work. For example, any recent five furlong bullet workout (which means the fastest by any horse at that track, for that distance, on that day, is signified in *Daily Racing Form* by a heavy dark circle next to the time) will entitle the horse to a plus.

We have repeatedly stated that, to be considered relevant, any five furlong workout must be recent—it must come within a proper time frame to be counted. Let us study a good example of what not to overlook.

Good Property ✱ — Ch. c. 3, by Rise High—Commercial, by T V Lark
Br.—Factor S (Cal) — 1982 9 2 1 0 $16,515
Own.—Perillo Mrs J — **114** — Tr.—Hess R B — $25,000 — 1981 3 1 0 0 $6,600
Lifetime 12 3 1 0 $23,115 — Turf 1 0 0 0

27May82-9GG	1$\frac{1}{16}$	:46^4	1:11^4	1:45^{1}ft	4$\frac{1}{4}$	114	3^3	2^1	2^{hd}	2$\frac{3}{4}$	Munoz E^5	20000	76	FrofCrton,GoodProprty,CombtEch	7
13May82-7GG	1$\frac{1}{16}$	:47^4	1:12^2	1:46^{3}ft	*2$\frac{1}{4}$	114	66$\frac{1}{2}$	65$\frac{3}{4}$	66$\frac{1}{2}$	4^{12}	Munoz E^4	25000	58	MuchaRis,CombtEcho,Michi'sSilor	8
28Apr82-8GG	1 ⓣ	:47^2	1:12^1	1:37^{4}fm	8$\frac{1}{2}$	115	2$\frac{1}{2}$	3$^1\frac{1}{2}$	6^8	6^{11}	Caballero R^7	Aw16000	67	TheBrginHunter,ThreDocs,Cvllrizzo	7
16Apr82-8GG	6f	:22	:45	1:10 ft	26	120	10^{12}	9^{11}	89$\frac{1}{2}$	77$\frac{3}{4}$	Munoz E^3	Aw13000	81	JetTravel,SirMacmillion,CyneWho	11
26Mar82-7GG	1	:47	1:11^3	1:38^{2}gd	3	113	21$\frac{1}{2}$	2^{hd}	2^1	1no	Munoz E^3	Aw13000	76	GoodProprty,ChnPuzzl,FblosFghtr	7
11Mar82-7GG	1$\frac{1}{16}$	:47^4	1:12^4	1:46^{1}sy	3	114	11$\frac{1}{2}$	1^4	1^6	1^{12}	Winland W M^1	c20000	72	GoodProprty,RnndGrn,CombtEcho	7
3Mar82-1SA	6$\frac{1}{2}$f	:21^3	:44^2	1:17^{2}ft	9	111^5	87$\frac{3}{4}$	88$\frac{1}{2}$	86$\frac{1}{2}$	87$\frac{1}{4}$	Steiner J J^{10}	28000	76	IndinO.,SndsofVegs,ClonmelArms	10
18Feb82-9SA	1	:45^3	1:10^4	1:37^{1}ft	6	116	7^8	6^7	65$\frac{1}{4}$	55$\frac{1}{2}$	Guerra W A^6	32000	77	OneBoldReason,Attempt,ShdyCreer	7
15Jan82-2SA	7f	:22	:44^4	1:23^{2}ft	9$\frac{1}{2}$	120	8^8	109$\frac{3}{4}$	87$\frac{1}{4}$	76$\frac{1}{4}$	DelahoussayeE^8	40000	77	JetPirte,CptinTuffy,OutBeforDwn	12
27Dec81-4SA	1	:47^1	1:12	1:36^{2}ft	18	116	54$\frac{1}{2}$	6^4	66$\frac{1}{2}$	6^{12}	DelhoussyeE^1	Aw20000	75	BargainBlcony,Botrell,AlmoStrnger	8

Jun 12 GG 4f ft :47^1 h ● Jun 6 GG 5f ft 1:00^3 h May 21 GG 5f ft 1:01 h May 7 GG 5f ft 1:03^2 h

From the sixth race at Golden Gate Fields on June 16, 1982, we see Good Property, who has not run in 20 days. You can see that he has posted two workouts in the intervening period, the most recent being a four furlong effort four days before the upcoming race. Immediately preceding that, on June 6, six days before the four furlong workout, we see the five furlong bullet effort. While we do not know how many horses worked five furlongs that day, we could count on several at Golden Gate, and the bullet shows that Good Property went faster at that distance than any other horse working that morning.

While we prefer a five furlong workout as the last one before the race to be run, Good Property's record shows that if it is closely connected in time to an intervening workout, it can be counted. Because of the bullet, we would award Good Property a + for recency.

In order to give a + for the recency factor because of a five furlong work, however, the horse must have run within the past three weeks, or 21 days. If he has been away longer than that time, the five furlong workout would be worth only an N, since even with that kind of workout, a horse away more than three weeks may not have all the sharpness we would want.

An equally important time factor is that all five furlong workouts must be close enough to today's race in order to be counted. Usually, the cutoff can be drawn at 14 days from today's race. If a workout is more remote than that, it will have to be considered as ordinary and evaluated like any other in dealing with recency. You will notice that Good Property's sparkling five furlong workout was ten days before his June 16 race.

Let us look at a quick example of a five furlong workout that would not qualify for any kind of rating, because of the poor time span. From the third race at Belmont on June 17, we have Brenda's A Star, who has not run in 34 days.

Brenda's A Star — Ro. f. 3, by Roanoke Island—Burning Bosun, by Bosun

Br.—Stancer C & Sandra (Md) — 1982 10 0 3 2 $18,040

Own.—Saldo Stables 114 Tr.—Sallusto Justin $47,500 — 1981 9 1 1 4 $10,870

Lifetime 19 1 4 6 $28,910 — Turf 2 0 0 1 $2,820

14May82-5Aqu	1	(T):4841:1331:382fm	12	111	62¾	53	55½	44	Migliore R4	(F) 75000	82	ExplodingWind,MystryWtnss,B•ndn	8
1May82-6Aqu	6f	:224 :471 1:11 ft	10	116	78½	66½	66¾	411	Migliore R4	(F)Aw19000	75	Dance Number, Belonging,Norznda	7
10Apr82-6Aqu	1	:472 1:121 1:39 ft	4¼	116	21½	21½	32	41¾	McCrronG4	(F)Aw20000	69	Brndin,NorthrnSprit,MystryWitnss	8
29Mar82-7Aqu	1	:471 1:123 1:392ft	9	112	64	1hd	2hd	2hd	McCarron G2	(F) 45000	69	AllMyMarys,Brenda'sAStr,Ebullient	7
14Mar82-5Aqu	1⅛	[•]:4921:1421:542ft	12	116	64½	53	54	54¼	McCrronG5	(F)Aw17000	70	Suspicious,MystryWtnss,FoolshSpn	6
3Mar82-6Aqu	1 1/16	[•]:48 1:14 1:461ft	4¾	112	66	32	33	34½	McCarron G4	(F) 45000	77	Decorous,FoolishSpin,Brenda'sAStr	7
13Feb82-9Aqu	170	[•]:4811:1341:444ft	5½	116	86½	67	815	716	MacBethD8	(F)Aw17000	62	ExplodingWnd,LurthLdy,MyGlPolly	9
30Jan82-3Aqu	170	[•]:4831:1321:444ft	5	112	67	45½	22	21¾	Beitia E5	(F) 45000	76	Decorous,Brend'sAStr,ChestrChims	7

May 30 Aqu 5f gd 1:043 b ●Apr 24 Bel 3f ft :343 h Apr 17 Bel 3f ft :383 b

While this filly has been bounced around a bit in her racing conditions, she is starting a new form cycle on June 17, because of the layoff and her substantial drop in class. Her most recent exercise consists of a five furlong workout on May 30, some 18 days prior to the race under review. This workout is thus too stale, and would not be counted at all. As you will see shortly, Brenda's A Star would get a O rating in the recency department as a most unlikely winner.

In addition to the + factor for a bullet workout, we can also give a + rating in one other situation only—when the five furlong workout, while not winning a bullet, is exceptionally fast. This is becomes tougher to judge, however. While we cannot evaluate and downgrade a horse for workouts at slow times, because of too many circumstances of which we know not, we can, however, more easily assess the blistering work. In the east and midwest, any five furlong workout in less than one minute flat, from :59.4 downward, is exceptional, no matter whether it gained a bullet or not. If an eastern horse worked in that kind of time, he merits a +, as long as his last race was within 21 days. If by the time you read this, you can still recall the 1982 Marlboro Cup at Belmont, where Lemhi Gold, an outsider, won decisively, this horse posted a five furlong workout of :57.4 a few days before the race. A work as fast as this did not even win a bullet, as some other speedball must have been flying over the dirt that morning. But it was slightly sensational, nevertheless, showing that Lemhi Gold was full of run, which he demonstrated when he destroyed his field by winning easily.

In dealing with California horses, where the faster surfaces always produce faster times, we require a five furlong work to be one full second faster. A horse must work in less than 59 seconds, which means :58.4 or less, to pick up a + for an exceptionally fast five furlong workout. On the other hand, if you are playing an extremely slow track, such as Calder or Oaklawn, you might want to extend the time for an exceptionally fast five furlong morning effort to less than 1:01, which would mean that a horse doing five furlongs in 1:00.4 or less would win a plus.

Would you put a bullet workout at six furlongs or seven furlongs in the + category? Not at all. No matter how fast a six furlong or seven furlong workout may be, I do not give a + for this kind of work, simply because its length serves a different purpose. Since six furlong and seven furlong workouts are very rare, a horse may pick up a bullet if he is one of only two running that day, and thus the bullet means almost nothing insofar as fast time is concerned. Accordingly, all six furlong and seven furlong workouts are treated like the ordinary five—a good preparation for today's race.

The N rating is our neutral, or non-applicable, rating, and it is far better than the O you will hear a lot about in this book. For all workouts of five, six, or seven furlongs in the last 14 days, if there is no bullet or exceptionally fast time, the N rating is awarded. This rating applies no matter how long the horse has been idle, even if for months. The key things we look for are positives that will show a very strong chance or negatives that will cause us to eliminate the horse altogether as a contender.

Let us repeat the two kinds of ratings we give for a five furlong workout (or six or seven) in the last 14 days before today's race:

+   For five furlong workouts only, where the horse has earned a bullet and has run within 21 days, or has turned in a very fast workout (:59.4 or faster in the east and in :58.4 or faster in California).

N   For workouts of five furlongs or longer that occur within the past 14 days, no matter what the time may be, and no matter how long the horse may have been away from the races. For five furlong workouts that are beyond 14 days from today's race, treat them as any other workout, which may mean they may not count at all.

Before we leave the five furlong workout, is there anything we can do with the very slow five furlong workout, despite our difficulties in evaluating it, and even assuming we know what a very slow five furlong workout is? The one area where it is most reliable is with younger, lightly raced horses, primarily two-year-olds. These juveniles are often worked five furlongs to help them get ready, and when they are pushed this distance, they usually are inclined to do about as well as they can. When a two-year-old shows a workout in 1:05 or slower, you can just about forget him. He is showing no life at all. Early in the three-year-old season, you can also treat lightly raced horses the same way. If they have run five races or less in their lifetime, and show only very slow five furlong works, they are not likely to do very much today, except for the rare situations where they may have shown something in some race in the past.

This is about as far as we can go with slow five furlong works. Older animals may loaf in their workouts, posting turtle-times, and yet the five furlong distance may be all they need to get ready.

How to Deal With Other Workouts

Are workouts other than five furlongs and longer worth evaluating? What do they mean? How do they fit into an analysis of recency for our form ratings?

Let us start with the ordinary four furlong workout, which is probably the most common, or near to it, of all workouts at the better tracks. At lesser plants, the three furlong workout is probably the most frequent. Standing alone, my research shows very little potency for the four furlong workout at better tracks, not much more reliable than the three furlong work as an indicator of what a horse might do. As for three furlong workouts, they simply do not matter, one way or another, as a predictor of how a horse will run.

An extremely fast four furlong workout in :45 and change in New York and :44 and change in southern California may be worth a second look, but because I am not yet persuaded that even this kind of run has the beneficial effect of the five furlong work, there is no basis for giving it any particular meaning.

On the other hand, as we descend the class level to the tracks where horses of lesser value are running, an extremely fast four furlong work may begin to assume some real significance. A bullet four furlong work, because it is the distance worked by so many horses, cannot be disregarded. Likewise, the very fast morning run (:45.4 or less in the east and midwest and :44.4 or less in southern California) takes on some of the same meaning. There is a real possibility that the outstanding four furlong work at the lesser value tracks may have comparable worth to a five furlong work at the top ovals, but again, I have not validated that possibility. Until I am sure about it, it is not safe to treat the fast four furlong workout at any greater level than what is accorded other four furlong workouts.

There is no question about the fact that four furlong workouts are useful conditioners and when we see them showing, they are entitled to some evaluation. We will integrate them into our recency ratings a few paragraphs from now.

But back to the three furlong workout, which I am not sure is worth more than a warmup for a horse. Many trainers use them, of course, for conditioners, particularly as a final tuneup a day or two before the race. While I am sure they are beneficial, and I would never quarrel with any trainer that uses them, when we come down to serious handicapping, there is no evaluation that we can give them as such.

The Potency of the Seven-Day Horse

As we turn from workouts to the fundamentally more important area of when the last race was run, we may begin by looking for positive factors. Is there any time-line from a horse's last race that will tell us something affirmative, or that will give us a strong indication that he will run well today? Indeed there is.

A horse in good enough condition and sufficiently geared to race again within seven days, or less, is easily worth a plus for recent action.

A return to the races within a week may mean several things, all of them positive. You can be reasonably sure of the horse's good condition. The trainer, sensing that his horse is "ready for action" again, is out to take advantage of good form to try to win, and the horse is likely to be placed correctly within the conditions of the race.

You may ask, what about eight days after a race? Again, the line must be drawn somewhere. A trainer may not find the exact race he likes for his horse within a week, but may sight a race on the eighth day where the conditions are more favorable. This surely happens over and over again, but for the purpose of statistical study and sound consideration, let us stay with the seven day "rule." For one thing, it works.

Fewer days than seven are also within the + range. If a horse is coming back in six days, it is the equivalent of a return in seven days. And what my handicapping sons and daughter have always shared with me as the "five-day horse" is even better. For some reason, a return in five days is a sparkling sign of something favorable on the horizon.

And in major stakes races particularly, a strong horse coming back in five days is a definite threat. Many of you may recall a few years back when Summing won the Pennsylvania Derby at Keystone on Memorial Day and came back five days later to beat Pleasant Colony in the Belmont Stakes. A few years before that, Pass Catcher finished a fast closing second in the Jersey Derby on Memorial Day at old Garden State and then moved on to the Belmont five days later to score a convincing victory. I have seen it happen over and over again.

While horses returning in seven days or less are always worthy of strong consideration, you must also be aware that horses coming back off poor form will not be miraculously converted into champions by the mere event of a seven-day return effort. This is particularly evident with horses coming back in five days, where it appears that the trainer is trying to rapidly run the horse back into condition, using the five-day race as a public workout. In my own handicapping, any five-day horse that does not possess other form qualifications set forth in this book is easily discarded. Look at what the form cycle shows and take care not to allow enthusiasm for an early returner to dim your good handicapping judgment.

To test the statistical value of the seven-day horse, I looked at all favorites in my 433 race study. In the entire project, favorites won 31.6% of these races. Any group figures that are better than the overall average ought to have some validity, and the higher the rating the more potent should be the factor.

In these 433 races, there were but 48 favorites returning in seven days or less. This is approximately an 11% frequency, meaning you may average only one per racing card—and of course, on many days, you will find none. Among these 48 favorites returning in seven days or less, 21 of them scored a victory, for a 43.7% return. This, as you can imagine, turns into a solid flat bet profit. For place, there were 29 successful tickets, for a 60.4% return, far better than favorites would normally he expected to do. Among the group of 433 favorites, if we subtract, for comparison purposes, all the seven-day horses from the total, leaving 385 remaining favorites that have not run in seven days, and subtract the 21 victories from the total, the winning percentage of the remaining favorites would be at an almost even 30%. Thus, you can see that the 43.7% winning return for seven-day favorites is far superior to the 30% return for all other favorites in the study. This is why you may easily award a + for seven-day horses.

Results involving horses returning in seven days or less varied from track to track. Second choices in the betting did not make out nearly as well as favorites, but some of this had to do with other form defects they brought along with them. Bear in mind that these figures on horses returning in seven days or less are based solely on recency. Thus, even if their form was poor or they had other form defects, or were lacking in class, they were included. There were also some good long shot winners coming back in seven days or less, particularly at Keystone and Bowie, as you might expect. Even at Meadowlands, almost 10% of all winning horses that were not among the top two betting choices were showing a seven-day return or less. At Belmont, however, the five furlong workout with more valuable animals somewhat takes the place of the quick return to the races. But even there, among the 97 favorites, 12 of them were running back in seven days or less and seven of them won—a very strong showing indeed.

As far as the recency factor is concerned, we will give a + only for a horse returning to the races within seven days or less and to the horse returning in 21 days or less with a bullet five furlong workout or an exceptionally fast five furlong workout. We can now move to some of the neutral and negative factors in the recency area.

Where to Draw the Line on Last Race Recency

Now that we have elevated the horse returning to the races within seven days by giving it a + factor for recent action, we can deal with all other horses and get back to the difficult question of where the line can be drawn for acceptability on the recency factor. How is this affected by class and value of the horses? When is it safe to entirely throw out a horse for lack of recent action?

We want to look at these horses with two objectives in mind. We want to try to include as contenders all those whose recent action still leaves them with a reasonably good chance of winning. And equally important, we want to eliminate and throw out altogether those runners whose lack of recent action renders them poor possibilities for victory today. In *Investing at the Racetrack*, my throw-out rule was 28 days. If a horse had not run in four weeks, he could not be considered (with exceptions for stakes horses with workouts). Of course, if he showed a race within 28 days of today's race, he would be considered.

A lot of subsequent experience and research convinced me that the 28 day line was far too generous in retaining horses as contenders, unless there were some significant workout factors included. There is little doubt that the nearer in time to today's race, the more likely a horse will perform well.

At some point, however, we are compelled to come down to arbitrary line drawing. After considerable experimentation, I began to draw some rigid lines and then began the long testing process. Along with these lines, there was the additional problem of integrating workouts into racing activity to approach the final question of how recent action, or lack of it, affected how the horse would perform today.

This most deliberate line-drawing began with an experimental two weeks, or 14 days. As a matter of fact, relating all recent action in tiers of weeks, from one week to two to three and then to four made a great deal of sense. It was also relatively easier to factor in workouts within these tiers of weeks between races. After considerable tabulation, I began to notice that a number of horses were winning who were returning in 15 days, 16, and even up to 21 days, without any intervening workouts. At first, I placed a doubtful symbol, which I portrayed with the zero and a diagonal through it, like this: ∅. This meant that the horse was not weak enough to throw out altogether, but that extreme caution was required in considering him as a contender. This worked well for a while, but as the research went on and on, and the steady flow of winners falling within the third tier between two and three weeks continued, it began to make less and less sense to place a doubtful tag on the horse returning to the races in 15 to 21 days. While I still prefer my contender to have run as recently as possible, there were enough winners in the 15 to 21 day range so that they could not be dismissed automatically. In our rating method, this meant that an N would have to be applied.

A perfectly good example of the horse coming back in the third tier of weeks from his last race is shown in the fifth race at Hollywood Park on June 16, where the favorite Gringo Jim at 2-1 odds.

5th Hollywood

6 FURLONGS. (1.07¾) CLAIMING. Purse $12,000. 3-year-olds. Weight, 121 lbs. Non-winners of two races since April 18 allowed 3 lbs.; a race since then, 6 lbs. Claiming price $25,000; if for $22,500 allowed 2 lbs. (Races when entered for $20,000 or less not considered.)

Gringo Jim ✲					Dk. b. or br. c. 3, by Gallant Romeo—Zonta, by Dr Fager							
					Br.—Tartan Farms Corp (Fla)			1982	5	1	1	0	$12,950
Own.—Tartan Stable				**115**	Tr.—Lukas D Wayne	$25,000		1981	0	M	0	0
					Lifetime	5 1 1 0	$12,950					
30May82-5Hol	6f :221 :452 1:112ft	27 117	6¹ 66½ 52½ 2ʰᵈ	Pincay L Jr⁹	40000	80 Nat's Penny,GringoJim,Insearchof 10
3Apr82-5SA	6f :22 :452 1:093ft	42 120	75¼ 8¹² 7¹⁷ 8¹⁸	Lipham T⁵	Aw20000	72 B.RichGeorg,Polly'sRulr,Accousticl 9
31Jan82-2SA	1₁₆:454 1:102 1:432ft	28 116	2ʰᵈ 3½ 79¾ 9¹⁸	ValenzuelPA⁹ Aw20000		66 Turbulation, Ask Me, Keno Hill 10
20Jan82-6SA	6½f :22 :454 1:192sy	10 118	2¹ 1½ 12½ 1²	McCarron C J⁵	Mdn	73 Gringo Jim, Idaho, Sir Pele 8
10Jan82-6SA	6f :214 :451 1:094ft	17 118	83¾10¹¹10¹⁵10²²	McCarron C J³	Mdn	67 JournytS,Htmoto,ConsciousEffort 10

May 27 Hol 4f ft :512 h   May 21 Hol 4f ft :492 h   May 14 Hol 3f ft :364 h

He has not run in 17 days or worked in the intervening period. Any experienced handicapper would quickly recognize, however, that this horse showed all the signs otherwise of a very juicy play at odds of 2-1. This lightly raced colt was trained by Wayne Lukas, one of the top handlers in the Los Angeles area, was dropping in class (almost suspiciously so, in fact), and had run extremely well in his last race.

You simply could not eliminate Gringo Jim from consideration because he had not run or worked in 17 days.

In this kind of race, it always pays to take a look at what the competition reveals. Gringo Jim was well ahead of the second choice on the board, Extra Quick, who went off at 4-1.

Extra Quick — Ro. g. 3, by Messenger of Song—Trishlyn, by Performance
Br.—Humes Mr-Mrs W A (Cal) — 1982 6 1 0 0 $6,950
Own.—Four D Stable **115** Tr.—Hartstone George D $25,000 — 1981 4 1 1 0 $8,900
Lifetime 10 2 1 0 $15,850

30May82-5Hol	6f	$:22^1$	$:45^2$	$1:11^2$ft	8	116	$9^{1\frac{3}{4}}$	$5^{3\frac{1}{2}}$	$6^{5\frac{1}{2}}$	$7^{7\frac{1}{4}}$	Castaneda M^5	40000	73	Nat's Penny,GringoJim,Insearchof	10
15May82-2Hol	$1\frac{1}{16}$	$:46^4$	$1:11^3$	1:44 ft	*$2\frac{1}{4}$	116	$2^{\frac{1}{2}}$	3^1	3^3	$10^{9\frac{1}{4}}$	McCarron C J^1	c32000	66	Jam Man, Carrie's Ten, ClubFlush	11
29Apr82-5Hol	6f	:22	$:44^3$	$1:09^4$ft	$3\frac{1}{4}$	115	$2^{\frac{1}{2}}$	2^{hd}	$1^{\frac{1}{2}}$	$1^{4\frac{1}{2}}$	Guerra W A^4	20000	88	ExtrQuick,OleKingTuck,Jo'sTribut	10
8Apr82-2SA	6f	$:21^4$	:45	$1:09^2$ft	35	117	$4^{4\frac{1}{2}}$	4^6	$4^{6\frac{1}{2}}$	4^6	Guerra W A^1	[S] 20000	85	Chris's Lad,Vavavavoom,BrightIsle	9
5Mar82-1SA	6f	$:21^4$	$:44^4$	$1:10^3$ft	13	118	5^4	12^{15}	12^{19}	12^{12}	Sibille R^2	20000	73	Mchll'sDrm,Prt'sOvr,Chcr'sOrphn	12
12Feb82-1SA	6f	$:22^2$	$:45^3$	$1:11^4$gd	13	116	$4^{1\frac{3}{4}}$	8^{13}	8^{17}	9^{25}	Sibille R^1	32000	54	L'Cap, Ima Sizzler, Supercede	9
11Dec81-2Hol	$6\frac{1}{2}$f	$:22^2$	$:45^4$	$1:18^3$ft	$3\frac{1}{2}$	117	3^{nk}	2^{hd}	1^2	$1^{1\frac{1}{4}}$	Sibille R^7	M25000	77	ExtrQuick,ARoylWlcom,ToughTim	12
27Aug81-3Dmr	6f	$:22^3$	$:46^1$	1:12 ft	$5\frac{1}{2}$	118	1^{hd}	$2^{\frac{1}{2}}$	7^6	11^{16}	Lipham T^4	M40000	62	Dena Jo, Smuggler's Gold,SirBoss	12
19Jun81-4Hol	5f	:22	$:46^4$	$:59^3$ft	3	116	2^1	2^3	2^{hd}	$2^{2\frac{1}{4}}$	Lipham T^2	Mc32000	79	Subdivide,ExtraQuick,Cpt'nArphy	10
6Jun81-6Hol	5f	$:21^4$	$:45^4$	$:58^1$ft	$8\frac{3}{4}$	116	$3^{\frac{1}{2}}$	3^4	$4^{7\frac{1}{2}}$	5^{11}	Lipham T^4	[S]Mdn	77	DistntHrt,B.RichGorg,SwtndNturl	10

Jun 11 Hol 4f ft $:47^2$ h **May 25 Hol 4f ft :48 h**

This horse likewise has not run in 17 days, but with his four furlong workout on June 11, he has not been idle quite as long as Gringo Jim. But looking at the form cycle, you can see that Extra Quick was recently claimed for $32,000 on May 15, and after one foray at the obligatory higher price, his owners are now offering him for $25,000, apparently willing to take a quick loss on their investment. This is never a good sign, unless the trainer is a mass mover of horses, like Frank Martin in New York, who will make frequent and precipitous drops to win a purse and willingly lose money on the purchase price, confident that he will make it up the next time.

As long as we are comparing contenders in the race, the third betting choice was Capt'n Arphy, who had won only a maiden race back in January in his last start.

Capt'n Arphy * — B. c. 3, by Gaelic Dancer—Sharon Market, by To Market
Br.—Giuliano & Sons (Cal) — 1982 1 1 0 0 $5,500
Own.—Bernstein-G Giuliano & Sons **115** Tr.—Bernstein David $25,000 — 1981 2 M 0 2 $3,750
Lifetime 3 1 0 2 $9,250

21Jan82-3SA	6f	$:22^2$	:47	$1:13^1$m	*9-5	118	$6^{2\frac{1}{4}}$	$5^{\frac{3}{4}}$	$2^{2\frac{1}{2}}$	1^{nk}	DelhoussyE^4	[S]M25000	72	Cpt'nArphy,FunnyCrr,InspirdAgin	12
3Jly81-6Hol	6f	$:22^1$	:46	$1:12^3$ft	*2	117	2^2	$2^{2\frac{1}{2}}$	1^1	$1^{1\frac{3}{4}}$†	Pincay L Jr^3	[S]M40000	74	‡Cpt'nArphy,CpturthSpirit,Crr'sTn	11
† 3Jly81—Disqualified and placed third															
19Jun81-4Hol	5f	:22	$:46^4$	$:59^3$ft	*$2\frac{1}{2}$	116	$3^{2\frac{1}{2}}$	3^5	$4^{3\frac{3}{4}}$	$3^{6\frac{1}{4}}$	Castaneda M^8	M32000	75	Subdivide,ExtraQuick,Cpt'nArphy	10

●Jun 11 Hol 5f ft :59 h **Jun 5 Hol 6f ft $1:16^3$ h** **May 30 Hol 5f ft $1:00^4$ h** **May 24 Hol 5f ft $1:00^4$ h**

His best advertisement was that sparkling bullet five furlong workout just five days previously. That is enough to keep us from automatically eliminating him because of the long layoff. But when you apply any kind of handicapping rules, you can see that this youngster has never performed at near the quality level of Gringo Jim's last race. Not only that, but his two good efforts were with weaker competition in state-bred races, a factor not likely to make him shine in an open event. Thus, even though he would earn a + for recency, he was suspicious on other grounds. The result chart shows what happened.

FIFTH RACE
Hollywood
JUNE 16, 1982

6 FURLONGS. (1.07⅖) CLAIMING. Purse $12,000. 3-year-olds. Weight, 121 lbs. Non-winners of two races since April 18 allowed 3 lbs.; a race since then, 6 lbs. Claiming price $25,000; if for $22,500 allowed 2 lbs. (Races when entered for $20,000 or less not considered.)

Value of race $12,000, value to winner $6,600, second $2,400, third $1,800, fourth $900, fifth $300. Mutuel pool $185,727. Exacta Pool $310,673.

Last Raced	Horse	Eqt.	A.	Wt	PP	St	¼	½	Str	Fin	Jockey	Cl'g Pr	Odds $1
30May82 ^{5}Hol^{2}	Gringo Jim		3	115	6	7	$3^{1\frac{1}{2}}$	$1^{\frac{1}{2}}$	$1^{\frac{1}{2}}$	$1^{\frac{3}{4}}$	Shoemaker W	25000	2.10
30May82 ^{5}Hol^{8}	Spectacular Bee	b	3	115	5	9	$7^{\frac{1}{2}}$	5^{2}	2^{hd}	$2^{2\frac{1}{2}}$	Toro F	25000	9.70
11Jun82 ^{2}Hol^{1}	Quick Response		3	118	4	6	$5^{\frac{1}{2}}$	4^{1}	$3^{\frac{1}{2}}$	$3^{2\frac{1}{2}}$	Castaneda M	25000	11.00
30May82 ^{5}Hol^{5}	Familiar Tune		3	115	2	8	2^{hd}	2^{2}	4^{3}	$4^{\frac{1}{2}}$	Ortega L E	25000	13.80
31May82 ^{3}Hol^{4}	Carrie's Ten	b	3	115	1	12	9^{1}	6^{2}	5^{2}	$5^{\frac{1}{2}}$	Valenzuela P A	25000	13.30
29May82 ^{2}GG^{1}	Reb's Outlaw	b	3	118	8	3	10^{1}	7^{hd}	$6^{\frac{1}{2}}$	$6^{1\frac{1}{2}}$	Hawley S	25000	51.30
6Jun82 ^{3}Hol^{5}	Ramble on John		3	115	9	11	12	10^{5}	7^{1}	$7^{2\frac{1}{2}}$	Ramirez O	25000	72.00
24Mar82 ^{1}SA^{8}	Stacy Jo		3	110	3	10	$11^{1\frac{1}{2}}$	8^{2}	8^{hd}	8no	Steiner J J^{5}	25000	85.90
21Jan82 ^{3}SA^{1}	Capt'n Arphy	b	3	115	11	5	6^{hd}	9^{2}	$9^{\frac{1}{2}}$	9^{1}	Delahoussaye E	25000	4.80
30May82 ^{5}Hol^{9}	Murtazz	b	3	115	12	1	$1^{\frac{1}{2}}$	$3^{\frac{1}{2}}$	10^{3}	10^{1}	Hansen R D	25000	107.30
30May82 ^{5}Hol^{7}	Extra Quick	b	3	115	7	2	8^{2}	11	11	11	McCarron C J	25000	4.20
5Jun82 ^{2}Hol^{2}	Gravitas	b	3	118	10	4	$4^{\frac{1}{2}}$	—	—	—	Pincay L Jr	25000	6.50

Gravitas, Lame.

OFF AT 4:09. Start good. Won driving. Time, :22, :45, :57⅗, 1:10⅘ Track fast.

$2 Mutuel Prices:			
6–GRINGO JIM	6.20	4.60	3.60
5–SPECTACULAR BEE		10.00	6.00
4–QUICK RESPONSE			6.20

$5 EXACTA 6–5 PAID $135.00

Gringo Jim did what he was supposed to do, as Bill Shoemaker racked up another in his long string of victories. Capt'n Arphy, despite his good five furlong workout, was not yet up to competing with this level of stock. Poor Extra Quick showed why his owners were offering him at a cut-rate price, as ten other horses finished ahead of him.

But this is about recent action, not other handicapping factors. The race was presented to show how it would be foolish indeed to eliminate a horse by drawing a line of two weeks for required recent action. There are too many situations like this one that come up every day.

Thus, any horse that has run within the past 21 days, even without a workout, can obtain an N in our recency ratings. Now we are back to line-drawing again.

Why not continue to use the 28-day rule that was set forth in *Investing at the Racetrack*? When I went back to check again on those horses that had not run in three weeks, but came in within the 28-day line, I began to see that those who were the winners had some workouts in their records, and the losers were those who showed no action at all. This was indeed a revelation, and the more I checked, the more it became apparent that any horse that is idle three weeks or more without a workout is in deep trouble, unless all his rivals are loaded down with form defects.

The best measuring device from my 433 race study was again the favorites, because of the statistical expectancy that they show, and because the one favorite in every race is easily defined (unless two horses are tied in the final odds breakdown). Of these 433 first choices in the betting, there were 74 of them that had not run in 21 days or worked in the intervening period. This was the form defect of zero, or O, that would cause us to eliminate them if the figures held up. How did they perform? Of these 74, only eight were able to win, a meager 10.8%. That tells you something right there. And when you subtract the 74 zero recency horses from the total of 433, there are 359 horses with either a + or an N, which leaves these remaining favorites winning at a rate of nearly 36%, which is far better than the 31.6% overall rate for favorites in this particular study.

We must also pay careful attention to the tracks involved. In New York, for example, a horse lacking recent action is likely to be competing against some reasonably strong horses that will show both recent action and the highly favorable five furlong workout. Horses lacking in recent action, as you might expect, fared far worse at Belmont than at any other track, which is consistent with expectancies where higher priced horses are concerned. Among the 97 favorites at Belmont, 12 had a lack of recent action as defined by the 21-day requirement. Not a single one of them returned a winner!

At Meadowlands, the next stop in the class ladder, 29 of 130 favorites were deficient in recent action to the point of a O disqualifying rating. Of this number, only three came home as winners!

Go down to the next rung to the slightly lower level of Keystone and Bowie, and the percentage picks up only slightly. At Keystone, three out of 21 favorites who had not run or worked out within 21 days came home as winners. At Bowie, there were two winners out of 12 horses with zero recent action.

When I was considering the gray area of between 14 and 21 days, I began to see again the wisdom of awarding an N for the horse that had run within the three weeks' period. There were 41 such horses that fell within this category, and 15 of them won. Much of this statistical strength came from results at Bowie, where the winners in several races showed strong class advantages. But nonetheless, there was little doubt that a horse running within three weeks, even without a workout, did not deserve to be eliminated, and thus was entitled to the N rating.

In reviewing the form defect of lack of recent action, it must be stressed again that no one is saying that horses with this deficiency never win. Some of them manage to get there, again most likely because of defects in their opposition.

Looking at the longer priced winners to see how they fared insofar as recent action is concerned is also highly instructive, even though we may expect to find some of them who would not meet our form standards.

Once more, we must take into account the level of track under consideration. At Belmont, just as among first betting choices no horses with a recency defect won, second choices in the betting were likewise shut out when they, too, lacked recent action. But even more astonishing, among all other winning horses at Belmont that were neither first nor second choices in the betting, which numbered 40 all told, only one horse with a recency defect managed to win!

This is truly one of the most remarkable figures in this book. Over any longer period of time, I would expect to find more than one winner out of 97 with a lack of recent action, but the mere fact that a span of 97 races showed only one such winner is about as eloquent a testimonial as we could find to our 21-day rule. Even the first time starter winners came in off workouts. Repeated studies of results in New York over the years confirms again and again the wisdom of the rule of three weeks.

Suspecting that Hollywood Park would show about the same recency reality as did Belmont, I did a careful review for four successive days in 1982, from June 16 through June 19, from the west coast edition of *Daily Racing Form*. There were 36 races in these four days—not one winner had a recency defect. And, just as at Belmont, there were not too many horses entered at Hollywood Park without some recent action, as trainers there realize as well that good stock ought to have sufficient preparation for any race to have a good chance to win.

Now that we have drawn a firm line behind 21 days as the longest period of time since its last race which we can accept to qualify a horse for recent action, are there any exceptions relating to workouts other than the five furlong work, which we will accept as a qualifier, no matter how long a horse has been away?

Turning to the sixth race at Belmont on June 18, 1982, a filly maiden special weight on the turf, how would you handle Scuff?

Scuff — Ch. f. 3, by Forli—Meccasin, by Nantallah
Own.—Claiborne Farm — **114** — Br.—Claiborne Farm (Ky) — Tr.—Stephens Woodford C
1982 4 M 2 1 $7,270
Turf 4 0 2 1 $7,270
Lifetime 4 0 2 1 $7,270

22May82-9Bel	1⅜ [T]	:48^{4}1:40^{1}2:18	fm	*1	113	6^7	4$^{2\frac{1}{2}}$	2$^{\frac{1}{2}}$	2^{hd}	Maple E^7	ⒻMdn	67	Kanduit, Scuff, Katyusha	8
7Apr82-10GP	a1 Ⓣ	1:38^3	fm	3	121	5^6	4^3	3^{nk}	2$^{1\frac{3}{4}}$	Saumell L^3	ⒻMdn	86	Zoophile, Scuff, Plum Ten	10
15Mar82-6GP	1$\frac{1}{16}$ Ⓣ	:46^{4}1:12^{1}1:45	fm	3¾	121	6$^{5\frac{3}{4}}$	1$^{\frac{1}{2}}$	1^{hd}	3$^{2\frac{1}{4}}$	Maple E^5	ⒻMdn	73	Famous Sis, Treaty Oak, Scuff	12
26Feb82-6Hia	a1⅛ Ⓣ	1:51^4	fm	*6-5	120	9^{12}	9^{15}	8^{12}	5$^{9\frac{1}{4}}$	Maple E^8	ⒻMdn	64	Lindoy,RoylAgreement,ExcitbleGl	11

Jun 15 Bel 4f ft :51^2 b Jun 10 Bel 4f ft :50^1 b ●Jun 5 Bel 3f gd :35^1 h May 31 Bel 5f gd 1:02^1 b

She last ran on May 22, some 27 days before the race under consideration. Running across the bottom of her past performances, look at the workout line. You find no five furlong works at all after May 31. The first question arises—will the work count to give her an N rating because it was followed by other works of five days apart? While a good argument can be made for it, a far safer way is to not count any five furlong workout that was more than 14 days from today's race. Applying that standard, we will still have to look to see if Scuff is worth a play, or should be discarded for lack of recent action.

Here is where the four furlong workout can help us, as long as it was a recent work, and as long as the horse ran within the four weeks time tier. We can modify the strict 21-day rule in this fashion: if a horse ran within 28 days and shows a four furlong workout in the week prior to the race, that will barely avoid the zero rating which would lead to disqualification.

Scuff is about as good an example of this observation as you will find. Here there were four works between races, and any time any horse works four times in less than four weeks, you can be reasonably sure that there is substantial readiness. In the race involved, Scuff was a winner.

While other tracks do not show the same consistency as does Belmont in any area of racing, we can take a quick peek at longer priced winners at the other three under consideration, to see how these victorious runners fared in the recency factor. Meadowlands, for example, showed a surprising number of recency defect winners, as 16 of 68 who were not among the first two betting choices and who did not qualify under our recent action rules still came home in front. Over a longer period, I would not expect this figure to be nearly so high. At Bowie and Keystone, there were only 13 out of 55 long shot winners without recent action at those two tracks. Because of the high run of favorites winning at Bowie, this held down the number of longer priced winners. At Bowie, among the favored horses, there were four winners out of 28 without qualifying recent action.

We may now set forth in summary review how we will rate horses for the first form factor of recent action.

+   Horses running within seven days or less of today's race.

+   Horses running within 21 days of today's race who have a five furlong workout in the last 14 days that earns a bullet or is at very fast time (:59.4 or less in the east and midwest and :58.4 or faster in southern California).

N   Horses running within 21 days of today's race.

N   Horses running within 28 days of today's race who have worked four furlongs within the past week.

N   Horses, regardless of how long they have been away, who have worked five furlongs or longer within the past 14 days.

O   Horses that have not run in 21 days without a qualifying workout. This is a serious form defect that will require us to disqualify the horse as a contender in today's race in most all circumstances.

4 The Second Form Factor: Last Useable Running Line

ALMOST EVERY PERSON who has ever looked at a *Racing Form* has taken into account a horse's last race. This most common handicapping factor has an almost certain influence on your thinking of whether a horse "looks good" today or "does not look too good." Any horse off a strong last race, unless he is totally outclassed in the field today, is a likely factor to be considered.

But is there a level at which a good performance rates some positive credit above the ordinary? And likewise, how "bad" does a race have to be before we can consider the horse a sure enough loser to throw him out of our handicapping consideration?

From this time-worn and universal factor, can we put some new insight into it and develop some solid points of view to help us determine how our horse will run today?

Before we start trying to unravel this common form factor, I do want to point out that in *Investing at the Racetrack* there were some rather sound rules for correct form set forth in that book. They are, for the most part, still useable, as they should be if they were sound originally. You could still use them completely with satisfactory results. But subsequent research has made some major changes to improve these form rules even more and to integrate them into the method of rating form that is at the heart of this book. And I can assure you that you will indeed find some new nuggets here that have not been revealed before anywhere. Consequently, there will be some tightening of the form rules that were used in *Investing at the Racetrack*, with rearrangements that will add greatly to what you learned there.

To make the necessary evaluations, even before we consider whether a horse's last race is always the "last useable running line" from which we will rate the horse, it is necessary to set some standards to help us determine the "good" from the "bad," or lead us to the plus and minus form ratings that are so crucial in guiding us to what our horse will do today. As we do this, you will see the first departure from form rules developed in the past, this time with new versions that have a considerable impact.

Establishing "Up Close" as a Basic Working Standard

A horse, to show good form, must rather obviously be close to the front at some time in his last race, preferably at the end, where it counts most. The term, "up close," was used in *Investing at the Racetrack*, and it is still an essential element in looking at a running line of a horse. As of now, we are only seeking a definition of the term that we will use over and over again in this book.

What is "up close?" We said that, for any given point of call in a race, if a horse was less than three lengths behind the leader at that point, then at that call the horse was up close. In *Investing at the Racetrack*, this meant in any race a horse had to be within two and three-quarter lengths or less of the lead at one of the four points of call in a race to get an up close designation.

This was used in all races, regardless of distance. We can now improve upon that somewhat.

In sprint races, those of six and a half furlongs and shorter, constant speed is vital. If a horse falls too far behind in a shorter race, you can usually forget about his chances. If he cannot keep up with the leaders, or near to the lead, he is not showing good form, or else he is outclassed. Thus, the less than three lengths from the lead rule in races of five furlongs, five and a half furlongs, six furlongs, and six and a half furlongs is still a sound definition for what up close means at any particular call of these shorter distances. In other words, to qualify as having been up close in a sprint race, a horse must have been less than three lengths from the lead, or not more than two and three-quarter lengths behind, at some point of call in the race.

But as races lengthen out, being a little farther behind than three lengths is not quite so serious. There is more time to make up ground. And running styles begin to vary.

While the seven furlong race is universally considered a sprint race, it is a sprint race of a far different variety. While there is more time and space in which to run, and thus slightly less of a premium on raw speed, there is also a much greater demand made upon the horse. Most veteran players have long recognized that there is literally a world of difference between a seven furlong race and a six furlong race. Therefore, after considerable thought and experimentation, it seemed wiser to put the up close stamp at less than four lengths behind (instead of at less than three) in seven furlong races. This means that at any call where a horse was within three and three-quarter lengths or closer to the lead, he has earned an up close call.

And when you come to think about it, the one mile distance is not that much different from the seven furlong race. Where one-mile races are run out of a chute, such as in New York, there is still some premium on speed and the need to stay up with the front-movers. On the other hand, at a one mile track such as Santa Anita, races at that distance start near the first turn. Getting out of the gate and near to the lead becomes vitally important. A slow horse on the rail can quickly find himself lost behind a wall of horses. A runner on the outside may be pushed wide at the first turn, and thus lose valuable ground. So, no matter where a one mile race begins, there is always some premium on speed, just as there is in a seven furlong race, but not as much as in a true sprint event. Therefore, we can safely use the same less than four lengths standard, or within three and three-quarter lengths of the lead at any call in one mile races just as we do in seven furlong events.

As the distance of the race lengthens, not only is there more territory in which to make up lost ground, but the running style continues to change. There is no longer an emphasis on early speed as such, as pace and position assume more importance in the running of the race. Consequently, the up close standard can be opened up a bit more, this time to within less than five lengths, or four and three-quarter or less, from the lead. In races longer than one mile, which includes distances of a mile and forty yards, a mile and seventy yards, a mile and a sixteenth, and on up through the long races, where a horse is less than five lengths from the lead at any call, there will be an up close designation at that particular call.

Summarizing up close rules for distances, here is what we have:

● Less than three lengths, or two and three-quarters or less, from the lead at any call in races of six and a half furlongs and shorter

● Less than four lengths, or three and three-quarters and less, from the lead at any call in races of seven furlongs and one mile

● Less than five lengths, or four and three-quarters and less, from the lead at any call in races longer than one mile

Now that we have defined "up close," we will consider the significance of the number of up close calls in the race and the points in which they occur.

Form Ratings for the Running Line

THE POSITIVE PLUS FACTOR. Our first goal is to find out if there is any kind of running line performance that is powerful enough to lead to a positive, or + factor comparable in strength to the plus for recency. There is one, and one only.

A horse that is up close at all four calls in his last race is entitled to a plus for running line. While, as we will discuss later, a horse's most recent race may not always be its useable running line for evaluative purposes, the definition of "last race useable running line" does not matter here, since the requirement for a plus can be met only from the last race. The logic is obvious: a horse that stays close to the lead from start to finish in his last race is running well, and if he returns to the races within the proper time frame (which brings us back to recent action), his form is thus positive enough to merit respectful attention and brand him a strong contender, if all other factors are in place. But we can not be so positive about the horse's current form if we are looking only at its second or third most recent race. Thus, to deserve the significant plus rating, a horse must earn it off its last race.

In dealing with the up close requirement, the distance of today's race is not a guideline. We consider only the last race at the particular distance at which it was run. It is simply logical to evaluate the potency of a horse's most recent effort by the distance, and the resulting strategy and premium on speed, of that race, rather than the conditions of a future race. A typical example comes from the *Daily Racing Form* of June 19, where Zany was the second betting choice in the seventh race at Belmont.

7th Belmont

7 FURLONGS. (1.20⅘) ALLOWANCE. Purse $20,000. 3-year-olds and up fillies and mares which have never won two races other than maiden, claiming or starter. Weights: 3-year-olds, 114 lbs.; older, 122 lbs.; non-winners of a race other than maiden or claiming since May 15, allowed 3 lbs. Of such a race since May 1, 5 lbs.

Zany — Ch. f. 3, by Foolish Pleasure—Zenda, by Graustark
Own.—Greentree Stable — **111** — Br.—Greentree Stud Inc (Ky) — Tr.—Reinacher Robert Jr
1982 7 2 0 2 $22,570 — Turf 1 0 0 0 $130
Lifetime 7 2 0 2 $22,570

2Jun82-7Bel	$1\frac{1}{16}$	:46^2	1:11^2	1:43 ft	$7\frac{1}{4}$	112	6^4	4^3	3^2	$3^{2\frac{1}{2}}$	Fell J^2	Ⓕ Aw21000	84	Broom Dance, Doodle, Zany	6
9May82-7Aqu	7f	:23^2	:47	1:26^{1}ft	10	116	$8^{5\frac{1}{2}}$	5^5	$3^{2\frac{1}{2}}$	1^{hd}	Fell J^8	Ⓕ Aw19000	70	Zany, Alzabella, Wimbledon Star	8
23Apr82-5Aqu	6f	:22^3	:46^2	1:12^{2}ft	24	116	$11^{8\frac{1}{4}}$	$11^{9\frac{3}{4}}$	9^6	$6^{2\frac{1}{2}}$	Fell J^2	Ⓕ Aw19000	76	FireinthSky,LdyLothrio,SyrinSnds	12
16Mar82-7GP	a1	Ⓣ		1:38^{2}fm	9	116	4^3	$3^{2\frac{1}{2}}$	$8^{6\frac{3}{4}}$	$7^{7\frac{3}{4}}$	BrumfildD^4	Ⓕ Aw13000	81	Malapropism,Banker'sFvorite,Gulf	11
1Mar82-4Hia	7f	:23^2	:47^2	1:26 ft	*9-5	120	$5^{2\frac{1}{2}}$	$4^{1\frac{1}{2}}$	$1^{2\frac{1}{2}}$	$1^{6\frac{1}{2}}$	Velasquez J^{12}	Ⓕ Mdn	73	Zany, Now It's Nicky,ChapterSeat	12
15Feb82-10Hia	7f	:23	:45^4	1:25^{2}ft	*8-5	120	$9^{8\frac{1}{2}}$	$7^{9\frac{1}{4}}$	$4^{5\frac{1}{2}}$	3^6	Velasquez J^9	Ⓕ Mdn	70	Catch Nana, Tailwind Ms., Zany	12
5Feb82-7Hia	6f	:22^2	:45^4	1:12^{1}ft	9	120	11^{14}	9^{14}	8^{11}	$5^{3\frac{1}{4}}$	Velasquez J^2	Ⓕ Mdn	79	Rebeautess,BloodRelation,CtchNn	12

● Jun 15 Bel 4f ft :46^2 h — May 31 Bel 4f gd :47^3 h — May 26 Bel 6f ft 1:14^4 h

While today's race is at seven furlongs, Zany must be rated off the mile and a sixteenth distance of her last race. Up close at seven furlongs is less than four lengths, while at distances of more than a mile, it is less than five lengths from the lead. Zany was four lengths behind at the first call of her last race which was good enough for an up close rating at one mile and a sixteenth, but it would not have qualified had the last race been at seven furlongs. Now, you can see that she was up close at all four calls of her last race at a mile and a sixteenth, which allows us to give her a plus for her last race running line when rating today's event at seven furlongs. The fact that she had won both her lifetime victories at the difficult seven furlong distance also did not hurt her chances.

While this made Zany a very strong play, there was some other good competition in the race. The favorite was Mochila, a very good, lightly-raced filly with splendid breeding.

Mochila — Dk. b. or br. f. 3, by In Reality—Ride The Trails, by Prince John
Own.—Nerud J A — **114** — Br.—Nerud J A (Fla) — Tr.—Nerud Jan H
1982 2 1 0 0 $11,400 — 1981 2 1 0 0 $9,240
Lifetime 4 2 0 0 $20,640

22May82-4Bel	6f	:23^1	:46^1	1:10^{3}ft	$5\frac{3}{4}$	109	1^{hd}	$1^{\frac{1}{2}}$	1^{hd}	$1^{2\frac{3}{4}}$	Venezia M^3	Ⓕ Aw19000	89	Mochil,WimbledonStr,Momnt'sPryr	6
23Apr82-5Aqu	6f	:22^3	:46^2	1:12^{2}ft	20	116	8^5	6^6	$6^{4\frac{1}{2}}$	$7^{4\frac{3}{4}}$	Venezia M^3	Ⓕ Aw19000	74	FireinthSky,LdyLothrio,SyrinSnds	12
16Dec81-9Aqu	6f	⊡:23	:47^4	1:13^{1}sy	*2	117	2^{hd}	2^{hd}	$1^{1\frac{1}{2}}$	$1^{1\frac{1}{4}}$	Venezia M^3	Ⓕ Mdn	78	Mochila,LuretheLady,LadyLothario	9
18Oct81-4Aqu	6f	:22^3	:46^2	1:12^{3}ft	21	114^3	$9^{7\frac{1}{2}}$	$7^{6\frac{1}{2}}$	$7^{5\frac{1}{2}}$	$4^{3\frac{1}{4}}$	Foley D^{10}	Ⓕ Mdn	75	MyGlPolly,Bestowed,StrokofTwlv	10

Jun 13 Bel 4f ft :49^3 b — Jun 8 Bel 4f ft :50 b — May 31 Bel 3f gd :40 b — May 19 Bel 4f ft :49 b

Immediately, you can see that we have another plus for a running line rating, as Mochila was in front, and thus obviously up close at every call of her last six furlong sprint. You still will have to rate Mochila for recency, because she has not run in 26 days. But off our four furlong workout qualifying rule, she would get an N for recent action, because she has been away less than 28 days and worked four furlongs within the past week. This is the same recency rating that Zany has.

As you will see later in this book, both these good fillies qualified in every respect insofar as form factors are concerned. Even in the revised ability time ratings that I use to separate contenders, these two came out equal. This was a very tough choice to make. Any time you see the top two betting choices with + running lines, you can be reasonably sure that one of them will win. But which one?

Perhaps the only real advantage for Zany was the fact that she had won twice at seven furlongs, and surely liked the distance. Yet, Mochila was still untested at this demanding distance. I have observed that any previous winner at seven furlongs is not to be taken lightly when that distance is at issue.

Here is what the chart revealed:

SEVENTH RACE
Belmont
JUNE 19, 1982

7 FURLONGS. (1.20⅘) ALLOWANCE. Purse $20,000. 3–year–olds and up fillies and mares which have never won two races other than maiden, claiming or starter. Weights: 3–year–olds, 114 lbs.; older, 122 lbs.; non–winners of a race other than maiden or claiming since May 15, allowed 3 lbs. Of such a race since May 1, 5 lbs.

Value of race $20,000, value to winner $12,000, second $4,400, third $2,400, fourth $1,200. Mutuel pool $199,063, OTB pool $133,334. Exacta Pool $290,663. OTB Exacta Pool $192,246.

Last Raced		Horse	Eqt.	A.Wt	PP	St	¼	½	Str	Fin	Jockey	Odds $1
2Jun82	7Bel3	Zany		3 113	1	7	6½	4hd	1½	18¾	Fell J	2.20
28May82	1Bel8	Forever Fair	b	4 117	2	6	5hd	6½	51½	2no	Samyn J L	5.60
31May82	5Bel1	Town Majesty	b	3 114	3	5	2½	1hd	3½	3no	Graell A	8.30
22May82	4Bel1	Mochila		3 114	6	2	41½	31	2hd	4nk	Cordero A Jr	1.30
7Jun82	5Bel1	Sugar Tart		4 122	4	1	1hd	21	43	52½	Miranda J	12.30
4Jun82	6Bel1	Sassy 'n Bright	b	3 114	7	3	7	7	7	61½	Velasquez J	13.40
6Jun82	7Bel5	Silent Film	b	3 109	5	4	3½	52	61½	7	Montoya D	18.30

OFF AT 4:19 Start good, Won ridden out. Time, :22⅘, :45⅗, 1:10⅖, 1:22⅘ Track fast.

$2 Mutuel Prices:

1–(A)–ZANY	6.40	3.60	2.80
2–(B)–FOREVER FAIR		5.00	4.00
3–(C)–TOWN MAJESTY			4.80

$2 EXACTA 1–2 PAID $35.60.

Ch. f, by Foolish Pleasure—Zenda, by Graustark. Trainer Reinacher Robert Jr. Bred by Greentree Stud Inc (Ky).

ZANY moved up along the inside approaching the turn, came out to continue her bid nearing the stretch and drew off after catching the leaders. FOREVER FAIR, wide into the stretch, finished with good energy to gain the place in the final stride. TOWN MAJESTY saved ground while vying for the lead to midstretch and weakened. MOCHILA rallied from the outside to reach the front approaching the final furlong but weakened.

Of all the running line ratings, the + factor is the easiest to apply, since it is simple enough: up close at all four calls at the distance of the last race, regardless of the distance of the race before you. There is a qualifying recency factor, of course, which we will discuss shortly, but it would not hurt to set it forth here and repeat it again later. In the absence of recent workouts, the last race must be within the past three weeks to be counted toward a + rating. If the horse has worked four furlongs within the past week, or five furlongs (or longer) within the past 14 days, the last race may be within four weeks, in order to be used for a + rating. For any race farther back in time than that, you will have to ignore the last race running line altogether.

Now we can come to the big question of how effective is the + form factor for last race running line.

To test its strength as a positive factor, we will now use two simple handicapping rules. First, a horse must not have other form defects at all, neither in recency nor in any of the remaining factors that will be discussed in later chapters. If a horse has any other form defect, it will likely cancel out the strength of his + factor for running line. Second, and this is also crucial, a horse must not be rising in class off his last race. Many horses that win their last race do so with impressive up close running lines, and then return at a higher class level. This is often their undoing.

Using these two handicapping rules to test the effectiveness of the strong up close running line, I looked at every first and second choice in the wagering in the entire 433 races that have been so fully studied. Third choices in the wagering were also added only if the odds on the third horse were very very close to those of the second favored animal. For example, if the second choice's odds showed 2.6-1 and the third choice was at 2.8-1, there was obviously little difference between the two insofar as money on the board was concerned. If the third choice odds of the horse were approximately a half number higher, he would not be considered, such as where the second choice may have been 3-1 and the third choice 7-2.

In these 433 races, out of the first, second, and very close third betting choices there were 105 horses with a + running line who had no other form defects and were not rising in class. This study covered some 47 racing cards, which means a horse in this category would show up approximately two times per racing card—not a great deal, but nothing to be downplayed, either.

Now, get set for the good news. Of these 105 horses, even where there were two in a race and taking both of them without any other handicapping, there were 51 winners—an incredible 48.5%! No one has to tell you what a lovely flat bet profit would result from figures like that. Equally impressive, 71 of these horses came in for a place ticket, for a 67.6% return. Even better, some of the place prices were in the upper $4 and low $5 range—a booming profit all the way.

The most impressive group of performers in this category were in the maiden races. Any time you see a well-played maiden with four calls up close in the last race and no form defects, you have a very strong proposition. There were 13 of these among the 105, and nine of them won and 11 were second or better.

Again, the question arises whether this was a sufficient number of maiden races to form a valid sample. Thirteen maiden races out of a study of 433 is not a great deal, but when you group the horses in these races together with the others sharing the same characteristics, you still have the considerable number of 105 horses over 47 cards, which can be enough to become the flagship of your profit flotilla.

This is why, without hesitation, you can award a + running line rating for any horse that was up close at all four calls in its last race. When you apply the two critical handicapping rules that we have phased into this factor, you have a powerful play indeed. My research showed that the exclusion of horses rising in class is quite necessary. There were 39 horses with the + running line factor that were stepping up in class, and two others which I put in a special category because, as you will learn more about later, they scored enormously impressive victories in their last races (both of them won their next outing). But taking the 39 horses, only five of them managed to win and only 14 placed! This win percentage dwindles to 12.8%, a brutal loss at the windows.

Now you can see that this form factor possesses enormous

strength, as does the + for recent action. When these two elements come together in the same horse, you are looking at very wholesome possibilities for success at the window. And when we add our third + factor a little later on, you will see plays that should always produce profits, even without the good handicapping that could make them work even better.

THE N FACTOR: NEUTRAL, NEITHER, OR NON-APPLICABLE. When we get past the positive factor of up close at all four calls, we next need to establish a rating that is neither positive nor negative, which leaves a horse to be evaluated further. When applying a rating of N, we are essentially looking at the same kind of rating that was considered Qualified in *Investing at the Racetrack*. In addition, there was a form rating in that book that we called Unknown, for which we gave a "U," which was neither positive nor negative, and that will have to be used here, at times, as well.

To warrant the "Q" rating in my last book, under ordinary circumstances, a horse had to be up close at any two calls in his last race. While that is helpful, an enormous amount of subsequent research has convinced me that we can make a very important change in this requirement as we look to see what is required for an N rating for last race useable running line.

Being up close at one call might be enough, provided we can select the right call. And, as in the past, much of this depends upon the level of competition. Using horses returning at approximately the same class as a standard off which to work, my investigation led me to the conclusion that the stretch call was the most important one of all for measuring up close, thus giving a horse a qualified last race running line, or an N for this form factor.

This may surprise you. Originally, after deciding that the two calls used in *Investing at the Racetrack* could be improved upon, I thought that an up close at either the stretch call or the finish would do. After all, a horse that is up close at the wire is putting it where it counts, and is most likely in or near the money.

But there is a distinction, and I began to see the importance of it as I probed deeply into both the 433 races in the 1981 group and the races in 1982. Let us take an example from a sprint race, where a horse is closing and is four lengths behind at the stretch call. He finishes only two lengths out. This looks like a very good race. But a sprinter who closes in the stretch is always at a disadvantage. In his next race, which will be the one you are considering today, he may not be there in time if he is an habitual closer. In distance races, since the up close standard is liberally fixed at four and three-quarter lengths or less, a horse that is not that close to the lead at the stretch call, even if he is making up ground, is simply too far behind to show the kind of form that we want.

This requirement that, to earn an N rating, a horse must have been up close at the stretch call of its last race works in all kinds of races. Other factors of stretch performance may affect it, as you will see at a later point in this book, but for now, we are talking only about a sufficient measurement for an N rating. Here is an example that meets the stretch call standard, out of the third race at Belmont on June 16.

Read and Deed		B. f. 3, by Semillant—La Heredera, by South Pole					
		Br.—Hemphill H H (NY)				1982 5 M 0 0	
Own.—Windinghill Stable	**114**	Tr.—Papa Louis				1981 1 M 0 0	
		Lifetime 6 0 0 0				Turf 1 0 0 0	
27May82-6Bel	7f :23 :462 1:254ft	18e 113	85½ 76½ 43½ 57	Molina V H7	ⓔⓢMdn	66	BrzenDne,ReglAmethyst,LmonSky 14
13May82-5Aqu	1⅛:49 1:143 1:524gd	7 113	11½ 1½ 421 529	Attanasio R7	ⓔⓢMdn	42	Tara K., Ever Higher, Sister Sunny 7
3May82-3Aqu	1⅛ⓣ:4821:1311:523fm	43 113	16 14 33½ 614	AttnsioR2	ⓔⓢAw27500	67	TopOfTheBrrel,CludiS.B.,SillyHeels 8
19Apr82-1Aqu	1⅛:503 1:161 1:561ft	5e 1057	1hd 31½ 712 718	Buscemi S3	ⓔⓢMdn	36	Claudia S. B., Slightly Sly,Katyusha 8
8Apr82-6Aqu	1 :482 1:143 1:412gd	14e 1075	98½ 813 713 713	White J R3	ⓔⓢMdn	46	Wise'NWilling,TrK.,BrookvillTr-or 10
13Jly81-4Bel	6f :23 :464 1:122ft	56 117	1121 924113011131	Venezia M2	ⓔⓢMdn	49	Cupecoy'sJoy,GrndOldFlg,DmL:ttl 13
● Apr 29 Sar tr.t 3f ft :372 h							

While you may want to argue that this horse's form is lousy (and I would be inclined to agree), the record of Read and Deed is shown for one purpose only—to illustrate that at the stretch call of her last race, at seven furlongs, she was less than four lengths from the lead, and would thus get an N for her last race running line. The N does not necessarily mean anything positive about the horse—it simply means that for this form factor she does not exhibit negative or positive signs, and we must consider the other factors. Indeed, she exhibits a glaring form defect on another factor, which would throw her out as a contender, even if she were well played, which she was not, but that will be shown later.

Let us contrast Read and Deed's up close rating with that of Breyer Patch from the second race at Belmont on June 17, 1982.

This horse would not qualify for a neutral rating.

Breyer Patch — B. g. 9, by Creme Dela Creme—Inviting, by My Babu
Br.—Combs L II (Ky) — 1982 1 0 0 0
Own.—Winpress Stable — 113 — Tr.—Gullo Thomas J — $10,500 — 1981 10 1 2 2 $12,570
Lifetime 71 9 11 15 $95,466

10Jun82-2Bel	7f	:23^{2}	:46^{1}	1:24 ft	8¾	114	3^{3}	3^{nk}	2^{4}	$6^{6\frac{3}{4}}$	Fell J^{9}	10500	75	PokieJoe,Residuary,PrtingGesture	10
22Nov81-3Aqu	6f	:23	:46^{3}	1:11^{4}ft	11	113	3^{2}	$4^{2\frac{1}{2}}$	$6^{5\frac{1}{2}}$	$7^{5\frac{1}{2}}$	Beitia E^{5}	10500	77	Whmbng,FstAndAlrt,DistinctivKing	7
25Oct81-9/.qu	6f	:23	:46^{4}	1:11^{2}ft	6	117	$5^{1\frac{1}{2}}$	$5^{1\frac{1}{4}}$	$4^{3\frac{1}{2}}$	$5^{5\frac{1}{4}}$	Beitia E^{5}	10000	79	Jill Believes, Golfer, Wimpfybell	10
27Jly81-2Bel	6f	:22^{3}	:45^{3}	1:10 ft	5	117	7^{7}	6^{6}	6^{7}	$6^{4\frac{3}{4}}$	McCarron G^{9}	10000	87	Perceptable,Whmbng,PuntDelEste	9
17Jly81-9Bel	6f	:22^{4}	:46^{1}	1:11^{1}ft	8	117	$6^{2\frac{3}{4}}$	5^{2}	7^{8}	$7^{7\frac{1}{4}}$	McCarron G^{6}	12500	79	RiverInvader,RightNRedy,SpecilFlir	8
24Jun81-1Bel	7f	:23^{1}	:46	1:23^{3}ft	5½	117	$5^{2\frac{1}{2}}$	3^{3}	2^{3}	$3^{4\frac{3}{4}}$	McCarron G^{4}	12500	79	Urisha, Sunderance, Breyer Patch	7
12Jun81-1Bel	6f	:23	:46^{1}	1:10^{4}ft	11	117	6^{6}	$4^{7\frac{1}{2}}$	$3^{8\frac{1}{2}}$	$2^{6\frac{3}{4}}$	Martens G^{7}	12500	81	Bold ReRe,BreyerPatch,Whambang	9
27May81-1Bel	6f	:22^{3}	:46^{1}	1:11^{1}ft	4	112^{5}	4^{2}	4^{2}	5^{4}	4^{6}	Migliore R^{3}	12500	80	Sunderance, Gale At Sea,Winrightt	7

May 2 Bel tr.t 5f ft 1:03^{2} b

In this old gelding's last race at seven furlongs, at the stretch call, he was shown as four lengths behind. Now, he may have been three and three-quarter lengths back, as far as we know, since the chart maker could have been a portion of a length off. But those of us who live and die by what we read in *Daily Racing Form* have to stay with what we see there. The horse shows four lengths behind, and we will not award an N for a running line like this one, despite the early lick that he displayed.

A quite common example of a running line that merits an N, or neutral, comes from the first race at Hollywood Park on June 17, where Bebito is entered at the same distance and same class as in his previous effort.

Bebito — Dk. b. or br. g. 4, by Flying Magician—Lucky Roz, by Lucky Mel
Br.—Rex C (Cal) — 1982 7 0 1 0 $5,412
Own.—Four Star Farms — 116 — Tr.—Happe Peter R — $12,500 — 1981 6 1 2 1 $3,295
Lifetime 13 1 3 1 $8,707

6Jun82-1Hol	1 1/16	:47^{1}	1:12^{4}	1:46 ft	14	115	6^{11}	$4^{4\frac{1}{2}}$	3^{3}	$4^{1\frac{1}{2}}$	Hansen R D^{9}	12500	63	Arribeno, On the Prowl,InTriplicate	9
29May82-9Hol	1 1/16	:46^{4}	1:11^{3}	1:44^{1}ft	13	117	$6^{7\frac{1}{4}}$	5^{6}	2^{3}	$2^{3\frac{1}{2}}$	Pincay L Jr^{11}	10000	70	Great Cloud, Bebito, Star Career	11
20May82-5Hol	7f	:22	:44^{4}	1:23^{1}ft	31	115	$8^{7\frac{1}{2}}$	$6^{3\frac{1}{2}}$	5^{5}	$5^{5\frac{1}{2}}$	Olivares F^{3}	12500	75	Geoff'sDncr,ThMthod,ProfssorGrn	10
25Apr82-2Hol	7f	:21^{4}	:44^{2}	1:22^{4}ft	22	116	$7^{8\frac{1}{4}}$	7^{11}	6^{9}	$4^{5\frac{1}{2}}$	Aragon J^{6}	12500	77	Fancy Guy, The Lonier, Reverb	9
25Feb82-2SA	6½f	:21^{4}	:45	1:17 ft	19	115	7^{8}	$6^{4\frac{1}{2}}$	$5^{3\frac{3}{4}}$	$4^{2\frac{1}{2}}$	Guerra W A^{5}	10000	82	CountCrlcio,EmprorJohn,Mschvous	9
17Feb82-1SA	6f	:22	:45^{1}	1:11 ft	52	115	11^{12}	11^{11}	10^{11}	9^{12}	Sim M C^{4}	12500	71	Kpfu'sNtive,RisingEcho,ShrthGold	12
29Jan82-1SA	6½f	:22^{2}	:45^{1}	1:17^{4}ft	57	115	6^{3}	$4^{5\frac{1}{2}}$	3^{5}	$4^{5\frac{1}{4}}$	Sim M C^{1}	10000	76	PuebloPlsur,MrktChmp,ArrntDriv	10
3Sep81-1Dmr	6f	:22^{3}	:45^{3}	1:10^{2}ft	17	115	$5^{2\frac{1}{2}}$	5^{7}	5^{10}	$4^{8\frac{3}{4}}$	Valenzuela P A^{3}	12500	77	ItsaTall,Gatlin'Gunner,Mr.Reactor	12
23Aug81-9AC	6f	:22^{2}	:45	1:10^{3}ft	*3-2	115	$8^{9\frac{1}{4}}$	$7^{6\frac{3}{4}}$	$6^{4\frac{3}{4}}$	$6^{2\frac{3}{4}}$	Vilches M H^{5}	Aw3000	83	DarkMster,LordThurber,ChngingSe	9
16Aug81-9AC	6f	:22^{2}	:45	1:10^{1}ft	12	110^{5}	$5^{4\frac{1}{2}}$	$5^{5\frac{1}{4}}$	$5^{3\frac{1}{4}}$	2^{2}	Vilches M H^{5}	Aw3000	86	Mr. Matt, Bebito, Changing Sea	8

●May 6 SA 5f ft 1:00 h ●Apr 23 Hol 3f ft :34 h Apr 17 Hol tr.t 5f ft 1:05^{1} h

This horse was actually up close at his last three calls in a mile sixteenth effort. But because he was not up close at the first call, he cannot obtain the + rating for his running line.

While the stretch call is a prime indicator of a qualifying up close effort, it is obviously not the final word. The position of a horse at the finish is also extremely important. If we would award an N to a horse who was up close at the finish of its last race, as the equal of an up close call at the stretch, there would be little need to discuss the matter further. But, if being more perceptive about the use of the finish will help us throw out an occasional loser without getting burned, then we have to find a way to do it.

Our research has shown that the stretch call should be the primary qualifying call, but under certain meaningful exceptions, the finish may be used as an alternate source.

Exception Number One: When a horse fails to be up close at the stretch, but won the race, or finished less than a length from the winner, we will use the finish call as an alternate qualifying position to award a neutral.

The reason for this exception is that any horse that won his last race certainly qualifies on form. If he is not up close at the stretch and still wins the race, you can be sure he was putting on a healthy stretch drive. While he may have been passing tired horses, the final result of a winner cannot be overlooked.

But, as you will see in the next chapter, this is only part of the story. We have noticed tremendous problems with horses that won their last races, and you will find a full discussion, with guidelines that will enable you to deal with these difficulties. At this point, however, we are concerned only with what kind of running line rating the horse gets, and in this case, it is a neutral.

The same general theory applies to a horse that closes well enough to be within less than a length of the winner, even though he is not up close at the stretch. While we are even more fearful here of the passing-tired-horses syndrome, when an animal is able to move alongside the body of a winning rival, he is close enough at the wire to merit respectful attention. He should receive an N, and then be evaluated carefully on other factors.

Exception Number Two: The fall back–gain pattern: when a horse loses more than one length from the second call to the stretch call, and then comes back again to register up close at the finish, this horse is fully qualified and should get a neutral. The fall back–gain performance, which has been mentioned in one of my previous works, is always a strong factor and whenever you see it, take a serious second look at the horse, for you can be sure that you have a ready contender today.

We can get two for the price for one when we look at Flying Jen out of the eighth race at Golden Gate on June 17, since she demonstrates both the exception for finishing less than a length from the lead and the fall back–gain pattern.

```
Flying Jen *                        Ch. m. 6, by Leonardo III—Inventory, by Bobillard
                                    Br.—Factor S (Cal)                 1982  1 0 1 0    $2,925
Own.—Santucci G               113   Tr.—Pollard Damon                  1981 13 4 1 2   $32,579
                              Lifetime   33  8  4  7   $70,449         Turf  3 0 1 2    $5,305
30May82-6GG   1     Ⓣ:484 1:132 1:391fm  6½   114  66   63½  56   2¾   Baze R A1   ⒻAw15000 70 ForgottnRulr,FlyingJn,HltoBoldnss 8
7Sep81-7Bmf   1 1/16 :471 1:121 1:45 ft  *3-2 115  711  54   57   58   Munoz E5    Ⓕ 20000  66 PeeWeeBarb,BagofChrm,Kitty'sBy 7
21Aug81-11Stk 1 1/16 :46 1:103 1:423ft   2½   113  713  47½  47½  412  MnzE1  ⒻM Dotson H 81 RomanRockette,Legere,TorndoRed 8
6Aug81-11SR   1 1/16 :453 1:092 1:414ft  10   107  510  67½  54   31½  WinickD6 ⒻL Burbk H 95 Coul Victress,Here'sHow,FlyingJen 7
25Jly81-10Sol 1     :464 1:11 1:373ft    *2¼  116  1010 97¼  43½  1¾   Munoz E7    Ⓕ 20000  89 FlyingJen,Kitty'sBay,Ms.Attababe 10
26Jun81-6GG   1 1/16 Ⓣ:473 1:123 1:444fm 4½   114  48   33   33   34   Munoz E1    Ⓕ 22500  74 Miki F., Safesilver, Flying Jen 7
21Jun81-1GG   1 1/16 :472 1:113 1:44 ft  3½   114  54¼  1hd  11   13   Munoz E2    Ⓕ 16000  83 FlyingJen,PeeWeeBrb,Slri'sOlympis 8
7Jun81-3GG    1 1/16 :463 1:104 1:431ft  *2¼  114  67¾  64¼  44   42½  Munoz E1    Ⓕ 16000  84 NoMrEnmy,‡RpOffSkr,Slr'sOlymps 7
17May81-1GG   1     :454 1:104 1:362ft   2½   117  69   33½  21½  23   Munoz E6    Ⓕ 18000  83 Ms. Attababe, Flying Jen, JayJ.May 7
10May81-7GG   1 1/16 :453 1:101 1:434ft  *2¼  117  917  911  56   4nk  Mena F8     Ⓕ 16000  84 FntsticLiz,Ms.Attbbe,NoMorEnmy 10
   ●Jun 10 GG 7f ft 1:262 h     May 21 GG 7f ft 1:27 h     May 14 GG 6f ft 1:15 h     May 7 GG 4f ft :49 h
```

As you can readily see, she was not up close at the stretch call in her last race, but she finished less than a length behind. She thus gets an N for her running line. This was easy to spot, so let us concentrate on the fall back–gain aspect. At the second call, Flying Jen was only three and a half lengths off the lead. She fell back at the stretch to six lengths behind, which would not have been close enough to qualify her in her next outing. But she came on again, charging down the stretch to gain far more than enough to make her up close at the finish. Even if she had not closed the gap to less than a length, as long as she was within less than four lengths from the lead at the finish of the one mile race, she would have been up close, thus registering the fall back–gain pattern.

We will look again at Flying Jen in a later chapter, and you can find out then how she fared against the competition she faced in that race.

While our rule of play is limited to horses that fell back between calls and then moved up enough to obtain an up close call at the finish, the fall back–gain move itself is so strong that whenever you see it at other points in a race, you may want to seriously consider the horse that revealed it in its last race as a potentially very strong play for today.

CLASS AND DISTANCE AS ELEMENTS OF THE N FACTOR. Thus far, in determining the neutral, or N, rating that is quite commonly given, we have dealt only with horses coming back in the same class and at the same distance. But since changes in distance and class are daily staples of handicapping life, we must take into account how these changes affect a horse's form for his next race. We can start with distance, which is rather easy to handle.

If a horse is running today at a distance that is at least one full furlong shorter than his last race, we can shift our requirement for up close to the second call, instead of the stretch call. Therefore, in his last race he must have been no more than the requisite number of lengths behind, according to the distance of the last race, at the second call, rather than the stretch call. If so, he merits a neutral. If the horse was not within the required number of lengths of the lead at the second call in a shorter race, and if he made up enough ground to qualify at the usual stretch call, that would be sufficient. In other words, a horse that is up close at the stretch call will always merit an N rating.

The reason for this guideline should be obvious. A horse that is falling back in the stretch in a race longer than he is called upon to run today may do much better at the shorter distance. The shorter distance is not nearly so demanding, and as long as he is up close at the second call, we will give the horse the benefit of the doubt and not remove him as a qualified competitor.

But if a horse is running a longer distance today than he ran in his last race, we will leave the required up close call at the stretch. Consequently, in dealing with changes in distance as they affect the particular call for measuring the up close requirement, we are concerned only about shorter races, not longer ones.

Bear in mind again that the shorter race must be at least one furlong shorter. A horse running at a mile and a sixteenth today after tackling a mile and an eighth last time will not be judged according to the second call. Nor will a horse shortening up from six and a half furlongs to six furlongs. It must be one full furlong.

A good example of a horse qualifying at the second call of its last race, although shortening up today, comes from the seventh at Hollywood on June 19, as we look at Explosive Kingdom.

Explosive Kingdom
Own.—Flying Zee Stables **118**

Dk. b. or br. f. 4, by Key to the Kingdom—Explosive, by Speak John
Br.—Woodford & Zent (Ky) 1982 9 1 2 0 $31,250
Tr.—Vance David R 1981 10 3 0 3 $60,204
Lifetime 31 7 2 5 $133,134 Turf 3 0 0 1 $2,640

27May82-8Hol	1 1/16	:462	1:103	1:423ft	5½	117	45	44	610	511	Hawley S4	ⒻTypecast	71	SatinRibera,Beachcombing,Aduana	8
7May82-7Hol	1	:47	1:111	1:362ft	5½	115	21½	2½	2½	11¼	McHrgDG3	ⒻAw35000	84	ExplosiveKingdom,TrckJestr,Rihun	5
16Apr82-8Aqu	6f	:241	:473	1:121ft	3½	121	21	22½	22½	22¼	Vergara O6	ⒻAw25000	78	Andy'sActon,ExplosvKngdm,Bstwd	6
5Apr82-7Aqu	7f	:232	:464	1:242ft	15	121	46½	47	34½	24	Vergara O6	ⒻAw25000	75	Rs'NDnc,ExplosvKngdom,GltdFlwr	7
21Mar82-7Aqu	7f	:224	:46	1:251ft	3¼	115	68½	57	57	55¾	Vergara O4	ⒻAw29000	69	Willnt,PowerStreet,GoodHevn'sGirl	6
26Feb82-8Aqu	6f	⊡:222	:454	1:11 ft	30	115	43½	53	42	55	Vergara O8	ⒻAw29000	84	Viva Sec, Anti Phil, Coprincess	8
22Jan82-8Aqu	1⅛	⊡:484	1:133	1:521ft	20	115	2½	2hd	43½	69½	Tejeira J8	ⒻAw32000	75	AutumnGlory,SinisterQueen,Quantr	9
15Jan82-7Aqu	6f	⊡:223	:451	1:10 ft	4½	1125	56½	69	69	613	Gomez ER3	ⒻAw29000	81	TheWheelTurns,TogaTog,LivelyStr	8
9Jan82-8Aqu	6f	⊡:221	:452	1:101ft	13	112	43	43	56	68	McCrrG4	ⒻIntrboroH	85	LaVue,SweetRevenge,SproutedRye	7
14Dec81-8Aqu	6f	⊡:221	:451	1:103ft	10	114	43½	43	32½	53¾	Migliore R4	ⒻHcp0	87	Sissy'sTim,ALittlAffction,InOurTim	6

Jun 17 Hol 4f ft :462 h Jun 10 Hol 5f ft :594 h May 26 Hol 4f ft :494 h May 19 Hol 5f ft 1:02 h

Her last race was at a mile and a sixteenth, and today she is shortening up to seven furlongs. Thus, you can move your qualifying call from the stretch to the second call. At the second call, she was four lengths behind in a distance race, which is less than the five lengths required to establish an up close for an N rating. Consequently, by using the second call, we can consider Explosive Kingdom as a bona fide form contender in today's race.

Now, let us take a shorter race that also qualifies. We have Waterford Billy running in a six furlong sprint on the same Hollywood card on June 19.

Waterford Billy
Own.—Purner & Mizrahie **116**

Ch. g. 5, by Fleet Allied—Fiji Native, by Native Charger
Br.—Mook & Blanchard (Cal) 1982 5 0 0 0 $2,225
Tr.—French Neil $32,000 1981 12 2 5 0 $49,100
Lifetime 22 3 7 1 $64,625

31May82-5Hol	7f	:214	:442	1:221ft	12	1115	41¼	31	44½	56	Steiner J J7	40000	80	Sam'sComet,Incorportor,HrdtoLee	8
21May82-5Hol	6f	:211	:441	1:092ft	11	1115	78	810	65½	42¼	Steiner J J1	32000	88	Sam's Comet, Sami, Valentine Lew	9
18Apr82-3SA	6½f	:212	:441	1:142ft	11	116	43½	65¾	68½	613	Asmussen C B2	50000	85	NaynoBay,BeachWalk,Incorporator	6
4Apr82-2SA	6½f	:214	:443	1:152ft	7¾	116	3½	53	612	613	Valenzuela P A7	62500	80	Fingal, Amen Brother, Tellaround	8
6Jan82-7SA	6f	:22	:46	1:123hy	4	116	31	2½	34	55½	Valenzuela P A5	62500	69	GrayDandy,HardtoLee,Incorporator	6
♦ 6Jan82—Dead heat															
13Nov81-7Hol	6f	:22	:443	1:084ft	3	118	31	41	41½	67	Pincay L Jr8	Aw26000	86	Hcwind,KngrooCourt,PompiiCourt	8
27Oct81-8LA	1 1/16	:444	1:103	1:432ft	*2-5	120	53	32½	33½	46¾	McCarronCJ1	Aw22000	85	Maw'sPappBre,VictorE.,Embermtic	6
9Oct81-7SA	6f	:22	:443	1:091ft	3	118	12½	12½	12½	1nk	Pincay L Jr3	Aw24000	92	WtrfordBilly,MidnghtMn,FormulOn	6
30Jly81-7Dmr	6f	:224	:452	1:102ft	*6-5	118	53¾	66	55½	65¼	DelhoussyeE4	Aw18000	81	Sli'sRoylDrem,BondRullh,BronzStr	8
3Jly81-3Hol	7f	:22	:442	1:212ft	*1	119	11	12	16	17	McCarronCJ4	Aw20000	90	WtrfordBilly,MstrCrmonis,JromPrr	7

Jun 11 Hol 4f ft :474 h May 12 Hol 4f ft :464 h May 3 Hol 5f ft :59 h

If this race at Hollywood had been a seven furlong race, Waterford Billy would not have had a sufficient up close call to obtain an N rating. But since he was running one full furlong less today than in his last race, from seven furlongs down to six furlongs, we can use the second call. At this call he was one length behind, which is indeed up close, and that is sufficient to get the neutral rating.

This adjustment in the standard for shorter distances is relatively easy to apply and should seldom cause any problems.

But changes in class, or levels of competition, are somewhat different and require considerably more fine tuning. First, as we mentioned with form cycles you have to make certain that a horse is either rising or dropping in class to a sufficient degree to place him in a different level of competition. If that is not so, then you will be misleading yourself.

When dealing with claiming races, dollar signs are still an excellent measure of levels of competition. To assess whether a different level of competition is involved, one safe guideline is to require a 20% change in dollar value, up or down or close to it. Mathematically, this is very easy to do. Start with ten percent of the value of the claiming price of the last race. We do this version of quick math because finding ten percent of any number is as easy as dropping the final zero. If a horse entered in a $12,000 claiming price in his last race you can quickly find the ten percent figure by dropping the last zero, which gives you $1,200. Twenty percent is twice ten percent, so merely double the $1,200 to get $2,400, which is a full 20% of the $12,000 claiming price. Subtract the $2,400 from the $12,000, and you get $9,600, which is the 20% level downward. If you were moving upward, you would add the $2,400 to get a $14,400 price.

But you are not likely to see either figure as an actual claiming price, because these prices are only thousands, not hundreds. Thus, you may find the dropping horse entered at $10,000 and the rising horse entered at $14,000. Neither figure meets the full 20%. What do you do?

Remember, the 20% figure is a sound guideline in most cases, but only that. We are not wedded to it. We are still searching for levels of competition. If at the track where you play, there is very little difference in levels of competition between $10,000 and $12,000 horses, you would not consider a horse moving from the higher figure to the lower price to be dropping in class. You will have to make that judgment based upon your knowledge of purses and levels of competition at your track.

For the most part, I would prefer to be safe and not consider the slight drop from $12,000 down to $10,000 as a move to a true lower level of competition. If the $12,000 horse drops to $8,500, then you have something. If the $10,000 horse drops to $8,500, you have a closer question.

At the major New York tracks, and in southern California, where you can have claiming races for as much as $100,000, the 20% guideline is often of very little use. A horse that last ran for a claiming price of $100,000 and today is entered for $75,000, while falling more than 20%, is very likely running against the same level of competition.

In these high-priced claiming races, which often have a range of prices at which a horse can be entered, it is vitally important not to make the mistake of rating your horse's dollar value off the claiming price at which he is entered today rather than the claiming price of today's race itself. This is equally important in the other claiming races. Look at the second race at Belmont on June 17, 1982, and ask yourself whether the fact that he last ran for a price of $12,500 and today is entered for $10,000 means that Emperor's Lad is dropping in class.

2nd Belmont

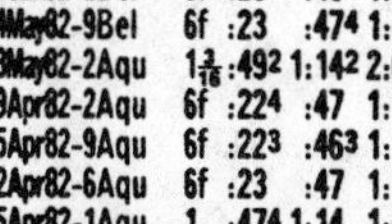

6 FURLONGS. (1.08$\frac{4}{5}$) CLAIMING. Purse $10,500. 4-year-olds and upward. Weights, 122 lbs. Non-winners of two races since May 15 allowed, 3 lbs. Of a race since then, 5 lbs. Claiming price $12,500; for each $1,000 to $10,500, 2 lbs. (Races when entered to be claimed for $8,500 or less not considered.)

Emperor's Lad — Dk. b. or br. g. 4, by Bombay Duck—Gala Lady, by Bold Tim
Br.—Ocala Stud Farms Inc (Fla) — 1982 9 1 0 2 $8,610
Own.—Allen H — 115 — Tr.—Jacobs Eugene — $10,500 — 1981 14 M 2 3 $10,360
Lifetime 28 1 2 5 $18,970 — Turf 4 0 0 1 $1,000

2Jun82-2Bel	6f	:23^{1}	:46^{3}	1:11 gd	$3\frac{3}{4}$e	119	$4^{2\frac{1}{4}}$	4^{6}	7^{11}	8^{16}	Bailey J D^{8}	12500	71	Dvl'sAdvoct,PolrPont,LSuprSonq	11
24May82-9Bel	6f	:23	:47^{4}	1:14 sy	$4\frac{3}{4}$	120	$4^{6\frac{1}{2}}$	3^{4}	$2^{\frac{1}{2}}$	$1^{3\frac{1}{2}}$	Bailey J D^{5}	M13000	72	Empror'sLd,Commodity,BoldVnntt	8
13May82-2Aqu	$1\frac{3}{16}$	:49^{2}	1:14^{2}	2:00^{3}m	9	117^{7}	1^{hd}	$1^{\frac{1}{2}}$	5^{4}	6^{11}	Ocasio L Jr^{8}	M15000	48	Solar Salute, All Cash, Angus Lane	8
29Apr82-2Aqu	6f	:22^{4}	:47	1:12^{1}gd	*$2\frac{1}{4}$	124	2^{3}	2^{5}	3^{8}	$4^{9\frac{3}{4}}$	Cordero A Jr^{2}	M15000	70	BroadwayBrvo,PinkPrty,OurWyOut	7
25Apr82-9Aqu	6f	:22^{3}	:46^{3}	1:13^{2}ft	*3-2	124	4^{4}	$4^{4\frac{1}{2}}$	2^{2}	3^{3}	Cordero A Jr^{3}	M15000	71	BigIzzy,DeebTheArab,Emperor'sLd	9
12Apr82-6Aqu	6f	:23	:47	1:13 ft	$8\frac{3}{4}$	115^{5}	$6^{2\frac{1}{4}}$	7^{9}	$7^{9\frac{1}{2}}$	$6^{7\frac{3}{4}}$	Puckett H^{1}	M35000	68	ChrstophrStr,GmblrEd,WhtMrTSy	10
5Apr82-1Aqu	1	:47^{4}	1:14	1:40^{2}ft	*$2\frac{1}{2}$	124	6^{5}	5^{7}	5^{5}	4^{8}	Cordero A Jr^{7}	M35000	56	EasternMusic,Gottgetup,FewPence	8
25Mar82-4Aqu	6f	:22^{3}	:46	1:13 ft	4	124	$5^{5\frac{1}{2}}$	$6^{9\frac{1}{2}}$	3^{9}	3^{8}	Samyn J L^{12}	M35000	68	OvrndEsy,ChrstophrStr,Emprr'sLd	13

Jun 10 Bel tr.t 5f ft :59^{3} h   May 11 Bel tr.t 4f ft :50 b   Apr 22 Bel tr.t 4f ft :49^{1} b

Experienced players will not be fooled by this one. You must always first look at the conditions of the race to see that the actual ceiling claiming price of the race is $12,500. Then you note the weight off allowances, which enable a trainer to reduce the price on his horse (therefore making a claim somewhat more probable) in exchange for carrying less weight, which presumably would give him a better chance to win. Trainers do this all the time. Emperor's Lad is not dropping in class at all, since he faced horses valued at $12,500 in his last race and is competing against the same level of stock in today's race at Belmont. Thus, there is no reason to consider judging him for the up close standard at any other than the stretch call, and as you can see, he was not up close.

From this same race, you can get a far more exact line on a true class drop when you look at Cliff Hanger.

Cliff Hanger

Dk. b. or br. c. 4, by Mr Prospector—Nana Blanch, by Sherluck
Br.—Heinen P & Patricia (Fla)   1982 7 2 0 0 $12,600
Own.—Sommer Viola   **117**   Tr.—Martin Frank $12,500   1981 10 1 0 2 $15,480

				Lifetime	17	3	0	2	$28,060		
12Jun82-9Bel	6f :223	:454 1:104ft	7¾ 117	11 2½	33	55¼	Miranda J2		16000 82	Truce, Soudan, Greene Go	9
26May82-3Bel	6f :23	:462 1:104ft	3e117	11½ 31½	64	89¾	Rivera M A1		16000 78	Whambang, Clodion,RajaTheGreat	11
14May82-9Aqu	6f :221	:453 1:112ft	*6-5 119	22½ 2½	13	1nk	Vasquez J9		c12500 84	CliffHanger,PowerMster,PokieJoe	10
8May82-9Aqu	1 :47	1:12 1:38 ft	6¾ 115	11½ 21½	711	815	Vasquez J4		19000 61	Sprink, Click Off, Marlago	10
30Apr82-2Aqu	6f :223	:462 1:111ft	*3-2 117	22½ 1½	13	15½	Russ M L1		c10000 85	Cliff Hanger, Born Great, I'm Vital	7
21Apr82-7Aqu	6f :222	:453 1:104ft	*8-5e117	21 25	37½	611	Velasquez J5		25000 76	WstgtBrnswck,MstrMgcn,Whmbng	8
3Apr82-4Aqu	6f :223	:451 1:11 ft	7 117	31½ 56	611	613	Vergara O6		35000 73	El Bombay, Assension, Royal Jove	6
28Dec81-7Aqu	6f ⊡:23	:4611:113gd	8-5e115	64 73¾	62½	64	Migliore R5		Aw16000 82	Grand Felice, FountainofGold,Rigid	8

Jun 3 Bel tr.1 4f ft :473 h   May 6 Bel 6f ft 1:19 b

Cliff Hanger is entered for a tag of $12,500—the same as the standard claiming price of the race itself. Therefore, you can use the $12,500 figure to assess the class level, but remember that you use it because it is the claiming level for today's race, and not necessarily the price at which the horse was entered. Cliff Hanger is moving downward from a $16,000 race. Twenty percent of $16,000 is $3,200. Subtracting this 20% figure gives you a price of $12,800 as the threshold below which Cliff Hanger must fall in order to register a true drop in class. Thus, because today's race is for less than $12,800, Cliff Hanger is truly running at a lower level of competition.

Now that we have learned how to identify a true class dropper in claiming races, we can establish variations in the up close measurement to apply to horses descending the class ladder.

When a horse is running at a lower level of competition, he needs only to have been up close at any call in his last race—just one—to get an N rating. Cliff Hanger was up close at two calls, both the first and second, which is a common pattern. He would thus get an N for his last effort because of the class drop today even though he was not up close at the stretch call in his last race. He was the second choice in the race under examination, and came through with a handsome victory. You may have noted that he was coming back in five days, a powerful sign in and of itself along with the + for recency that it merits, and this made Cliff Hanger a prime selection for the victory be turned in.

The discussion thus far has dealt with measuring class in claiming races. Allowance races are much less difficult to deal with since 1982 because the *Racing Form* has made the helpful improvement of showing the purses in allowance races. Now you can use purse values as a dollar measure device to often determine the level of competition in these races. A drop in purse value of 20% is thus a very useful guide, but it must be at the same track in the same racing circuit.

The "same circuit" is very important, since a horse may ship in from a track that does not pay high purses in allowance races and yet have sufficient class to compete against runners who have been accustomed to seeking bigger payoffs. This factor, however, is usually only critical when purse values are going up.

Far more important in allowance races, however, are the conditions themselves, which give you some idea of the level of competition required. Any serious student ought to become familiar, if not already, with James Quinn's analytical work, *The Handicapper's Condition Book* (GBC Press, 1981), which provides excellent examples of the class ladder in allowance races. Typically, after winning their maiden races, allowance horses compete thereafter in races where the conditions limit entries to horses fitting into "non-winners other than maiden, claiming or starter." The next level is usually for non-winners of one race other than maiden, claiming or starter, and so on up the· ladder. The young allowance horse that won his last race in limited company is almost certainly moving to the next level on the conditions rung, and thus is usually rising in class.

After a maiden victory, almost every horse is rising in class, since he is in effect facing a level of competition that he has never previously encountered. One cardinal exception is where young lightly raced two-year-olds may be competing in a field where nearly all of them are coming off their maiden victories, and here, of course, they are all at the same level of competition.

In open allowance races for older horses, however, the purse value may be your best indicator of class levels of competition.

When a horse is moving from an allowance race into a claiming race, the allowance purse level is also extremely useful in determining whether there is a true drop or not. You should not assume that a move from an allowance race to a claiming race represents a drop in class. Purses in many high-priced claimers outstrip many allowance purses and I have seen many situations where a horse going from an allowance race to a claiming race is actually rising in class, as far as the level of competition is concerned.

In assessing the move from allowance to claiming ranks, the player is often confronted with a move from one track or racing circuit to another. The ninth race at Hollywood Park on June 19, offers a prime illustration. Menotti had run in the Bay Area at Golden Gate in an allowance event for a $16,000 purse. He was entered at Hollywood for a claiming price of $40,000—was Menotti rising, dropping, or remaining above even in class?

Menotti *

B. g. 4, by Pia Star—First Time Out, by First Landing
Br.—Mamakos & Stubrin (Cal)   1982 5 3 0 0 $22,000
Own.—Mamakos & Stubrin   **122** Tr.—McAnally Ronald $40,000   1981 8 M 1 0 $5,475
Lifetime 13 3 1 0 $27,475   Turf 4 0 1 0 $4,175

31May82-9GG	1 :46⁴ 1:11² 1:37¹ft	3½ 117	14 13	11½ 12½	Sorenson D⁶	Aw16000	82	Menotti,ImaTrackStr,BornRestless 7
1May82-4GG	1 ⑦:45²1:10³1:36⁴fm	12 120	6¹¹ 9¹³	9¹⁵ 9²⁰	Sorenson D⁹	Aw15000	63	Winewood Host, Montera, Vizier 9
23Apr82-6GG	1₁₆:47 1:10⁴ 1:43¹ft	17 113	11½ 11	12 11	Sorenson D⁵	Aw13000	87	Menotti, Lark's Flight, Brightwell 6
13Apr82-8GG	6f :22¹ :45¹ 1:10¹ft	12 120	7⁵¾ 6⁷½	6⁹ 6¹¹	Sorenson D⁶	Aw14000	77	Im Full of Joy,Hematite,YoungFella 9
2Apr82-5GG	6f :22³ :45⁴ 1:12 sy	4 119	1¹ 1³	1⁴ 1⁶	Sorenson D⁷	Mdn	79	Mnotti,BurstofSong,APrsntofSong 8
30Oct81-3BM	1₁₆:47 1:12³ 1:45¹ft	2½ 116	3¹½ 4²½	5⁸ 6¹³	Baze R A⁷	Mdn	60	FbulousRson,Doon'sBy,PrciousTim 7
16Oct81-4SA	6½f :22¹ :45³ 1:17⁴ft	3½ 117	6⁵ 5²½	4²¾ 4¹½	Castaneda M²	M25000	80	HveGoodTim,FthrMc,NonTooSoon 8
27Aug81-6Dmr	1₁₆:46¹ 1:10³ 1:43 ft	5½ 116	7⁴¾ 7¹²	7¹⁶ 7²²	McHargue D G⁵	Mdn	63	Snacked, HonchoNotor,Calabonga 12
8Aug81-4Dmr	1₁₆⑦:47³1:12³1:44⁴fm	4½ 116	1ʰᵈ 1ʰᵈ	2½ 5³½	Ortega L E²	Mdn	84	PocktMn,HonchoNotr,YmnnSHwk 12
27Jly81-6Dmr	1₁₆:46¹ 1:11² 1:44 ft	4½ 114	8⁷½ 6⁵¾	7⁶½ 6⁶¾	Ortega L E⁷	Mdn	73	GoldenCircle,AnotherEgle,Clbong 12

Jun 10 GG 5f ft 1:02² h   ●May 23 GG 5f ft :59⁴ h   May 17 GG 5f ft 1:02² h   May 10 GG 4f ft :49⁴ h

The purse value is perhaps the major key, although California handicappers are well aware of the higher class of horse that races on the Hollywood–Santa Anita–Del Mar southern California circuit. The ninth at Hollywood on June 19 carried a purse of $23,000, as compared to the $16,000 offered to allowance horses at Golden Gate. Menotti was indeed rising in class against tough competition, and he ran out of the money, as you might expect.

THE DIFFICULT AREA IN BETWEEN: CLOSE, BUT NOT QUITE. In fixing absolute figures for the up close standard insofar as lengths behind are concerned, we must always be aware of the horse whose figures are just a shade on the borderline. In the six furlong sprint, where to be up close a horse must be two and three-quarter lengths or less from the lead, what do you do about the horse that is an even three lengths behind, and an even four behind in seven furlong races, or five lengths behind in distance races? Even three and a half or four and a half lengths behind, as the case may be, can be a troublesome issue.

Violating lines of demarcation in one instance leads to violations in other cases, and soon, there will be no lines at all. You simply have to stay within certain lines if you want a degree of precision in form-handicapping. But even so, when carefully handicapping a field of horses, you will always want to take a second look at the horse that is close, but not quite. An example is Playboy Jubilee, in the fourth at Hollywood on June 19.

```
*Playboy Jubilee                      B. h. 5, by Connaught—Paphos, by Vilmorin
                                      Br.—Berry Col J (Ire)                        1982  6  0  0  2      $7,500
Own.—Lambourne R                 116  Tr.—Palma Hector O             $40,000       1981  9  0  0  3      $9,168
                                    Lifetime    23  1  1  8    $47,861             Turf 18  1  1  6     $40,361
10Jun82-4Hol  6½f :22   :44  1:143ft   22  114  53½ 46  59½ 611  Guerra W A5   Aw22000 86 Okubo,StrikeItBig,LongLivethKing 7
14May82-5Hol  6f  :221  :444 1:09 ft    4  117  41  53½ 44½ 45½  Pincay L Jr3  Aw20000 86 Rawbone, Colonel Stu, Doon's Bay 7
 1May82-9Hol  1⅛ Ⓣ:452 1:101 1:47 fm  10  114  17  11½ 55½ 1218 Lipham T2     Aw22000 77 Peter Jones, Amrapour, Hansel   12
15Apr82-7SA   6f  :214  :444 1:09 ft    4  114  41½ 52¼ 64¼ 79½  Black K6      Aw19000 83 Never Tabled, Santir,TonysLanding 9
31Mar82-7SA   6f  :223  :45  1:081ft    3  117  31  32  22½ 34¾  Pincay L Jr3  Aw20000 92 Jnny'sDvid,TurnngWhls,Plyboy.Jubl 8
 3Mar82-5SA   6f  :22   :442 1:09 ft   *2½ 117  32  24  24½ 36½  Pincay L Jr9  Aw20000 86 Okubo,LukePadgett,PlyboyJubilee 10
15Oct81♦6Newmarket(Eng) 7f  1:274gd    8  137  Ⓣ  43½ StrkeyG          Fordham H  SharpCeleste,Azam,PlyboyJubilee 13
 3Oct81♦3Newmarket(Eng) 1⅛  1:52 gd   28  120  Ⓣ  17  McKW      Cambridgeshire H  Braughing, Baronet, Lulav        28
 9Sep81♦2Doncaster(Eng) 1   1:391gd   6½  133  Ⓣ  8   StrkeyG     Julio Mariner H  Tugoflove,HillsdownGold,HrbiQuyl 10
 2Sep81♦1York(Eng)  7f      1:261fm   *3  140  Ⓣ  43  StrkeyG  Gilby Slvr Trphy H  TopO'Th'Lne,SecrtGill,ShowofHnds 9
    Jun 4 Hol 4f ft :472 h       May 28 Hol 4f ft :474 h      May 22 Hol 5f ft 1:001 h      May 9 Hol 4f ft :481 b
```

He is moving from an allowance race with a purse of $22,000 down into a claimer for the first time in his record, running for a tag of $40,000. The claiming purse, as shown in the conditions of the race, is $21,000. So, again you see that there is hardly any difference in the level of competition involved, even though a horse running for a claiming price is normally not as valuable as the animal entered in an allowance race. If there were a true drop in class, you would then take up the question of whether the three and a half lengths behind at the first call would be close enough for a second look. Actually, this horse fails all around. The fact that he twice came close, both on the class drop and the lengths behind, but not quite, removes any doubt at all. Playboy Jubilee would get a O for his last race running line.

Another close, but not quite, area is when a horse finishes second without being up close at any call. In *Investing at the Racetrack* any horse, no matter how far back he finished, was considered as qualified on form if he finished second. The reason was that he might have faced a very outstanding animal that ran off from the field.

For more precise handicapping, however, we have to take a second look at the horse that finished second, without being up close. What should we do about Speak Amour out of the first race at Belmont on June 17?

Speak Amour ✻ — Dk. b. or br. m. 5, by Royal John—Skip Amour, by St Amour II
Own.—Tresvant Stable — 112^5 — Br.—McKee J D (WVa) — Tr.—Sedlacek Sue — $25,000
Lifetime 62 10 10 8 $105,857
1982 11 2 4 1 $33,540
1981 21 5 1 5 $38,565
Turf 2 0 0 1 $825

9Jun82-5Bel	7f	:22^4	:45^4	1:23^{2}ft	9	108^5	8$^{8\frac{3}{4}}$	8$^{7\frac{1}{2}}$	5^5	2^7	White J R^4	Ⓕ 35000	78	WinsomeSky,SpekAmour,SnkrStrkr	8
20May82-9Bel	7f	:23	:46	1:24^{1}ft	7½	108^5	10^9	10^{12}	8^{10}	5$^{7\frac{1}{4}}$	White J R^6	Ⓕ 45000	74	Nor'sLss,HrlemQueen,WinsomSky	10
8May82-2Aqu	7f	:23	:46^2	1:25 ft	5½	112^5	7$^{4\frac{1}{2}}$	6$^{7\frac{1}{4}}$	3$^{3\frac{1}{2}}$	1$^{7\frac{3}{4}}$	White J R^3	Ⓕ 30000	76	Speak Amour, Cognito,DawnOfLife	8
1May82-3Aqu	1	:46^4	1:12^3	1:38^{4}ft	5½	108^5	8^{17}	8^8	5^6	5^4	White J R^5	Ⓕ 30000	68	ExctlyTricky,EdistoEpic,HrlemQun	8
10Apr82-4Aqu	1	:47^2	1:12^4	1:39 ft	4¾	108^5	6$^{9\frac{1}{2}}$	6$^{8\frac{1}{2}}$	4$^{3\frac{1}{4}}$	1$^{\frac{1}{2}}$	White J R^3	Ⓕ 30000	71	SpekAmour,WinsomSky,EdistoEpic	7
28Mar82-1Aqu	1⅛	:49^4	1:16^1	1:55^{4}ft	4¼	110^7	3$^{1\frac{1}{2}}$	4$^{\frac{3}{4}}$	3$^{2\frac{1}{2}}$	2$^{1\frac{1}{4}}$	Buscemi S^5	Ⓕ 25000	55	WinsomeSky,SpeakAmour,GallntBo	8
20Mar82-1Aqu	1	:46^4	1:12^1	1:39^{3}ft	6¾	112^5	3^2	4^5	3^4	4$^{1\frac{3}{4}}$	Gomez E R^5	Ⓕ 35000	66	ExactlyTricky,DwnOfLife,RedSprite	7
7Mar82-5Aqu	1⅛ ⊡	:49	1:15	1:54 sy	*2¾	108^5	2^{hd}	1$^{\frac{1}{2}}$	1^{hd}	2$^{\frac{3}{4}}$	Gomez E R^3	Ⓕ 20000	75	ClssicGl,SpekAmour,Tinsley'sDrem	7

She shows a second place finish only eight days before, followed by a substantial drop in class. Speak Amour was unable to be up close at any call in her last race, and off the standards we have set in this book, she would not be entitled to an N for her last race running line. But does the second place finish allow for an exception? Now, we will ask the new question of whether the winning horse in the previous race turned in an outstanding performance. If there was such a high powered effort, then the second place finisher ought to be given respectful attention in the next race. The winning time was 1:23.2, not bad at all, but not of extraordinary caliber. Speak Amour's speed rating, which is based on final time, was only 78, and while again, the performance was not really a bad one at all, we are looking for something more spectacular. I would not want to give Speak Amour an N off her last race because it simply was not good enough. You will have to make judgement calls in situations like this, guided by the winner's time and margin.

Another kind of horse that has its weak points but cannot be disregarded altogether is the animal whose running line comment in the eastern edition of *Daily Racing Form* says, "evenly." Since comment lines are not used in the midwestern and western editions, it is necessary to determine the sort of running line that would warrant the "evenly" comment. If a horse remained approximately the same distance back at every call of his last running line, with only slight gains or losses, this kind of race, while not always the kind we are looking for, is worth keeping under consideration.

An example of this kind of running line is shown by Effortlessly in the first race at Hollywood Park on June 16.

1st Hollywood

6½ FURLONGS. (1.14) CLAIMING. Purse $9,500. 4-year-olds and upward. Weight, 121 lbs. Non-winners of two races since April 18 allowed 3 lbs.; a race since then, 6 lbs. Claiming price $10,000; if for $9,000 allowed 2 lbs. (Races when entered for $8,000 or less not considered.)

Effortlessly * — Dk. b. or br. g. 7, by Windy Sands—Honey Im Lucky, by Lucky Mel

Own.—Goode & Biermann — **118** — Br.—Hemming Brothers (Cal) — Tr.—Pew Karl — $10,000

1982	12	1	2	1		$9,975
1981	10	1	3	0		$8,990
Lifetime	47	5	10	3	$54,955	
Turf	1	0	0	0		$325

3Jun82-1Hol	6f	:22^{1}	:45^{1}	1:10^{4}ft	11	119	6$^{3\frac{1}{4}}$	5^{5}	5$^{3\frac{3}{4}}$	3$^{4\frac{1}{4}}$	McHargue D G^{8}	10000	79	RmmbrMyDrm,Gtln'Gnnr,Effrtlssly	9
27May82-1Hol	7f	:22^{2}	:45^{1}	1:23 ft	7$\frac{1}{4}$	118	2$^{\frac{1}{2}}$	2^{hd}	6$^{5\frac{1}{2}}$	7$^{8\frac{1}{4}}$	McCarron CJ^{8} Ⓢ	10000	74	Don's Dancer, Paintec, Tragic Bell	11
15May82-9Fno	6f	:22^{2}	:45^{3}	1:10^{4}ft	*1	114	1^{hd}	1$^{\frac{1}{2}}$	1^{2}	1^{3}	Hamilton M^{9}	10000	86	Effortlessly, Bathymetry, Cajoje	9
7Apr82-1SA	6f	:21^{4}	:44^{3}	1:09^{2}ft	3$\frac{3}{4}$	116	9$^{6\frac{1}{2}}$	10^{11}	10^{13}	9$^{9\frac{1}{4}}$	McCarron C J^{7}	10000	82	Pintc,RllySombody,BulldogPrntic	11
31Mar82-1SA	6f	:21^{4}	:44^{3}	1:09^{3}ft	8	116	7$^{6\frac{3}{4}}$	5$^{5\frac{3}{4}}$	6$^{8\frac{1}{2}}$	4$^{4\frac{3}{4}}$	DelahoussayeE^{5}	12500	85	ImFullofJoy,TrgicBll,FirstGrndson	10
17Mar82-1SA	6f	:22	:45^{2}	1:11 sy	4	116	6^{5}	6$^{6\frac{1}{4}}$	6$^{7\frac{3}{4}}$	5$^{4\frac{1}{2}}$	DelahoussayeE^{2}	12500	78	Prkinthedrk,Tulse,ProfessorGreene	8
4Mar82-1SA	6f	:21^{3}	:44^{1}	1:09^{1}ft	7$\frac{1}{2}$	117	9^{11}	7$^{7\frac{3}{4}}$	6$^{4\frac{1}{4}}$	4$^{1\frac{3}{4}}$	Pincay L Jr^{3}	12500	90	Tulsea,RisingEcho,ImmanentIssue	11
25Feb82-1SA	6$\frac{1}{2}$f	:21^{4}	:44^{3}	1:17 ft	9$\frac{1}{4}$	116	6$^{3\frac{1}{2}}$	6$^{6\frac{1}{2}}$	6^{5}	2no	DelhoussyeE^{9} Ⓢ	10000	85	CaliforniFig,Effortlessly,SirDvidR.	11
19Feb82-2SA	1$\frac{1}{16}$	:45^{2}	1:10	1:42^{2}ft	19	116	5^{5}	4$^{7\frac{1}{2}}$	4$^{9\frac{1}{2}}$	5^{12}	McHargue D G^{2}	12500	77	Concussion, SeaRide,Protectorate	12
12Feb82-9SA	1$\frac{1}{8}$	:47^{3}	1:12^{4}	1:51^{3}ft	13	116	2^{hd}	3$^{1\frac{1}{2}}$	9^{17}	10^{26}	Fernandez A L^{6}	16000	45	The Big T., PacificMorn,Umaticca	11

Jun 11 Hol 3f ft :35^{2} h

This horse was reasonably close in his last race on June 3, but he was not quite close enough to the lead to earn an up close rating at any call. At the stretch call, effortlessly was three and three-quarter lengths from the leader. But, in this six furlong race, the horse would have had to have been two and three-quarter lengths or less from the leader at the crucial call. Yet he ran rather evenly, never more than five lengths back and never closer than three and a quarter. This is about as far as we can stretch the lengths behind from call to call when determining whether to give a horse the benefit of the doubt. Nevertheless, because the last race was an even effort within hailing distance, we would not want to eliminate him as a potential contender in today's race. Thus, rather than imposing a O for unqualified on the horse, we can assign a "doubtful but not completely out of it rating." This is indicated by marking the zero with a diagonal through it, like this: Ø.

In any of these running line situations where the horse is almost, but not quite, up close, such as the situation where it is only slightly past the qualifying number of lengths behind, or where it has finished second, or has demonstrated an "evenly" running line, it is wise to weigh the horse against the other contenders, based upon whatever method you use for rating horses. For me to consider any horse in the close, but not quite category, as a contender worthy of being played, the horse must show stronger ability points than any of the other horses.

However, where a horse is dropped in class to a lower level of competition you can see that the close, but not quite, horse could be formidable indeed in his next race. The lower level of competition may be all he needs to convert the up close, not quite, performance in the last race into a significant victory against today's weaker competition. When a horse shows an "evenly" running line in its most recent effort, the class drop is most effective. That is when you should pay careful attention.

In *Investing at the Racetrack*, a horse that gained five in its last running line, whether in lengths made up or in horses passed, or a combination of the two, was considered qualified on form. While this "gain of five" rule still has its virtues, they can rather easily be wiped out by other deficiencies identified by the new research. Out of the sixth race at Hollywood Park on June 16, 1982, the powerful old gelding, No No, was favored in a six furlong race against some very impressive foes. How does he look to you?

No No *

B. g. 7, by T V Commercial—Cuba Bound, by Sunrise Flight

Br.—Marydel Farm (Md) — 1982 8 3 1 0 $82,366

Own.—Bacharach B — **119** — **Tr.—Frankel Robert** — **$62,500** — 1981 11 2 1 1 $63,000

Lifetime 51 12 7 5 $326,746 — **Turf** 5 0 1 1 $10,590

3Jun82-7Hol	6½f	:22	$:44^1$	$1:15^3$ft	*9-5	118	$7^{4\frac{3}{4}}$	$7^{8\frac{3}{4}}$	$6^{9\frac{1}{4}}$	$4^{4\frac{1}{2}}$	Ortega L E^2	72500	87	WalterOsborne,FlyingChick,StndPt	8
15May82-3Hol	7f	$:22^1$	$:44^2$	1:22 ft	2¼	116	$5^{9\frac{1}{2}}$	$5^{5\frac{1}{2}}$	$1^{\frac{1}{2}}$	$1^{\frac{3}{4}}$	Ortega L E^2	62500	87	No No, Perry Cabin, Philip E.	6
8Apr82-9OP	6f	$:22^2$	$:46^2$	1:12 ft	*7-5	118	$8^{5\frac{1}{4}}$	$5^{4\frac{1}{2}}$	5^5	5^2	Snyder L^3	Count Fl'th	83	Sandbagger,BlueWterLine,Lockjw	10
19Mar82-9OP	6f	$:21^4$	$:45^4$	$1:11^4$ft	18	114	10^{15}	10^{12}	$8^{5\frac{3}{4}}$	2^{hd}	Ortega L E^7	HcpO	86	Smokite, No No, Blue Water Line	11
20Feb82-9OP	6f	$:21^3$	$:45^3$	$1:11^3$ft	4	120	$5^{9\frac{1}{2}}$	6^7	$6^{7\frac{1}{2}}$	$6^{6\frac{1}{4}}$	Ortega L E^6	HcpO	81	Sandbagger, Skate, Vodika Col'ins	8
6Feb82-8OP	5½f	:22	:46	1:05 gd	11	117	$9^{7\frac{3}{4}}$	$9^{7\frac{1}{4}}$	$6^{5\frac{1}{4}}$	1no	Ortega L E^6	HcpO	93	No No, Smokite, Sandbagger	11
23Jan82-8SA	6½f	$:21^3$	:44	$1:14^4$ft	11	115	5^7	5^8	$4^{5\frac{1}{2}}$	$4^{6\frac{1}{4}}$	DlhossyE^3	Sra Mdre H	90	To B. Or Not, Bold Ego, Solo Guy	7
7Jan82-8SA	6½f	$:22^3$	:46	1:18 sl	*1	117	4^2	$3^{1\frac{1}{2}}$	2^{hd}	$1^{\frac{3}{4}}$	DelhoussyeE^3	Aw32000	80	No No, Foyt's Ack, Pirate Law	7
19Dec81-8Hol	7f	$:21^2$	$:43^4$	$1:21^3$ft	5½	115	1^{hd}	1^{hd}	4^5	$4^{7\frac{3}{4}}$	VlenzulPA[2]	Yuletide H	81	Shanekite, FlyingChick,IslandWhirl	5
15Jly81-8Hol	6f	$:21^4$	$:44^2$	1:08 ft	5	116	5^3	$5^{7\frac{1}{2}}$	$5^{8\frac{1}{2}}$	$5^{8\frac{1}{2}}$	DlhssyE^6	Hol Exprs H	88	I'mSmokn,SmmrTmGy,Rb'sGoldnAl	6

Under my guidelines in my previous book, No No would have qualified on form because he showed at least a gain of five in his last race running line. From the stretch call to the finish, he passed two horses and picked up more than four and a half lengths, for a gain of six and a half, which was enough to keep him under serious consideration. Under what is set forth here, he would not have qualified at the stretch call, since he was hardly sufficiently up close at nine and a quarter lengths behind. Because No No is returning at the same class and today's race is only half a furlong shorter than the June 3 effort, the stretch call remains the critical call for measuring whether No No was up close. Despite the difference in the claiming prices at which he was entered in the two races, there is not really a class drop here for No No, since a fall-off of $10,000 against such high priced claiming horses is hardly a drop at all. The 20% general guideline would require a $15,000 drop in price before No No could be regarded as a dropper in class. Actually, subsequent research has shown that the gain of five that I previously considered so effective was potent because most horses gained enough to get up close at the stretch call. When they do not get up close at the stretch, as No No failed to do, the new form rules set forth here indicate that the gain way back in the field will not in and of itself qualify a horse.

However, do not discount a big gain from one call to the next, when a horse is making one big, quick move. I have not tried to make a rule here for dealing with such a move, but when you see it, it is easily worth the doubtful symbol of ∅ to keep a horse under further consideration. In fact, if you will turn back several pages in this chapter to Zany's past performances in the seventh at Belmont on June 19, 1982, you can see an excellent illustration of this point down in her past performances. Look at the third line down, to her race on April 23 in the fifth at Aqueduct. She made a very big move from the stretch to the finish, passing three horses and gaining three and a half lengths. A gain this substantial from one call to another—here it was six and a half—is just about what it takes to continue considering a horse as qualified. Indeed, you will usually want to see more of the gain in terms of lengths, rather than horses passed. Zany came back 16 days later, stretching out to the longer seven furlongs. An extra furlong or more is especially likely to benefit the horse that made a large gain in its last race, but fell short of getting up close. While going off at 10-1, Zany got up to win. I am sure you would have liked to have had that one?

But back to our friend, No No, who had heavy money laying on his nose. The reality, under the form insights that I have learned, is that he simply did not have a chance. There are two imposing reasons for this, the first of which we have just discussed—failure to be up close at the stretch call. The second we will come to in a few more pages, when we will recall No No one more time.

THE O RATING FOR THE RUNNING LINE. From what has been said thus far, we are now left to deal with the O rating. This rating is highly unfavorable, and it is used to indicate a form defect that will serve to eliminate the horse altogether. When a horse fails to meet any of the other standards for a +, an N, or even a $\emptyset$, he gets the plain and unfancy zero. A running line that is bad across the board has always been obvious to handicappers as something to be avoided. But, in the long study of so many races, I have tried to document its real effect, protected by the kinds of exceptions that can be used to show that the horse might actually run well today.

In spite of what is generally considered as "traditional wisdom," many horses with the O form defect for a poor—or unqualified—running line, get astonishingly good play at the windows, and wind up as favorites more times than you may suspect. A horrendous example is shown from the second race at Belmont on June 19, 1982, where Cerro Indio, while not the favorite, was well played as the third choice in the betting. When any horse receives enough dollars in the win pool in New York to be the third betting selection, you may be sure that a considerable number of people are lining up for the privilege. How confident would you feel with your money on this horse?

***Cerro Indio** — B. h. 8, by Hyphen—Solvencia, by Theseus

Own.—Ponton J — 117 — Br.—Haras Los Prados (Arg) — Tr.—Hernandez Marcos — $16,000

1982	3	0	0	0		
1981	10	2	1	0	$19,552	
Lifetime	40	6	6	3	$57,767	
Turf	4	1	0	0	$11,079	

Entered 18Jun82- 3 BEL

4Jun82-2Bel	7f	:23^1 :46^2 1:24^{3}ft	38	117	5$^{4\frac{1}{2}}$ 5$^{6\frac{1}{2}}$ 7$^{7\frac{1}{2}}$ 5^8	Graell A^6	16000	71	Marlago, Inpenetrable, Souda:	9
23May82-4Bel	1	:46^2 1:10^4 1:36^{1}m	18	117	7^9 7^{14} 7^{19} 7^{21}	Beitia E^7	25000	64	RdMThNms,OurClticHir,Prthr'sImg	7
16May82-9Aqu	1	:46^3 1:11 1:36^{4}ft	20	117	6$^{7\frac{1}{2}}$ 7^{13} 7^{15} 7^{13}	Rivera M A^7	30000	69	Mr.Wilford,ShntyToCstl,Ficton.Chf	8
30Oct81♦8SanIsidro(Arg)	a1⅜	2:12^{4}fm	5$\frac{3}{4}$	119	Ⓣ 8^{22}	GllsR	Premio Royal Top Hcp		‡DoesdeOro,‡TowerBridg,MuroAzul	8
23Sep81♦5Hipodromo(Arg)	a1¼	2:03 ft	2$\frac{1}{4}$	117	1$\frac{1}{2}$	GllosR	Pr.Bolivia Especial Hcp		Cerro Indio, Palafox, Bulliante	7
14Aug81♦6Hipodromo(Arg)	a1$\frac{9}{16}$	2:33^{3}ft	18	121	9^{26}	RssR	Premio Cordoba EspecialH		Morango, Tarot, Cinq Mars	11
24Jly81♦5Hipodromo(Arg)	a1¼	2:01^{2}ft	22	111	2$^{2\frac{1}{2}}$	RossR	Pr.Yatasto Especial Hcp		Avivato, Cerro Indio, Promenade	11
11Apr81♦4Hipodromo(Arg)	a1$\frac{9}{16}$	2:37^{1}hy	13	119	7^{26}	CntV	ClAmericaLatinoHcp		Frenesi Moon, Caledonia,CinqMars	9

May 12 Bel 5f ft 1:01^2 h　May 7 Bel 7f ft 1:28^1 h　May 3 Bel 4f ft :49 h　Apr 29 Bel 4f ft :50^2 b

This running line was as clearcut a O as you will find. The horse was hardly even almost up close at any call, and he steadily dropped back. Cerro Indio ran just as you might expect, back among the also rans.

There is not much more to say about identifying the O running line, since it is relatively easy when the requisite up close calls are not found. In other words, if a horse does not satisfy the rules for receiving a +, an N, or a Ø rating for its running line, the horse is dismissed with an zero.

What Is the Last Useable Running Line

In all the examples set forth in this chapter thus far, the running line from the horse's last race has been used. But you may also have noted that in each of these examples, the horse had no measurable defect for recent action. While it is always preferable to use the last race for rating form off a running line, every player knows that this is not always possible. The non-useable last race comes in two categories: (1) too far away in time to be reliable, and (2) under such different circumstances that it would not be effective to use it to try to decide how your horse will run today.

Take the easy one first. The old line of four weeks for a race is still very useful here. Thus, if a horse has not run within four weeks, no matter how well he may have worked at five furlongs or longer, the last race running line cannot be used to make a meaningful form rating insofar as up close calls are concerned. The race is simply too stale to be a reliable indicator of the horse's current form.

If the horse has not run within the past four weeks, and if he lacks requisite workouts, he gets a O for recency, of course. In these situations, when rating the running line factor, you can either use the U for Unknown, or fill in a small dash (–) to show that you cannot count the running line at all. On the other hand, if a horse that has not raced in more than four weeks has worked five furlongs, although it would qualify for recency, the horse is still short of a measurable last race running line. As earlier indicated, in these situations where the horse cannot be rated for its running line, you will have to rate the horse off other standards, such as ability times, or in any other manner you choose.

The rule for discounting last races that are not within 28 days causes little trouble when compared to the judgments you will have to make on whether to use a last race that was run within 28 days or to use the previous effort instead, or in some rare cases, even the race before that. But there are some rather solid standards that will help you make these judgments in a correct fashion often enough to put you in good position to answer our vital question of how your horse will run today.

The first situation where a changed circumstance will cause you to ignore the last race and turn to the prior running line, provided it is within the proper time frame of 28 days before the last race, is when a horse was raised to a higher class level in his last race, and today is being brought back down to the realistic level at which be previously competed. This is the old up-and-down dropper pattern where you are always advised to use the next-to-last race instead of the last effort. When a horse is raised to a class level that is simply too much for him, you would not expect a decent running line. And, of course, when he comes back to his own company, provided it is within the form cycle time frame, he may reasonably be expected to return to good form.

This kind of circumstance is demonstrated with Estoril, entered in the sixth race at Belmont on June 19, an allowance race on the grass with a purse of $25,000.

Estoril ✻

Own.—Seeligson A A Jr

114

B. c. 3, by Graustark—Brown Berry, by Mount Marcy
Br.—Seeligson A A Jr (Ky)
Tr.—Cantey Joseph B

| | | 1982 | 6 | 3 | 0 | 0 | $36,175 |
| Turf | 2 | 1 | 0 | 0 | $12,100 |

Lifetime   6   3   0   0 $36,175

5Jun82-8Bel	1½:47¹ 2:03¹ 2:28¹sy	9½	126	6¹⁰ 7¹¹ 7¹⁸ 7³⁰ Fell J⁶	Belmont 49 ConquistdorCilo,GtoDlSol,Illumint 11
24May82-7Bel	1¼:47⁴ 1:37³ 2:03 sy	*3	113	2¹ 1⁴ 1¹½ 1¹ Fell J²	Aw21000 85 Estoril, Lejoli, Caps And Crowns 7
6May82-5Hol	1¹⁄₁₆ ①:47⁴1:12¹1:42¹fm*7-5	120	6³¾ 4ⁿᵏ 2½ 1½ Pincay L Jr⁷ Aw22000 88 Estoril, Georgios, Forebear 10
14Apr82-8SA	1¹⁄₁₆ ①:46³1:11⁴1:48 fm	9¾	116	5⁸ 6⁴ 9¹² 9⁹½ DlhoussyE⁸ La Puente 77 RcinglsFun,BrginBlcony,RoylCptv 12
27Mar82-5SA	1½:46² 1:11 1:49 ft	3	118	9⁵½10⁸½ 5⁶ 47½ DelhoussyeE⁹ Aw21000 76 RoylCptive,Berbru,FbulousMystic 11
7Mar82-4SA	1¹⁄₁₆:45⁴ 1:10³ 1:42²ft	6½	118	2⁵ 2³ 1ʰᵈ 1ʰᵈ Delahoussaye E⁵ Mdn 89 Estoril, ConsciousEffort,Chargeur 11

Jun 15 Bel 6f ft 1:13² h   ● May 31 Bel 1 gd 1:40 b   May 20 Bel 6f ft 1:11³ h   May 13 Hol 1 ft 1:40¹ h

Estoril's last race was in the Belmont Stakes, where he was badly outclassed by Conquistador Cielo, Gato Del Sol, and a few others. He ran a wretched race. But today, he is back in more comfortable allowance company, where he has performed reasonably well. The May 24, 1982 effort was was only 12 days prior to the Belmont, and thus you can use that running line for Estoril today. Since that was a good + running line, are we free to give Estoril a + for running line form factor in today's race? Not at all, since any + rating must come only from the last race. We would give Estoril an N in his running line rating for today's race, no matter how good his semi-final effort was. The reason: there is always some tinge of doubt after a horse runs badly, no matter what class or surface or kind of race it was. We play safe and award only the neutral rating.

The second major changed circumstance we have to deal with is when a horse goes from dirt to grass or from grass to dirt. If a horse's last race was on a different surface from what he will run on today, this will usually make the last race not a useable one for running line rating purposes (although there can be some exceptions to this observation). When you are confronted with a grass-to-dirt or dirt-to-grass shift, you have to compare the races, evaluate the horse's general consistency on the surface of today's race, and decide which past races running line is properly useable.

A prime example of the reasoning that must be used came in the third race at Belmont on Father's Day, June 20, 1982, where I enjoyed a happy and most profitable day in the company of my Number One son, who is a most keen handicapper.

3rd Belmont

1 MILE. (1.33) CLAIMING. Purse $20,000. 3-year-olds. Weight, 122 lbs. Non-winners of two races at a mile or over since June 1 allowed 3 lbs. Of such a race since then 5 lbs. Claiming price $50,000; for each $2,500 to $45,000 2 lbs. (Races when entered to be claimed for $40,000 or less not considered.)

Chapter One — B. c. 3, by Nostrum—Empormila, by Emporium

Own.—Sommer Viola — 117 — Br.—Twin Eagles Farm Inc (Ky) — Tr.—Martin Frank — $50,000

1982	11	1	4	2	$29,480
1981	6	M	2	1	$7,510
Turf	2	0	0	0	
Lifetime	17	1	6	3	$36,990

31May82-7Bel	1	Ⓣ:48 1:142 1:41 sf	6¾	114	67	87½	109¾	1011	Cordero A Jr2	80000	49	Whippin, Full Concert, Class Hero	10
17May82-7Aqu	1⅛	Ⓣ:49 1:13 1:511fm	4½	117	11	11	33½	64¾	Fell J3	Aw20000	83	FourBss,VictoryZon,ThYoungSqur	12
10May82-4Aqu	1⅛	:501 1:154 1:53 ft	3	117	43½	3½	2½	2¾	Vergara O6	Aw20000	69	CosmicReson,ChpterOn,ShyGroom	7
14Apr82-7Aqu	1	:47 1:122 1:374ft	2¾	117	75½	42½	42¼	21½	Vergara O5	Aw20000	75	Illuminate,ChpterOne,WhtAChrger	7
3Apr82-1Aqu	1	:464 1:111 1:372ft	3½	114	41½	21½	2½	2nk	Vergara O2	80000	79	ClassHero,ChpterOne,JsonTheRcer	6
27Mar82-3Aqu	6f	:23 :472 1:13 ft	4½	119	64½	55	36½	23½	Venezia M5	c50000	72	StoneNess,ChapterOne,MajorFrank	8
8Mar82-7Aqu	170	⊡:47 1:1211:422gd	4½	115	34½	43½	44	37½	Venezia M5	55000	82	Starhitch, David K., Chapter One	7
2Mar82-6Aqu	6f	⊡:222 :4541:112ft	20	117	64¾	64¾	65¼	64¾	Venezia M7	57500	82	Pleasure Bid, Irish Waters, Mingo	9

Jun 15 Bel tr.t 4f ft :49 b   Jun 8 Bel tr.t 3f gd :36 h   May 26 Bel tr.t 5f gd 1:013 h   May 7 Bel tr.t 4f ft :49 h

You can see that the race on June 20 was at one mile on the dirt. Chapter One had been claimed back in March by Frank Martin, and after a string of second place finishes, Martin tried this colt in two grass races.

Chapter One was not making it at the level where Martin was running him, especially on the grass. A good conclusion would be that Chapter One was not quite ready for the turf. And since today's race is back on the dirt where Chapter One has been competitive, can we go all the way back to the May 10 race for a "last useable race running line?" Since his races have been regularly spaced, there is no great time difficulty involved.

The answer is that we should use the May 10, 1982 race. If Chapter One had run badly on May 10, we would give him a O rating for running line. But because the race was a good one, he can get an N for his running line for today's race. Again, note that although Chapter One would have received a + for this running line, where he was up close at all calls, we can give him only an N because it was not his immediate last effort. His competition was a little weak and Chapter One romped to an easy victory .

The same general situation would apply to a grass horse running back today on his favorite surface after a bad showing on the dirt. If his semifinal race was on the grass, you could use that as a rating and, in the opposite of Chapter One, if the horse's two most recent efforts were on the dirt and regularly spaced, and its race before those two was also at a regular interval but on its favored turf surface, you could use that most recent turf race. But what if the horse has not run on the grass in some period of time? If he shows good consistency in his turf record, you may want to give him an unknown rating even off bad dirt races. But if he has also shown good form on the dirt in the past and his last race on the dirt was bad, he is likely going off form and would get a O from me, even if he is returning to grass today. A horse out of form is not likely to be too rejuvenated by a return to the turf.

A third kind of circumstance is even more difficult to evaluate. Some horses simply cannot handle off tracks, even though most of them run about the same whether the track is fast or muddy. A bad last race in the mud or slop, or on a soft grass course if a horse is a turf runner, may be something that you will want to disregard. Then you would rate the horse off his semi-final race on a more compatible surface. The danger in this one is you cannot be sure whether the off track resulted in bad form or whether the horse is naturally tailing off. If past performances show that the horse cannot handle an off track, then you can usually ignore the last race and go back to the semi-final one if we have a dry surface today. All of us have heard stories of great "mudders" who could only win when the track was gooey, and likewise, have heard a great deal about some outstanding horses that cannot "stand up in the mud."

Most past performances will not show more than one race on an off track. What would you do about Laddy's Luck in the fourth at Belmont on June 19?

Laddy's Luck *

Dk. b. or br. g. 6, by Wig Out—Chitty B, by Chieftain

Own.—Falcone M J **117** Br.—Wolosoff J K (Fla) Tr.—Van Wert Robert G $35,000

1982	12	2	2	3	$28,440
1981	21	4	3	1	$46,820
Turf	1	0	0	0	

Lifetime 77 12 10 10 $155,200

6Jun82-2Bel	1 1/16	:46^4 1:12 1:44 sy	*3-2	117	4^6	3$^{3\frac{1}{2}}$	4^7	6$^{9\frac{1}{4}}$	Velasquez J^6	c25000	73	OurClticHir,PrfctBiddr,ThrMorWks	9
19May82-5Bel	1⅛	:46^4 1:11 1:48^{4}ft	*6-5e	115	1^{hd}	2^{hd}	1^{hd}	2no	Velasquez J^1	37500	83	KtchnCommndr,Lddy'sLuck,Advntr	8
29Apr82-5Aqu	1	:48^1 1:13^2 1:38^{3}ft	5¼	108^5	7$^{6\frac{3}{4}}$	7^3	4^1	3$^{1\frac{1}{4}}$	White J R^8	c30000	72	Imaromeo, Funny R.J.,Laddy'sLuck	8
9Apr82-2Aqu	7f	:23^3 :47^1 1:24^{4}ft	*2	112^5	6^5	6^5	6$^{2\frac{3}{4}}$	1^{nk}	White J R^5	25000	77	Lddy'sLuck,DdictdBoy,RdMThNms	8
24Mar82-6Aqu	1⅛	:48^3 1:13^2 1:52^{4}ft	2e	108^7	4^4	5$^{4\frac{1}{2}}$	4^1	3$^{3\frac{1}{4}}$	White J R^3	32500	68	Wimpfybll,StyWithAcs,Lddy'sLuck	7
14Mar82-9Aqu	1 1/16 ⊡	:47^3 1:13 1:45^{3}ft	6½	108^5	6^6	5$^{2\frac{3}{4}}$	5^4	3$^{1\frac{3}{4}}$	Gomez E R^5	30000	83	LttrFromLucy,OsgChf,Lddy'sLuck	10
6Mar82-2Aqu	1⅛ ⊡	:48^4 1:13 1:51^{3}ft	*8-5	110^7	2^2	2$^{\frac{1}{2}}$	1^1	1^{nk}†	Milo R^5	25000	88	‡Lddy'sLuck,NtiveGroogle,DringBt	7
† 6Mar82—Disqualified and placed seventh													
25Feb82-2Aqu	1 1/16 ⊡	:48^2 1:13^1 1:45 ft	5	112^5	4^2	3$^{3\frac{1}{2}}$	3^6	2^5	Milo R^4	25000	83	Psychosis,Lddy'sLuck,CyrnoDBrgrc	9

Jun 16 Bel 5f ft 1:00^4 h Jun 2 Bel tr.t 5f sy 1:03^3 b May 27 Bel tr.t 5f ft 1:02^1 b May 13 Bel tr.t 5f sy 1:03 b

The last race was on a sloppy track. In that race the horse was favored off an impressive running line on May 19, but with a substantial drop in class. Yet he ran miserably. The question is whether the sloppy track on June 6 contributed to his bad race sufficiently for you to use the running line of May 19 for an N rating. But here we have some additional help. You can see a mud mark by Laddy's Luck (the large asterisk after his name), which tells us that he has run well in the past on off tracks. With this assistance, you should have little difficulty concluding that his last race must be used. But what if there had been no mud mark to give us a hand? For me, I would give the horse a O, because he ran poorly off a class drop after a good race. Moreover, he showed some good early lick in the June 6 race to be up close at the second call, which suggests he handled the off track sufficiently well. A bad last race is still something to be very concerned about.

The other area where you might not want to use the last race involves a shift in distances. Some horses do not respond well to distance shifts, and when you see one bad effort with a quick return to a more comfortable number of furlongs, you may be safe in using the semi-final race. This is especially so when a distance horse ran in a sprint race, where it was never up close at any call, and is being returned today to the same distance at which it has run well in the past. You should not hesitate to rate these types of horses off their running line from the previous distance race.

Therefore, within these situations described above you can by-pass the last race and go back to races that are at conditions more nearly like those the horse is accustomed to running. And this, of course, brings up the final point that we mentioned briefly in the opening chapter. What do we do about a horse off a bad trip? This, too, involves a lot of judgment. If you saw the last race where the horse was in deep trouble and are confident enough in your handicapping judgment, you could likewise ignore the last race. But this has its perils. For example, a horse that in its last race stumbles out of the gate and then turns it on to catch up with the field, only to come up short in the stretch, may have had an excuse in that race. But at the same time, its effort in catching up with the field may have taken enough out of the horse to throw it off form and

and start a downward trend in the form cycle. A horse in good form, even with a bad trip, is highly likely to show a requisite up close call at a proper point in the race, and this may relieve you of the judgmental problem. Our rule here, as long as we have to rely on what we see in the *Daily Racing Form*, is to stay with the up close call requirements in the last race even when we suspect that a bad trip may have thrown the horse off.

Now that we have determined how to evaluate a horse's last useable running line, we will go on to consider one overall pattern to look for in a horse's past performances that can be one of the most useful and outstanding tools in your handicapping arsenal.

Elimination For Lack of Early Speed in Sprint Races

This elimination factor is one of the most reliable that you will find in racing, regardless of what the last race running line shows. However, it applies in sprints only. It is most effective in races of six and a half furlongs and shorter, but it can also be applied in seven furlong sprints with the appropriate adjustments that will be set forth here.

This powerful elimination factor is lack of early speed. Now, it may not be such a great secret that horses with lack of early speed may have a difficult time of it in sprint races. But here we are going to draw a positive line that is extremely accurate and reliable, so you can know what degree of lack of early speed is fatal and in what circumstances.

An enormous amount of research has demonstrated that in a typical sprint race at six and a half furlongs, six furlongs, five and a half furlongs and shorter, a horse will almost never win if its total lengths behind at the first call of all ten races shown in the past performances add up to 60 lengths or more. Actually, a total of 55 lengths is almost as effective, but the rule of 60 is easy to follow, for it averages out to six lengths per race. This means that where a horse's past performances show fewer than ten races, you can multiply the number of races by six to get the total number of lengths behind that will eliminate that horse. Thus, a horse showing seven starts requires you to multiply the seven by the six length standard for each race, which in this case would mean 42. When the lengths behind at the first call are added to a figure of 42 or more, then the horse is in serious elimination trouble.

There is a corresponding standard that must also go with this rule. Before you definitely eliminate a horse for lack of early speed as demonstrated by its total lengths behind at the first call, you must check to make sure there is at least one or more other horses in the race with a good degree of early speed. To determine what is good early speed for guideline purposes, we are safe with a standard of less than 25 total lengths behind at the first call of all ten races or an average of two and a half lengths behind per race. If a horse is consistently that near the front, he is showing enough early speed for us to eliminate the slower starter who carries the 60 lengths or more figure. More than one early speedster in the race is an even better sign for eliminating the slow starting horse. This does not always mean that the early speed horse will win the race, or even finish ahead of the laggard horse. What is does mean is that the horse without sufficient early speed is not going to win. The reason is that with true speed horses present, you can be sure there will be an honest pace that is likely to leave the horse without early speed much too far behind to have a realistic hope of getting up in time.

Exhibit "A" is Valentine Lew, the favorite in a six furlong sprint at Hollywood on June 19, in the fifth race.

Valentine Lew ✳

Dk. b. or br. g. 5, by Windy Sands—Sleek and Sassy, by Coursing
Br.—Jarvis Mr–Mrs L (Cal)
Own.—Basler–Block–Fiore et al **116** Tr.—Bernstein David $32,000

									1982	8 1 1 2		$16,450
									1981	21 6 2 3		$64,275
			Lifetime	33 9 3 5	$87,888							
6Jun82-5Hol	6½f :22	:45 1:16¹ft	3¾ 116	72½ 72½ 42¾ 31½	McCarron C J⁷	32000	87	Grits¬dFritz,HrdtoLee,VlentineLew 9
21May82-5Hol	6f :21¹	:44¹ 1:09²ft	3 116	9¹⁰ 67½ 44½ 3²	McCarron C J⁴	32000	88	Sar᷉ , Comet, Sami, Valentine Lew 9
9May82-1Hol	6½f :22²	:44² 1:15²ft	2¾ 115	54¾ 44 2½ 2hd	Guerra W A⁶	25000	93	Emer̄matic,ValentineLew,Pat'sPet 8
28Apr82-5Hol	6f :21⁴	:44⁴ 1:09⁴ft	12 115	85¾ 63 3² 1hd	Guerra W A⁷	20000	88	VintnLw,Phl'sPhntsy,Trxton'sDobl 10
20Apr82-1SA	6½f :22	:44² 1:15²ft	15 116	98 9¹¹ 8¹² 77¾	McHargue DG¹⁰	25000	85	RoughRider,HeMnSm,Sm'sComet 10
27Feb82-5SA	6f :21⁴	:44² 1:10 ft	6½ 117	11¹⁴10¹⁵ 9¹³ 96¾	Hawley S⁴	20000	81	Varga, King Gonzo, Knight ofGold 11
15Feb82-1SA	6½f:21⁴	:44² 1:15³ft	19 116	72¾ 85¼ 74½ 54¼	McHargue DG¹¹	20000	88	Proud Duke,Devon,TurningWheels 11
7Feb82-2SA	6f :21⁴	:45 1:10¹ft	9¼ 117	11¹¹11¹¹10¹⁵10¹⁵	Pincay L Jr³	25000	72	Unalakleet, Shooting Wind, Taiyo 11
23Dec81-3Hol	6f :21⁴	:44⁴ 1:10¹ft	4¾ 122	85¾ 76¾ 66 44½	Pincay L Jr⁵	25000	82	McCutcheon,StblePt,WinwoodHost 8
25Oct81-2SA	7f :22²	:45² 1:22³ft	4¾ 117	96¾10¹⁵ 9¹⁸ 9¹⁷	Pincay L Jr²	Aw21000	70	RllySombody,Clonwlln,BrghtstRlr 10

Jun 13 Hol 4f ft :47⁴ h   May 28 Hol 4f ft :49² h   May 16 Hol 4f ft :48¹ h

When you see a lot of big numbers for the lengths behind figure in the first call of a horse's races you are alerted to the fact that you had better start counting total lengths behind. Note that Valentine Lew was actually up close at every call in his last race, where his running line would show a formidable plus rating. I would have to suspect, without even seeing the other horses, that in that race Valentine Lew was running against a gang of slow starters. At any rate, in the race before us, we have to add up the lengths behind at the first call of the horse's ten races showing, and you get a total of 71, well over the line of 60 that we use as a disqualifying factor.

But even with this tragic lack of early speed, we have our always necessary additional task before we can finally eliminate Valentine Lew. You can see that he did win a six furlong race at Hollywood Park back on April 28, 1982, even with his late-running habits. There again, it was likely that his competition had little if any early speed. What else is running against Valentine Lew today? Will some horse be out there to set an honest pace and put Valentine Lew far enough back that he will not be able to get up in time to win?

We can start with Dream of Fire, whose last race running line would rate a tentative Ø.

Dream of Fire ✱ — Dk. b. or br. h. 5, by Drum Fire—Dew Dream, by Mr Mustard
Br.—Rakow R R (Wash) — 1982 4 0 2 0 $10,150
Own.—Achar V — 116 — Tr.—King Hal — $32,000 — 1981 13 2 3 1 $17,545
Lifetime 38 8 6 5 $50,195

6Jun82-5Hol	$6\frac{1}{2}$f	:22	:45	$1{:}16^1$ft	$6\frac{1}{2}$	116	$85\frac{1}{4}$	$94\frac{3}{4}$	6^5	4^4	Guerra W A^6	32000	85	GritsndFritz,HrdtoLee,VlentineLew	9
3Mar82-7SA	6f	$:22^2$	:45	$1{:}09^1$ft	*6-5	118	2^2	2^1	2^2	$2\frac{3}{4}$	Hawley S^8	40000	91	BerPudding,DremofFire,Logrhythm	8
21Feb82-1SA	6f	$:21^3$	$:44^1$	$1{:}08^4$ft	23	118	$52\frac{1}{4}$	$42\frac{1}{4}$	$4\frac{3}{4}$	2no	Hawley S^3	40000	94	I vaPet,DreamofFire,BttenPocket	10
23Jan82-5SA	$6\frac{1}{2}$f	$:21^2$	:44	1:16 ft	15	120	$31\frac{1}{2}$	4^6	5^2	9^{15}	Gallitano G^1	c32000	75	WinewoodHost,BerPudding,Neely	11
23Nov81-9YM	$5\frac{1}{2}$f	$:23^2$	:48	$1{:}07^3$m	*2-3	115	2^{hd}	1^{hd}	$11\frac{1}{2}$	1^4	Moore K D^4	Aw1500	77	DrmofFir,ChrisCommndr,ChifYkim	6
25Oct81-9YM	$1\frac{1}{16}$	:47	$1{:}11^2$	$1{:}44^3$ft	*6-5	121	1^{hd}	2^{hd}	2^1	$56\frac{3}{4}$	Cooper B^5	HcpO	85	Fire N Eddy, Haggai, Lew	8
4Oct81-9YM	6f	:22	$:45^1$	$1{:}09^3$ft	3-2	123	2^1	2^1	$1\frac{1}{2}$	2^{nk}	$MorKD^4$ P Woodall H		97	J. W. Blade, Dream of Fire,TomToo	5
26Sep81-9Lga	$6\frac{1}{2}$f	$:21^4$	$:43^3$	1:15 gd	8	115	$1\frac{1}{2}$	2^{hd}	$21\frac{1}{2}$	$75\frac{3}{4}$	$MgnrnTM^3$ W G Mgsn		88	Foyt'sAck,Wahtahshee,SiennaSwps	7
18Sep81-9Lga	6f	$:21^3$	$:43^4$	$1{:}08^1$ft	11	119	$1\frac{1}{2}$	$1\frac{1}{2}$	1^{hd}	3^1	$MalgariniTM^2$	Aw11000	94	Foyt'sAck,Wahtahshee,DremofFire	6
26Jly81-9Lga	6f	$:21^4$	$:44^4$	1:09 ft	32	114	1^{hd}	3^2	5^9	6^{13}	$MalgriniTM^2$ Speed H		78	TrooperSeven,J.W.Blde,TrmmlLuck	7

Jun 17 Hol 4f ft $:47^2$ h — May 27 Hol 5f ft $1{:}01^1$ hg — May 19 Hol 5f ft $1{:}02^2$ h — May 13 Hol 4f ft $:49^2$ hg

The critical thing for determining whether we should keep Valentine Lew under consideration is not the last race of the speed horse above, but his habit of being up front early in his races. You can quickly count the lengths behind at the first call of the ten races showing, and even with the bad last race, his total is but 12. By separating form cycles, you can see that last out Dream of Fire was running after a considerable layoff, and will likely do better today, especially in the early speed department.

But in the range of getting out there early, we have another strong entry in Smokin' Native, who has not been in a race since back in February. But look at that early speed!

Smokin' Native *
Own.—Red Baron's Barn **116**
B. h. 5, by Native Royalty—You're a Wonder, by Monitor
Br.—Mulholland Bros (Ky)
Tr.—Cofer Riley S $32,000

1982	2	0	1	0	$4,900
1981	15	3	2	2	$40,485
Lifetime	27	5	4	4	$65,220
Turf	3	0	0	0	$875

13Feb82-9SA	1⅛	:47^{2}	1:11^{4}	1:49^{2}ft	2¾	117	1^{1}	1½	2^{hd}	2^{2}	Pincay L Jr^{2}	25000	80	Trbitn,Smokin'Ntive,PleseBeOnTim	8
6Feb82-9SA	1$\frac{1}{16}$	:45^{4}	1:10	1:41^{3}ft	15	116	3^{3}	3$^{2\frac{1}{2}}$	4$^{7\frac{1}{2}}$	4^{14}	Guerra W A^{5}	32000	79	SuprStrVincnt,SoftMrkt,RulthMrkt	7
2Aug81-9Dmr	1	:45^{3}	1:10^{1}	1:36 ft	3	115	1^{2}	1$^{1\frac{1}{2}}$	1½	1^{hd}	Shoemaker W^{2}	32000	88	Smokn'Ntv,FollwthJdg,TchfAblty	10
17Jly81-11Sol	1	:46^{4}	1:10^{2}	1:36 ft	*2	118	1^{1}	2^{hd}	2^{hd}	4$^{1\frac{1}{2}}$	GonzalezRM^{5}	Aw10000	95	BlackSaber,BridgeTwister,PinkRoyl	6
11Jly81-9Pln	6f	:22^{2}	:45	1:10^{2}ft	*3-2	115	4^{3}	3^{3}	4^{4}	4$^{7\frac{1}{2}}$	Gonzalez R M^{1}	40000	84	SirPortRu!er,BeuBlde,GorgeousGrk	5
11Jun81-8GG	1$\frac{1}{16}$	:46^{3}	1:10^{1}	1:41^{4}ft	4	115	4$^{4\frac{1}{2}}$	2$^{1\frac{1}{2}}$	3^{5}	4$^{8\frac{1}{2}}$	Diaz A^{4}	Aw15000	85	Zoot Alors,ActingFoolish,KingHark	6
30May81-4GG	1	:46^{1}	1:10^{1}	1:35^{1}ft	4	119	2^{hd}	2^{hd}	2^{1}	3^{2}	Diaz A^{4}	Aw15000	90	Cuchillo,ActingFoolish,Smokin'Ntv	6
21May81-5Hol	1⅛Ⓣ	:48^{3}	1:13	1:49 fm	22	119	1½	1^{1}	2^{hd}	6$^{4\frac{1}{2}}$	McCarron C J^{2}	50000	80	Vorlufer,RuletheMrkt,GrtGrndson	10
10May81-9Hol	1⅛Ⓣ	:48	1:12	1:48^{4}fm	33	117	1^{1}	1$^{1\frac{1}{2}}$	1^{hd}	5$^{5\frac{1}{2}}$	Diaz A L^{6}	55000	80	ThreeBits,LetsGotoEdwrds,BckBily	9
2May81-6GG	1	:45^{3}	1:09^{4}	1:35^{4}ft	4¼	119	1^{hd}	2^{hd}	1^{hd}	2^{2}	Diaz A^{6}	40000	87	ErlyTomtos,Smokn'Ntv,WstrnMndt	7

Jun 10 Hol 5f ft 1:00^{1} h **Jun 4 Hol 5f ft 1:00^{3} hg** **May 29 Hol 5f ft 1:01 h** **May 23 Hol 5f ft 1:01^{2} h**

His total lengths behind at the first call come out to ten and a half, as seven times he was in the lead or only a head behind. This horse not only shows the five furlong workout sign, but had four of them in a row. He was indeed ready, as he streaked out to a victory, paying $15.20. Valentine Lew fought on and did well to finish second, but this is not a victory. Dream of Fire held on to finish third.

At this point, we should put to rest one belief you hear of often, which is if there are two early speed burners in a race, a come from behind horse will take it all after the early runners wear themselves out. This theory has real validity in distance races, but it just does not work in sprints where early speed is always vitally necessary. Two early speed horses may get out and go head and head for most of the way, and one of them will almost always win. One of the two may fold under the pressure, but a late closer may never catch the horse that stays out in front. The race that Valentine Lew lost is a prime example. We repeat again, the theory is extremely important in distance races, but disregard it altogether in six and a half and six furlong races, as well as shorter sprints.

Before we leave the six furlong sprinters, let us hearken back to No No earlier in this chapter—another favorite whose backers were throwing their money away. Add up his lengths behind at the first call and you come up with 63¾, far too many to allow him to remain as a contender. Without showing you his competition, I will only say that there was plenty of early speed running against him, which doubly insured that he could not win.

When we deal with seven furlong races and even those at one mile, early speed, while still significant, does not dominate. But again, if a horse is an extremely slow starter and there are one or more horses in the race that have shown early speed and that they can sustain it in a tough seven furlong race, the closer again is going to have a very tough time of it. In seven furlong races, we can draw the line at 80 lengths behind, or an average of eight per race. Now, take a look at Soudan, who was the favorite in the first race at Belmont on June 16, carded for seven furlongs.

Soudan

Ch. c. 4, by Soudard—Denova, by Degage
Br.—Cashman E C (Fla)
Own.—Pic Stable **117** Tr.—Hertler John O $20,000

										1982	3	0	1	1	$3,740
										1981	24	3	1	2	$42,200
				Lifetime	37	4	2	5	$56,360	Turf	4	1	1	1	$17,000
12Jun82-9Bel	6f :22³ :45⁴ 1:10⁴ft	5½ 117	8⁷ 6⁵ 55¼ 23½	Fell J⁹	16000 85	Truce, Soudan, Greene Go	9
4Jun82-2Bel	7f :23¹ :46² 1:24³ft	11 117	4³ 41½ 33½ 34½	Samyn J L⁹	16000 75	Marlago, Inpenetrable, Soudan	9
26May82-3Bel	6f :23 :46² 1:10⁴ft	45 117	10⁹ 85½ 8⁶ 66½	Samyn J L⁹	16000 81	Whambang, Clodion,RajaTheGreat	11
17Dec81-5Aqu	1¹⁄₁₆⊡:47²1:12¹1:44²m	20 115	8¹⁹ 8¹⁶ 8¹⁹ 8²¹	McCarron G⁹	20000 71	FollowThtDrem,BornGret,WllP!sdII	9
8Dec81-8Med	1¹⁄₁₆:47³ 1:12³ 1:45³sy	3½ 115	7¹² 6¹⁴ 4¹¹ 4¹⁷	McCarron G³	25000 64	Choosey Beggar, Lolatzor,Lunamor	7
23Nov81-1Aqu	1¹⁄₈:47² 1:12² 1:52²ft	16 117	32½ 2¹ 3³ 42¾	Samyn J L³	25000 70	Funny R. J., Tonce, Larking's Run	9
8Nov81-5Aqu	1¹⁄₈:46⁴ 1:12 1:51 ft	22 113	8²⁰ 8¹² 9¹⁷ 9¹⁶	Samyn J L⁹	30000 64	BrnyR.,MyFrindWilli,GoldnProspcts	9
29Oct81-5Aqu	1¹⁄₁₆:47⁴ 1:13¹ 1:58 ft	7 117	43½ 3² 3³ 46½	Samyn J L³	25000 65	Importnce,Lrking'sRun,KicksndDls	7

May 20 Aqu 6f ft 1:16⁴ h   May 16 Aqu 5f ft 1:02² b   May 10 Aqu 4f ft :48¹ h   May 5 Aqu 4f ft :51 b

Alerted by the big numbers, you can total up 76 lengths behind for the eight races shown. Any number of 64 or higher would have met the non-qualified standard, because with only eight, rather than ten races shown for Soudan, you have to multiply the number of races by the average number of lengths behind per race that we will allow. For a seven furlong race this is eight, and multiplying that by the eight races gives 64. (The eight races shown, rather than the usual ten, comes out of the western edition of the *Form* which, although giving you the full ten for the California races, reduces the number down to eight for New York). Soudan, of course, faced with some decent early speed, had no chance to make it.

Whether you want to apply the seven furlong number to races of an even one mile is up to you. In most instances, early speed at one mile is about as important as at seven furlongs, and my view is that you should also use it in the same way as in seven furlong events. Any race longer than one mile, however, and especially those with two turns, does not fit this pattern.

In all the studies I have done over the past few years, I have not seen any rule of elimination as reliable as this one. Because I know of no absolute rule of complete infallibility, this one will some-times, but only rarely, let you down. It comes out as close to total reliability in the complex game of handicapping races horses as anything you can find. Following it hereafter ought to save you a great deal of money.

There is only one general situation in which it does not work effectively. When you encounter a pronounced track bias against early speed, and closers seem to be winning every race—as sometimes does occasionally happen—then this magnificent rule will have to be put on the shelf until the track returns to normal. But in every situation except this one, it remains the single most effective elimination rule I have ever encountered in my years of trying to analyze what makes horses win and lose.

How Effective Are Running Line Ratings

Now that we have defined the positive + factor, placed an N on running lines that meet the next level of standards, and even allowed a Ø in some doubtful situations, and assigned the unwant-ed O for horses that have a negative rating, how do these factors stand up over a long test period? How reliable are they? How do they help you know how your horse is likely to run today?

You have already been told in this chapter of the spectacular results from + running lines where horses have no other form defects and are not rising in class. That test dealt with first and second betting choices, along with third betting choices whose odds were very close to those of the second horse. How about the long shots? Do horses with a O running line win, and if so, how often and under what conditions?

While a + running line is one of the most effective positive form factors, a O running line, while surely to be avoided, is sometimes overcome, especially where class is involved. But never ignore it altogether, for if you try to play against it, losing will be your certain destiny.

Among favorites only, there were some 61 out of 433 in our major study that had a running line of zero. There were 15 winners, or 24.6%. While this is unusually high, the key ingredient, as I have already stated, was a distinct class advantage that allowed these O running line favorites to win as often as they did in this particular study.

In looking at the outside betting choices at all the tracks involved in the study, there were 58 longer priced winners out of 191 total winners that failed to show an N or a + for last useable running line. This represents 30.4% of the longshot winners. At Belmont there were but seven winners out of the 40 longer priced winners with a O last race running line. Of course, this number was whittled down somewhat because of lack of recent action on some of them, or no useable last race running lines. At Meadowlands, 17 out of 68 longer priced winners had running lines of zero. At Keystone, 16 out of 55 longshot winners had the weak line of O, and at Bowie there were seven of 28. The horses with the doubtful, or marginal running line symbolized by Ø, had some degree of success, with 11 winners at all four tracks.

I have not poured an enormous amount of analysis time into the "whys" of these winners, so accordingly, am not able to give you as many specific figures on why this 30.4% came home in front. But you can rest assured the single most important factor was the one that has been set forth already, that of a meaningful advantage in class level of competition. The reason why we cannot do more with these horses dropping in class is that so many of them do fail off O running lines, and when you play one of them, absent some powerful signs, you are gambling indeed. The O running line is still a sound elimination factor.

In summary, by far the most impressive feature of any last race running line is the + factor, where a horse with no other defects and without a class disadvantage is an enormously strong play. A weak last race running line is a severe handicap, although not a fatal one, especially when there is sufficient class to overcome it.

Summarizing Running Lines Rules

● WHAT IS THE LAST USEABLE RUNNING LINE?

The last race, provided it was run with 28 days of today's race, is to be used, except when the last race is not truly representative of a horse's form.

The common exceptions are:

1. When a horse was raised to a higher level of competition in his last race and is being returned today to a level approximately equal to his next to last race, we will use the next to last race, provided it was within 28 days of the last race.

2. When a horse's last race was on either grass or dirt and today's race is on a different surface, the next to last race can be used if it is on today's surface and within the proper time frame.

3. When some other unusual circumstances make it reasonably certain that the last race was not representative, then go back to the next to last race. A muddy track where a horse has demonstrated that it cannot handle mud is a prime example. You may also go back to the next to last race with a confirmed sprinter or router that may have been tried at the wrong distance in his last race, if the prior race was at the proper distance. But never casually throw out the last race because you do not like it or expect better things today. The circumstance must be truly unusual.

● THE STANDARDS FOR AN UP CLOSE CALL

To be up close at any call in a race, a horse must be within the required number of lengths from the lead, based upon the race distance, as follows:

1. Sprints up to and including six and a half furlongs—two and three-quarter lengths or less from the lead.

2. Races at seven furlongs and one mile—three and three-quarter lengths or less from the lead.

3. All races of a mile and 40 yards and longer—four and three-quarter lengths or less from the lead.

- THE PLUS (+) FORM FACTOR

A + is awarded only when the horse was up close at every call of his last race at the distance of that race.

- THE N FACTOR: NEUTRAL, NEITHER, OR NON-APPLICABLE

1. For horses returning at the same or higher level of competition and at the same distance or a longer distance:

   A horse must be up close at the stretch call of his last useable race, or;

   A horse must have won his last race, or finished less than one length from the winner, or;

   A horse must have a fall back-gain pattern by being up close at the finish after having lost one length or more from the second call to the stretch and gaining one length or more from the stretch to the finish.

2. For horses returning at a shorter distance of one full furlong or more, the horse may be up close at the second call.

3. For horses returning at a lower level of competition, the horse may be up close at any call.

- THE DOUBTFUL FACTOR

When a horse is very close to meeting the necessary standards for an N rating, but not quite, you may choose, if you wish, to call him "doubtful," and here, you are referred back to our discussion on doubtful earlier in the chapter. This is entirely discretionary with the handicapper.

- THE MINUS, OR O FACTOR

When a horse cannot qualify for either a + or an N, he is awarded a zero. This form defect normally eliminates him as a contender in the race.

- THE UNKNOWN, OR U FACTOR

When there is no basis for rating the second form factor off any running line, a horse must be given a U for unknown. A first time starter is obviously an unknown. A horse that has never run on the grass and is entered on the turf today is another unknown. While a horse that has not run in the last 28 days is also unknown, he would have a form defect for recency, unless he showed a recent five furlong workout. His running line would still be unknown.

● THE POSITIVE ELIMINATION FACTOR IN SPRINT RACES

In sprint races of six and a half furlongs and less, lack of early speed is almost always fatal when there is at least one or more other horses in a race with a reasonable degree of early speed. If a horse's total lengths behind at the first call of all his races shown in his past performances average six or more per race, or 60 for a ten-race showing, then he lacks sufficient early speed to win. A rival, to have enough early speed to eliminate the slow starter, must not show more than an average of two and a half lengths behind per race, or 25 lengths behind when ten races are shown.

In seven furlong races, lack of early speed is not so devastating. However, a horse that averages eight lengths or more behind at the first call, or a total of 80 or more in the ten races shown by *Daily Racing Form*, is almost sure to lose if there is some other early speed in the race.

5 The Third Form Factor: Performance Within the Form Cycle, Part I – Did Your Horse Win its Last Race?

EVERY PERSON WHO GOES TO THE RACETRACK is confronted with horses on the program that won their last race. It is doubtful that you would ever find a single racing card without at least one of this number, and most likely, you may see several. In the 433 races examined in my major study, there were 460 entrants that were coming off a last race victory, averaging better than one per race. And when you recognize that in every maiden race there can be no returning winners at all, you begin to see the added significance of this occurrence. In some of the better quality races you may even find as many as four or five returning winners.

Knowing how to deal with horses that won their last race thus becomes a critical handicapping factor, merely because of the high frequency of its occurrence. Many of these horses are well bet as favorites or second or third choices. Some that are rising considerably in class may be outsiders in the odds, but every one of them must be considered. If reliable standards for testing these horses can be devised, another important step can be taken on the way to answering the central inquiry of how your horse will run today.

Not only do we need to know something about the chances of these horses repeating their wins in the race we are considering today, but we need to know even more about what factors most influence whether they might win again or not. Likewise, are there certain factors that are likely to drag them down to defeat? If you can come to grips with this factor alone, you will have made great strides toward the profit line.

Because of the importance of class in determining how your horse will run today, all winning horses should be separated into four categories:

1. Those rising in class today.

2. Those running back at the same class.

3. Those that drop in class (yes, there are a few).

4. Horses that won their maiden race in their last start.

Winners Rising in Class

As you might expect, horses rising in class off a win have the most difficulty in repeating their victories. But even though this should hardly come as a surprise to you, there are an awful lot of people who bet these horses to win their next race, often making them favorites or near-favorites.

In New York, where class is an extremely strong factor, my study found 25 entries that had won their previous race and were rising in class the next time out. How many of them won? Not one—no, not even a single one. This is quite unusual, for a prolonged study over several months would uncover several. In fact, we will show you one very shortly.

While the figures at the three other tracks were better, they, too, showed the difficulty that returning winners face when they rise in class. Among the horses that won their last race and were rising in class, here are the results for all four tracks.

Track	Horses	Win	Pct.
Bel	25	0	0.0%
Med	55	4	7.0%
Key	39	5	12.8%
Bow	42	7	16.7%
Total	161	16	10.0%

A typical example of such a winner rising in class can be taken from the first race at Hollywood Park on June 18, 1982, where Summer Sailor is coming off a victory, although he dropped back a bit in the stretch in his last race.

Summer Sailor ✱   Dk. b. or br. g. 5, by Fleet Allied—Summer Chatter, by Helioscope
Br.—Allen & Thompson (Cal)   1982 9 1 4 0 $16,488
Own.—Steele V M   **116**   Tr.—West Ted $16,000   1981 10 0 3 3 $14,636
Lifetime 44 7 11 8 $84,499

11Jun82-1Hol	6f	$:22^1$	$:44^4$	1:10 ft	$4\frac{1}{2}$	115	2^{hd}	1^3	1^5	1^3	Guerra W A^5	S	12500	87	SummrSlor,Don'sDncr,TlofTrmph	12
3Jun82-3Hol	6f	$:22^2$	$:45^2$	$1:10^3$ft	*7-5	116	$4^{1\frac{3}{4}}$	4^3	$3^{6\frac{1}{2}}$	2^4	McCarron C J^1		c10000	80	SpdyTdor,SmmrSlor,OlympdProms	7
13May82-2Hol	6f	$:22^1$	$:44^3$	$1:09^2$ft	3	115	5^3	4^4	4^5	$5^{7\frac{3}{4}}$	McCarron CJ^7	S	12500	82	Tulsea, Don's Dancer, Gaffero	9
28Apr82-5Hol	6f	$:21^4$	$:44^4$	$1:09^4$ft	8	108^5	5^3	$8^{6\frac{1}{4}}$	9^{11}	9^{11}	Pedroza M A^{10}		18000	77	VlntnLw,Phl'sPhntsy,Trxton'sDobl	10
10Apr82-1SA	6f	$:21^4$	$:44^4$	$1:09^1$ft	7	114	$5^{2\frac{3}{4}}$	5^5	6^{12}	$5^{9\frac{1}{2}}$	Guerra W A^{11}		18000	82	Rough Rider, Embermatic, Graben	12
27Feb82-5SA	6f	$:21^4$	$:44^2$	1:10 ft	*3-2	115	$6^{3\frac{1}{4}}$	$4^{3\frac{1}{2}}$	8^{11}	$7^{5\frac{1}{4}}$	McCarron C J^6		c20000	83	Varga, King Gonzo, Knight ofGold	11
19Feb82-1SA	$6\frac{1}{2}$f	$:21^3$	$:44^1$	$1:14^4$ft	*8-5	116	1^1	$1^{1\frac{1}{2}}$	1^{hd}	$2^{2\frac{1}{2}}$	McCarron C J^6		c16000	93	RoughRidr,SummrSlor,Goff'sDncr	12
6Feb82-1SA	6f	$:21^1$	:44	$1:09^4$ft	$4\frac{3}{4}$	116	6^6	5^7	$4^{3\frac{1}{2}}$	2^{nk}	Asmussen C B^6		16000	89	Ws'sRb,SummrSlor,CounslorCcony	9
14Jan82-3SA	6f	$:21^3$	$:44^3$	1:10 ft	10	116	$6^{3\frac{3}{4}}$	$5^{4\frac{3}{4}}$	$4^{1\frac{1}{2}}$	2^{nk}	Asmussen C B^2		16000	88	Windy'sDuke,SummerSailor,Tu'se	11
30Dec81-1SA	6f	:22	$:45^2$	$1:11^3$m	*8-5	116	4^2	3^2	3^5	$3^{6\frac{1}{2}}$	DelahoussyeE^8		c12500	73	RghtOnTobn,RylAckAck,SmmrSlr	12

●May 6 Hol 5f ft $:59^1$ h   ●Apr 25 Hol 4f ft $:46^4$ h   Apr 18 SA 5f ft $:59^3$ h

This horse was strongly bet, going off at odds of 7-2 against a very respectable field of medium priced claimers. He had little chance at all, as he finished fourth behind Embermatic, who was dropping in class and had powerful credentials. A horse in the situation of Summer Sailor is a strong candidate to lose.

There are some limited situations, however, where the winner rising in class does come home in front. We can examine the 16 winners out of our study to determine what these factors are.

Not only with winners rising in class, but with all winning horses that manage to prevail in their next outing, there are two major positive signs that are found in the majority of these repeaters. A horse having these characteristics is not guaranteed to win, but it is terribly difficult to score unless one or more of them shows up.

The first key sign is that the horse must have at least two positive, or +, form factors, and *no* defects. A horse that won its last race is often a good candidate to have these credits, but not always. A winner returning to the races could be stale in recency, could have a running line that did not rise above an N, or could have one of the other form defects that will be discussed hereafter. Thus, do not always expect every returning winner to be loaded with + form factors.

The other important marker is a decisive, pull-away victory in the last race, which was tabbed by Tom Ainslie several years ago as a "Big Win." The horse should win by three lengths or more without losing ground in the stretch, and without having been so far out in front at the first call that the others gave up without a real fight. A Big Win must be earned. If a horse turns in that kind of performance, he at least has a reasonably good chance to win his next race. A Big Win in itself is one of the + form factors, as you will see in a later chapter.

To show you that a winner rising in class *can* triumph, let us turn to the seventh race at Belmont on June 17, an allowance race once around the big mile and a half track. Look at Jasamy, well backed at the windows.

Jasamy — Ch. f. 4, by Crimson Streak—No Holding, by Noholme II
Br.—Bass J K (Ark) — 1982 5 1 1 0 $17,800
Own.—Martin Gertrude A — **117** — Tr.—DeBonis Robert — 1981 5 2 1 1 $25,920
Lifetime 15 3 3 2 $48,800

14Jun82-2Bel	1 1/16	:46^3	1:10^3	1:42 sy	2¾	117	3^{1½}	2^3	1^{1½}	1^4	Venezia M^1	Ⓕ c50000	92	Jasamy, WellI'llSwan,HarlemQueen	7
26May82-5Bel	1 1/16	:45^3	1:09^3	1:41 ft	8	119	4^9	4^{11}	4^{12}	5^{14}	Venezia M^2	ⒻAw20000	83	TooChc,NcolMonAmour,SvdGrond	6
15May82-4Aqu	6f	:22^1	:45^3	1:11^{3}ft	7½e	119	9^{11}	8^8	5^{8¼}	4^{1¾}	Venezia M^9	ⒻAw19000	81	FvoredTimes,ExclusivFbl,HustlOn	10
15Apr82-5Aqu	6f	:23^1	:46^4	1:13^{1}ft	*1e	117	6^{4¾}	7^{8¼}	5^{5½}	4^{4½}	SantagatN^9	ⒻAw19000	70	Sharonna, BiggerEnough,Messalina	9
28Mar82-6Aqu	6f	:23^1	:47^3	1:13^{4}ft	6e	116	10^{10}	8^{10}	5^{5½}	2^2	SantagatN^1	ⒻAw16000	70	Caricatura, Jasamy, Messalina	10
8Apr81-1Aqu	1⅛	:49	1:13^3	1:53 ft	*3-5	118	1^4	1^4	1^7	1^7	Santagata N^1	Ⓕ 30000	70	Jasamy, Leak Proof, Gallant Bo	5
21Mar81-9Aqu	1⅛	:49	1:14^4	1:55^{1}ft	*2¾	116	3^{½}	1^{½}	1^4	1^{2¾}	Santagata N^6	Ⓕ 35000	59	Jasamy, Collect, Bread n' Water	8
1Mar81-6Aqu	1⅛⊡	:48^3	1:14^3	1:56 sy	9¼	122	2^{1½}	2^2	2^{1½}	2^3	Santagata N^1	ⒻMdn	63	Visual Effects, Jasamy, Jilly Pilly	11

Jun 9 Aqu 7f ft 1:29^3 h — Jun 4 Aqu Ⓣ 3f fm :39 b (d) — May 24 Aqu 4f sy :50^4 b — ●May 13 Aqu 3f ft :38 b

This horse was rising in class into an allowance race off a claim, although not by much. However, Jasamy had a superb race only *three days before.* Trainer DeBonis wanted a quick cash-in for his $50,000 purchase, and he was out to start racking it up without a delay. This filly's last race was what we would call a Big Win, because she pulled away from the field to win by more than three lengths. Likewise, she was showing three other + form factors in recency, last race running line, and in improvement in her form cycle, which we will get into in the next chapter. Not surprisingly, Jasamy repeated her victory with ease.

It takes powerful credentials like these to win when a horse rises in class. But to go with these credentials there needs to be one more vital element—back class. Back class means the horse has previously demonstrated competitive ability at or above the higher level it faces today. If the class-riser is returning to a level at which they have performed successfully in the past, the class rise is not too big a hurdle to overcome. Jasamy, for example, ran a strong second and an up close fourth in two previous allowance efforts. When this sign of back class is showing, your last race winner rising in class with the other necessary credentials can be a very likely repeater.

Of the 16 repeat winners rising in class in our study, 12 had two or more + form factors. Eight showed a Big Win as one of those two plusses. One of these repeat winners, however, came at Meadowlands, and showed neither of these ingredients. But this class rising winner caught a weak field where every other horse had one or more form defects. Obviously, very weak opposition can allow a horse rising in class off a win to become a repeater.

But the cautionary signals are out. A horse that won its last race and is rising in class today is a very poor bet, unless it has the necessary strong positive form factors, won impressively in its last race, and is running back at a class level of competition where it shows previous competitive ability.

Recognition of these facts of life can save you a lot of money!

Horses Running Back at the Same Class

When horses return off a winning effort and do not have to climb in class to run against a higher level of opposition, they fare much better. In those situations the key question always is: did they reach their peak in their form cycle when they won their last race, and consequently, will they start downhill today? First, let us look at how they fared, and then go on to analyze why.

There was a somewhat reasonable consistency among the four tracks with winners returning at the same class level. Likewise, the factors that came with those that did win were also reasonably the same. This similarity of winning factors is what we look for, since it teaches the strong lesson that certain elements *do* matter and that they *do* influence the outcome of horse races.

Rather than stringing out each track, let us use the same kind of short table that we used with winners rising in class.

Here are the results at the four tracks of all horses that won their last race and next raced at the same class.

Track	Horses	Win	Pct.
Bel	59	14	23.7%
Med	44	7	15.9%
Key	46	10	21.7%
Bow	41	12	29.2%
Total	190	43	22.6%

This is quite a respectable showing. Belmont and Bowie ran higher than the other two tracks, in keeping with their higher percentages of winning favorites. Meadowlands, with the lowest percentage of winning favorites, tracked the lowest figure for returning winners at the same class.

But here, like the situation with winners rising in class that managed to score successive victories, the presence of plus factors is all-important. A look at the 14 returning winners at Belmont shows how this works.

Eight of these victorious repeat winners had a + running line. This is further affirmation of this key element, where a horse won his last race by being up close at all four calls. Five returning winners showed a Big Win in their last race. Thus, you see again the same two dominant features that will be displayed in almost every returning winning horse. It may bear repeating once again that these two potent plus marks will not guarantee a second win. It does mean, however, that without them, your horse is fighting a very uphill battle.

Three of the 14 returning winners during the Belmont study were interesting cases, which will lead to another good observation. One was gallant old John Henry, winning the Jockey Club Gold Cup as expected. Another was No Neck in a turf race. For those racing fans outside New York, No Neck is an old gelding that is super-tough on the grass at anywhere near his class level—very hard to beat at any time. The third special case involved a gelding named Steelwood, who has to be one of the most consistent horses ever to run in the east. His lifetime victory record close to 40% of his starts. If this horse did not run in the money in any race, something had to be radically wrong. Like No Neck, he was nearly invincible at his class level.

In this discussion of the three "special" cases, you will have noted a common string by now. All three of these horses were very experienced geldings, extremely consistent. This is the kind of horse you would expect to come roaring back at the same class to win again and again.

I have continued to study winning horses in their next races, even after the research for this book had been completed. From hundreds more races, I have seen a pattern emerge of older geldings coming back to win as repeaters. This is not to indulge in any commentary on the sexual anatomy of the male horse, but merely to report observations gleaned from studying *Daily Racing Form*. A gelding aged five or over, riding a crest of good form, is always a serious candidate to repeat a victory in his next outing. This is not to say that colts and fillies never do, but the realities seem to show that the geldings repeat their victories more often. Perhaps a more intensive study is needed on that one, too.

As we move on to Meadowlands to look at the seven winners there, we see five of them displaying the same double-plus form pattern highlighted by the Big Win. This shows again how the Big Win, coupled with at least one other + form factor, is a power-house indicator of a possible repeater.

One of the other seven was a stakes winner returning at the same class without either the requisite + form factors or a Big Win. He did it on strong, consistent ability. The final returning winner, who also did not have two positive signs, was again facing a very weak field, where every other horse in the race carried one or more form defects.

The impressive feature of this study, as we move onward to Keystone, continues to be its lovely consistency. Eight of the ten winners at Keystone had two or more plus form factors. Six of the ten had a Big Win. All ten had at least one plus form factor or a Big Win, or both.

And at Bowie the pattern was nearly the same. Six of the 12 repeated victories off of Big Wins in their last race. Once again, the strongest plays were those that combined the elements of a Big Win and at least one other plus form factor. Three of the returning Bowie winners came in stakes races, where you have the highest quality of consistent horse. One of the returning winners that lacked either a plus form factor or a Big Win had sandwiched in a five furlong workout between races, and you have already been told about the power of this handicapping gem.

This portion of the study of returning winners may be the most important one of all. While the percentage of repeating winners is quite high—the 22% of those returning at the same class is better than one might expect—the real importance comes in the "Why" department. The two elements of at least one or more plus form factors and a Big Win, preferably combined, are the reliable essentials. Without them, your horse is not likely to win.

On the other hand, the kind of returning winner that will find it extremely difficult to score again is shown as we look at Drifting Dune in the seventh race at Golden Gate on June 18, returning at the same class and same distance off a victory in her last race.

Drifting Dune — B. f. 4, by Pleasure Seeker—Sand Picture, by Windy Sands
Br.—Ridder B J (Cal) — 1982 11 2 1 0 $14,986
Own.—Wright W J — 117 — Tr.—Lambert George — $12,500 — 1981 8 1 1 1 $8,050
Lifetime 22 3 2 1 $23,411

4Jun82-7GG	1 1/16	$:47^4$	$1:13^1$	1:48 ft	6 1/2	114	8^{12}	$7^{8\frac{1}{2}}$	$6^{2\frac{3}{4}}$	$1^{1\frac{1}{2}}$	Anderson JR[8]	Ⓕ 12500	63	DriftingDun,Brb'sOut,Plnum'sChick	9
26May82-7GG	1 1/16	$:48^1$	$1:12^4$	$1:45^4$ft	13	114	6^7	7^{12}	8^{18}	8^{24}	Howell W C[3]	Ⓕ 16000	50	Star Gem, Great Lou, Let's Party	8
12May82-7GG	6f	:22	$:45^2$	$1:11^3$ft	18	114	$9^{6\frac{1}{4}}$	$8^{5\frac{1}{4}}$	6^5	$4^{6\frac{1}{2}}$	Howell W C[9]	Ⓕ 16000	74	Tracey'sSteel,CrazyBby,FntsticLiz	10
28Apr82-9GG	1 1/16	$:46^3$	1:12	$1:45^1$ft	4 1/4	114	$4^{5\frac{1}{2}}$	3^3	4^3	$4^{6\frac{1}{2}}$	GonzlezRM[8]	Ⓕ c12500	70	She'saGal,Plenum'sChick,Brb'sOut	8
14Apr82-6GG	1 1/16	$:47^3$	$1:12^1$	$1:45^3$ft	4 1/2	114	$3^{2\frac{1}{2}}$	$3^{1\frac{1}{2}}$	$2^{\frac{1}{2}}$	2no	Gonzalez RM[1]	Ⓕ 12500	75	She'saGal,DriftingDune,PrideOPaul	6
6Apr82-5GG	6f	$:23^3$	$:47^2$	$1:13^1$gd	5 3/4	114	1^2	$1^{1\frac{1}{2}}$	1^{hd}	1^{nk}	Gonzalez RM[2]	Ⓕ 12500	73	Drifting Dune, Barb's Out, ‡NikkiC.	7
17Mar82-7GG	6f	$:22^4$	$:46^3$	$1:12^2$sy	14	114	3^3	5^5	$4^{6\frac{1}{2}}$	$4^{9\frac{1}{2}}$	Gonzalez RM[3]	Ⓕ 12500	67	Trcey'sSteel,Rosie'sBrt,SttlDuchss	8
4Mar82-2GG	1	$:47^3$	$1:13^4$	$1:40^2$ft	6 1/2	114	8^{11}	$6^{2\frac{3}{4}}$	2^4	3^4 †	Lamance C[3]	Ⓕ 12500	62	CariQueen,StingyLdy,‡DriftingDune	8
† 4Mar82—Disqualified and placed fifth															
24Feb82-2GG	6f	$:22^2$	$:45^3$	$1:11^1$ft	11	114	$1^{\frac{1}{2}}$	$4^{2\frac{1}{2}}$	7^{13}	7^{12}	Gonzalez RM[1]	Ⓕ 16000	71	Glad Nap, Bad Bad Lucy,Let'sParty	7
15Feb82-5GG	6f	$:22^3$	$:46^1$	1:14 sy	3 1/2	114	2^{hd}	$2^{1\frac{1}{2}}$	$3^{3\frac{1}{2}}$	5^6	Lamance C[5]	Ⓕ c10000	63	Nikki C., Windax, Book's Miss	10

Jun 13 GG 5f ft $1:03^3$ h — May 22 GG 4f ft $:50^1$ h — Apr 24 GG 5f ft $1:02^3$ h

This filly passed a pile of horses in the stretch to get up to win her last race, but not by nearly enough to even approach a Big Win. She was pounding and driving all the way, after being previously dropped in class to her more comfortable $12,500 level. If she had any kind of reasonably good competition, which she did have, it would be an astonishing upset form reversal if she could have pulled off two in a row at the same class.

Her last race, after her class drop, was immeasurably better than her previous effort, as she even won off a O rated running line to pay $15 or better. But, absent the double plus factors, her strong effort on June 4 was not likely to be repeated, and in fact, you could comfortably put her down as a loser. This happened, of course, because she lacked the necessary ingredients to score a repeat victory.

We could show you dozens of examples like Drifting Dune. These typical kinds of horses who won their previous races, without the necessary power factors, are very poor possibilities to win the next time out. Usually, there is a lot of money on the board backing them because, after all, they defeated horses of the same class the last time, and "ought to be able to do it again." Write it off as lost money. Your dollars need not be there.

On the other hand, let us look again at the kind of returning winner coming back at the same class that has a strong possibility of repeating his effort, even without a Big Win.

Stone of Scone — Ro. c. 4, by Blazestone—No More Bells, by Rapido
Br.—Brown D (Cal) — 1982 7 3 1 0 $15,438
Own.—Coleman-Fernandez-Welch **120** Tr.—McMeans Bill **$12,500** — 1981 9 1 2 0 $10,020
Lifetime 18 4 4 0 $25,971

31May82-3GG	6f	:22^{2}	:45^{2}	1:11 ft	*9-5	114	1^{hd}	1½	1^{2}	1^{2}	Lamance C^{5}	12500	84	StoneofScon,EdgofthBy,TimsT'mri	7
15May82-5GG	6f	:22^{1}	:45^{2}	1:11^{2}ft	4¼	117	41¾	3^{nk}	1^{2}	2¾	Baze R A^{1}	8500	81	SpclPoston,StonfScn,KntKtchK.lly	10
20Apr82-3GG	6f	:22^{3}	:45^{4}	1:10^{4}ft	*2	117	51¾	3^{2}	21½	52½	Baze R A^{9}	11000	82	BestofPlces,ChsMRound,TimHoldr	9
8Apr82-5GG	6f	:22^{3}	:46^{2}	1:11 ft	8½	117	1^{1}	11½	1^{3}	1^{5}	Lamance C^{12}	10000	84	StonofScon,Trstn'Dob,RpplngRvr	12
5Mar82-2GG	6f	:22^{1}	:45^{2}	1:11 ft	3½	114	1½	1^{hd}	2^{2}	74½	Baze R A^{1}	12500	79	WngdPhroh,ShdowWrror,Sbjet'.nOt	8
10Feb82-7GG	6f	:22^{2}	:45^{4}	1:12^{3}ft	*8-5	114	2^{hd}	1^{2}	1^{3}	1½	Baze R A^{4}	10000	76	StoneofScone,SpectculrCrr,QuitCrr	7
19Jan82-7BM	6f	:22^{2}	:45^{3}	1:12 sy	7¾	114	2^{1}	31½	5^{7}	9^{11}	Lamance C^{9}	12500	69	ShemTov,NativeRun,SubjecttonOut	9
31Dec81-7BM	6f	:22	:45	1:10^{4}m	9½	114	77½	7^{12}	12^{20}	11^{17}	Baze R A^{10}	20000	69	Coyotero,CutiousDecision,Mrimin	12
17Aug81-2Dmr	6f	:22^{1}	:45^{2}	1:11^{2}ft	42	113	3½	2^{2}	5^{6}	96½	Meza R Q^{12}	22500	74	PasstheBll,ImmnentIssue,Rosewlk	12
24Jly81-5Dmr	6f	:22^{2}	:45^{3}	1:10^{4}ft	11	116	1^{hd}	2^{hd}	3^{nk}	7^{7}	Shoemaker W^{8}	25000	77	RuledbyHoyle,TouchofGood,Gerldo	8

Stone of Scone was the favorite in the fifth race at Golden Gate on June 16. His last race was a model of a strong win, although his two length margin at the finish was not enough to rack up a Big Win.

But even without that important aspect this colt (and thus not a consistent old gelding) still had two plus form factors. He was up close at every call in his last race running line for one. The second comes in his improvement in his last race, a factor that we have not yet discussed, which comes in the next chapter. But look at the improvement he showed, since he ran a better and faster race against horses in a higher level of competition in his last effort than in the previous race. These two plus form factors gave him what we are looking for when we try to decide whether a horse can repeat a victory, which Stone of Scone did.

This is a good place to take up another element that is extremely important in trying to decide whether any horse will repeat a victory. We brought it out when discussing winners rising in class, but it is equally rewarding in dealing with winners returning at the same class. It is always necessary to search for "back class." If you see in a horse's past performances some evidence that he was able to compete successfully at a higher class somewhere back in his record, then his chances of repeating in today's race are all the more strengthened. Can we find this "back class" in Stone of Scone's record?

The first signs may be slightly negative. You will note that in the three victories before you, two were at the $10,000 level, with the last race at the same $12,500 for which he is competing in the race being considered today. Now look at the two bottom races in 1981, where he ran at Del Mar for $22,500 and $25,000. Neither of these races showed that he was a success at that class level. But the fact that he was running against much better horses tells you something quite important in this investigation. Del Mar, being a summer extension of the Santa Anita-Hollywood Park combine, would draw a much better quality of horses than those that compete regularly at Golden Gate.

But merely competing against a high level of horse still is not enough. There must be some degree of success at the higher class level if we are to consider it as true back class. Is there anything before us now to indicate that Stone of Scone had the necessary success? Let us extend our detective work a step further.

We have to go back to the three-year-old season. He ran nine times in 1981 and the three we see on the board are not impressive at all. But what about the six that we do not see? One of them had to be a maiden victory, since his career total wins are only four, as we consult that very helpful lifetime record box. Since Stone of Scone was running at Del Mar in July and August, we are now nearly certain that he was competing at Hollywood and Santa Anita before July, 1981. We also know that horses normally come down in class rather than go up, especially after they try high classes off their maiden victories and fail to win.

Now, to the next piece of evidence. Stone of Scone finished second twice in 1981, as his total earnings hit $10,020. A horse that finishes second in any race is considered competitive. Stone of Scone had two second place finishes in races where claiming prices were surely $25,000 or better. This is sound deductive reasoning from the evidence that we have before us.

Therefore, Stone of Scone shows back class. This fortifies his chances of winning again on June 16, running back at the same class. You can go through similar exercises when a horse is rising in class, always looking for success in the past at a higher level of competition, which means that your horse has the basic ability to come through today.

In summary, when horses are returning at the same class off a last race victory, their chances of repeating are highly influenced by whether they won their last race with a Big Win or with two or more strong + form factors, one of which can be a Big Win. If they show evidence of back class in their past performances, their chances are immeasurably strengthened.

The contrary consideration is whether they peaked in their form cycle by winning their last race, which is highly possible, and will thereafter start a decline in form, as so many horses do. Because the effort of winning a race is so great, it is quite natural for a horse to begin tailing off. We will have to rely on the plus signs, or otherwise reject the horse as a contender.

Horses Returning Off Their Maiden Victory

Horses who run their next race after having broken their maiden are almost always rising to a higher level of competition. About the only exception is where lightly raced two-year-olds compete in allowance races for non-winners of a race other than maiden, claiming or starter, and are competing against a group showing exactly the same characteristics. It is not uncommon to see a half dozen young leading contenders in any such two-year-old allowance race all coming off their maiden victories. Obviously there is no rise in level of competition for any of them. But outside of that exception, and the rare example of the horse that breaks its maiden against winners, most of the others are entering the new world of running against winners for the first time in their racing careers, where they find this far more difficult than competing against horses that have never won in their lives.

Consequently, you will not be surprised to know that figures for returning maiden winners closely parallel those for horses rising in class after scoring a victory against other winners.

Once again, the following table shows what occurred in the 433-race study.

Track	Horses	Win	Pct.
Bel	23	4	17.4%
Med	28	3	10.7%
Key	24	3	12.5%
Bow	18	2	11.1%
Total	93	12	12.9%

Once again, the prevalence of the Big Win and last race + form factors dominated among the winners. Ten of the 12 that emerged to score off their maiden triumphs had won their maiden races with a Big Win, revealing some unusual talent. Eight of the returning winners had two or more + form factors, once more showing the power of the combination of these elements. One of the returning maiden winners came off a layoff long enough to constitute a break in the form cycle, but had the highly desirable five furlong workout to prepare for the next victory.

But even this very slightly higher total percentage of winners repeating off of maiden victories above those rising in class comes out of the reality that we observed in two-year-old races, where so many of the horses have the same credentials. A horse, for example, returning off a maiden claiming victory in an open claiming race, almost never wins the next time out.

Additional Reflections on Returning Winners

In the racing cards under study, there were eight horses returning off victories that were dropping slightly in class. You may ask why a trainer would want to run his horse off a victory by moving backward to a lower level of competition. In almost every case, the class drop was very slight. One example was that of a horse that won a stakes race and returned in a high priced allowance event, which it also won. This slight class drop was more of a reflection of keeping the animal active than trying to drop him in class.

At any rate, among these eight horses, five were winners and a sixth came home first but was disqualified down to second. Another example in this group of winners was a horse shipping from one track to another, with the trainer "getting away with" a slight drop in class in the new surroundings. In two races at Meadowlands horses dropping in class after a layoff with appropriate workouts were able to win again at a lower class. So, you see, there were a variety of reasons, none of which seemed to indicate that the horse was declining in monetary value. If a horse is dropping considerably in class after a victory, and I have observed this phenomenon on a number of occasions, it is not a very likely candidate for a return victory. The trainer of such a horse is probably viewing a rash of infirmities that tells him to get rid of the horse while the animal is at peak value.

Leaving out the class droppers, we can summarize the overall study with a final table of figures, combining winners rising in class, winners returning at the same class, and winners coming back off maiden victories, for a total picture.

Track	Horses	Win	Pct.
Bel	108	18	16.7%
Med	130	16	12.3%
Key	111	20	18.0%
Bow	103	22	21.3%
Total	452	76	16.8%

An additional observation, which ought to be obvious, should be mentioned. A horse may win his last race and incur physical problems requiring a layoff, sometimes of an extended duration. When he returns to the arena, all the observations in this chapter are off, as the horse must be evaluated as any other horse coming back after a vacation period. The line to be drawn here, as in other form factors, is the four weeks, or 28 days, that we always use.

A Follow-Up Study

As I often do, when a concentrated study reveals certain figures and percentages, I will want to test a second time, where possible, to see if the previously discovered pattern still holds.

Accordingly, in 1982, I looked at scattered races at eastern tracks over several months, here and there. This random selection, somewhat like the technique of political pollsters, was not intended to have the precision of the inquiry into the 433 races that made up the master study, but was only geared to see if the same conclusions were still as valid as they appeared to be when first analyzed.

The bottom line simply is: even more so.

In doing the follow-up 1982 tabulations, I changed the rules only very slightly. Because I had learned from the previous study that very consistent horses were strong candidates to repeat, I omitted all bona fide stakes horses—which embraced those who ran regularly in stakes and had one or more stakes victories to their credit. By their class and ability, they are designed to be consistent runners, and to include them in a study which is directed more to maintenance of current form would surely distort the results.

Still keying in on consistent horses, I also noticed that some animals are streak competitors (back to our old geldings again, although a few mares occasionally showed the same tendencies). When they reach a peak of form, whether they are moving up the class ladder or not, some of them seem to pick up the habit of winning and winning. There are not many of these, but they are around and you can find the strings of victories in their past performances. Because they showed outstanding consistency— remember old Steelwood at the New York tracks—their records, too, might distort what we are trying to find out, which is, in most normal situations, how the horse will fare that won his last race.

With that in hand, I looked at some 539 winning horses that

were not dropping in class. (In this study, I came upon three that were dropping off a win, and all three of them won). I again divided them into the same basic three groups: (1) winners rising in class, (2) winners running back at the same class, and (3) winners off their maiden victories.

The class risers numbered 250 and 25 of them managed to win, or only ten percent of the total. This was precisely the same percentage that I found in the 433-race study, absolutely identical. Concentrating only on the Big Win as a dominant factor, 12 of the 25 winners had this characteristic.

Winners returning at the same class numbered 171 and 30 came home in front the second time in a row, for a 17.5% figure. This was slightly below the 22.6% of the previous study, but remember, stakes horses and horses with demonstrated consistent habits were omitted. Had those two groups been included, the results would again have been almost the same. In this survey, 14 of the 30 repeat winners did so off a Big Win.

With maiden winners, there were 118, and only 11 won again, or 9.2%. Five of these eleven had come off Big Wins. This was a little below the figures of the previous study, but there is probably greater reliability here because of the spread of the races. The late September–early October time period for the 1981 study of 433 races picked up many two-year-olds off their maiden victories, where they were running against competitors with the same drawback, and thus the higher figures in the 433-race study are to be expected.

Based upon more observation than what is contained in the tabulated figures, you should recognize by now that any horse that won his last race faces some difficult obstacles the next time out that may likely cause him to lose.

The realities tell us that these figures are tremendously reliable, but thus far, we have not dealt greatly in the why of this reality. Some of the explanation why horses have so much difficulty in winning a second or third successive time is undoubtedly due to the fact, which "trip handicappers" have discovered, that their winning trip was devoid of difficulty and such good fortune is not likely to occur twice in a row. Performing equally well two times in a row is a demanding assignment even for the human athlete. Horses are no exception. Obviously, when horses rise in class, winning thereafter is inherently more unlikely, because the competitive conditions are much more demanding. These are only some of the reasons, of course.

And from all this, we can now set forth some rather reliable guidelines when you are confronted with horses that won their last race.

Final Guidelines for Play on Returning Winners

Once again, we have to deal with the class level factor at the outset and make our rules for various levels of competition. When a winning horse is rising in class, knowing that he will likely lose nine times out of ten, we should eliminate him from consideration altogether unless he shows these characteristics:

- He must have at least two + form factors from his last race *and* a demonstration of back class, showing that he has performed competitively at the class level to which he is rising today, or

- He must have a Big Win + form factor in addition to at least one other plus form factor. Back class is always preferred, although not positively necessary, since the Big Win may be sufficient evidence that the horse is ready to take on a new level of competition today.

When a winning horse is returning at the same class, knowing he will likely lose four times out of five, we should eliminate him altogether unless he shows these characteristics:

- Two or more plus form factors in his last race, with a strong preference that one of them be a Big Win. If the horse does not show a Big Win, look for back class at a higher level of competition. If the horse shows neither a Big Win nor a demonstration of back class, and is not unusually consistent (showing a past history of an ability to win two races in succession), then out he goes.

When a winning horse is returning off a maiden victory, knowing that he will likely lose nine times out of ten, we should eliminate him altogether unless he shows these characteristics:

- Two or more plus form factors, which *must* include a Big Win. Those who score a victory after breaking their maiden and who do not show a Big Win usually do it when the remainder of the field is very weak. If you determine that the competition is therefore very thin, you can make an exception to the rule of requiring a Big Win, but be certain about the weakness of the others before you do it.

We can adopt easy symbols to mark our form ratings when horses won their last race. When a horse has won and is rising in class, we can put down an R for rising and place it inside the zero which is ordinarily used as a form defect symbol, and show it this way: Ⓡ.

When a horse won its last race and is returning at the same class, we can put a W for the win within the zero, and show it this way: Ⓦ.

When a horse won its maiden race and is running in his next outing, we can write an M, or maiden victory in the zero, and show it this way: Ⓜ.

If a horse has won and is dropping in class, there is no need for any symbol at all.

Dealing in this fashion with horses that won their last race is an entirely new handicapping development for me, growing out of the research that has gone into the writing of this book. Already, it has proved enormously helpful and extremely reliable. I expect it to do the same for you.

6 The Third Form Factor: Performance Within the Form Cycle, Part II – Improvement and Decline

WILL YOUR HORSE RUN BETTER TODAY THAN HE DID IN HIS LAST RACE? Or is he tailing off and is he likely not to do as well as in his last effort? These questions remain one of the great mysteries of handicapping, often presenting enough of a quandary to drive the most serene of prognosticators up against the paddock fence. Everyone can buy the old cliche: improving horses are better than declining horses. But how do you really tell? What are the reliable signals that a horse will do better today? Or can we see enough out of his past performances to be sure he is a poor candidate for success today and safely throw him out of contention? If handicappers had the correct answers to all these questions, their enjoyment and profits would be euphoric.

In Part I of this third form factor, which deals with performance within the form cycle itself, we first looked at horses that won their last race, and the difficulties they would encounter in the race that you would be looking at today. Horses rising in class brought with them the burden of competing against animals of a higher value level. Therefore, one would naturally not expect them to fare so well, except when they met certain exacting criteria. Even these attributes were far from enough to insure a victory. The second major area of concern was the victorious horse coming back at the same class under generally the same conditions, and there, the most important question is whether the effort in the last triumph took so much out of him that he is not likely to repeat. Or, did he win at the peak of his form cycle, making him likely to start a decline today?

In past writings, I have dealt with the improving horse and the declining horse. In *Investing at the Racetrack*, for purposes of form evaluation, I relied entirely upon a criterion of lengths nearer the lead or lengths farther from the lead in a horse's last race, compared to the previous race, if the performance met certain qualifying standards. In this way, we could label a horse as either improving or declining, or neither, and evaluate him accordingly. This method had the beauty of extreme simplicity, since all one had to do was measure the lengths closer or farther back and compare them. Fearful of bogging the reader down with complexity, I had hoped to blend simplicity and effectiveness together and produce something very useful. The effort was not at all unsuccessful—in fact, it is still workable, and thus forms the foundation for a deeper, more searching probe of the essential questions.

But it can be improved upon, and here we seek the most comprehensive guide we can find to good current form, or bad. In the past, I have also used modifications of times and track variants, which is bothersome for more than one reason: variants are not very reliable, as many researchers have shown, and even if they were, players outside the range of the eastern edition of *Daily Racing Form* were not provided them until 1983. Certain professionals make their own track variants, and while I am reasonably sure they are superior to the published ones, I am not yet convinced they are the total answer either.

Because predicting the outcome of horse races is one of the most complex and challenging endeavors that any sports fan will ever encounter (and that to me makes it the most rewarding), a good player simply cannot overlook every helping aid to discerning how a horse may run today. That is why we will try here to use every tool we can find to try to help us decide whether a horse will perform better or worse today. This is also why it was important to analyze horses that won their last race, because there are so many of them, and many of them are well played—wrongfully so, it seems.

When we start moving beyond lines of simplicity, the going gets tough. While it may be far better to rest upon the question, did a horse in his last race run "better" or "worse" than he ran in the race before that, we get thrown into subjective value judgments and these can often lead us astray, since we may like a horse enough for one reason or another to become blinded to his defects in another area.

Frankly, this is the most difficult part of evaluation of current form. But tackle it we must, and tackle it we shall. Here is where identification of the form cycle itself becomes so helpful. By separating and isolating past performances into form cycles, we are better able to evaluate the form cycle before us, and thus hopefully be in a position to make a wiser decision as to current form: is the horse improving within the form cycle or is declining within the form cycle?

Identifying form cycles may also tell us that we simply cannot compare the horse's two most recent efforts to determine whether it is improving or tailing off. For example, a horse with a recent race may have run that race after a layoff of four weeks or more. Drawing a line through the past performances shows this reality and tells us that the horse we are looking at is in the second race of a new form cycle and there is no next-to-last race with which to compare his last performance. Or, if today's race is the first outing after a layoff of four weeks or more, comparing the last two races before the horse's vacation is not likely to be very useful. In these circumstances we can use the N, neutral or non-applicable, rating for this form factor. But if the line through the past performances shows that today's race is the third one in a new form cycle, and the last one showed some improvement over the previous effort, we will be looking for a horse with an improving form cycle.

In addition to layoffs we are, as always compelled to deal with class levels of competition, different distances, and different surfaces. A great deal of study and research has persuaded me that when a horse is dropping to a lower level of competition, it is extremely difficult to determine whether an ostensible improvement is due to the lower class level. When horses face competitors of a lesser strength, their entire running behavior appears to change. Of course, when a running line is considerably better at a lower level, there indeed may be improvement in form of a horse, but we can never be sure. Because there are three other form factors upon which we can measure a horse, we can always retreat to safe ground here and put the neutral N in our rating line. If the horse qualifies on other factors or is eliminated on one of them, you can rely upon that and play your race accordingly.

Thus, we have adopted a safe and conservative rule: when a horse in its last race was dropping in class, and that last race appeared on the surface to be an improvement over the immediate prior effort, we will still award only an N because of the rather imposing possibility that the "improvement" was due largely to the weaker competition the horse faced. On the other hand, if a horse's running line is obviously "worse" while dropping in class, we can rate him on whether he has improved or declined. Usually, he will pick up a O form factor somewhere else in his record and we will not have to worry too much about him.

With that one resolved, let us now set forth the guidelines that we will apply to determine whether a horse is improving enough to be awarded a +, whether there are not sufficient standards to give him anything other than an N, or whether he is demonstrably declining in form which will bring a O and elimination as a serious contender.

We will always use the last two races for comparison purposes if they both fall within the proper recency time frames. The last race must have been run within 28 days of today's race. The next to last race, which we use for comparison purposes, must be within 28 days of the last race. We will make further reference to this in the specific examples that will be shown in later pages. They should be easy enough to follow at that point.

If, as with the examples given above, either of these two measuring races are not within the proper time frames, we cannot make a comparison for improvement or decline. This form factor then becomes a washout. We write down an N and proceed to rate the next and final form factor.

If either of the two measuring races were run on a different surface, such as grass or dirt, then we likewise are not able to make a reliable comparison, because horses do run differently on these surfaces. Here again, we write down an N for neutral.

Within the same level of competition, we are often confronted with different distances in the two measuring races, and we have to deal with this problem. There are two phases of it: sprint to route or route to sprint; and differing distances within either a sprint race or a route race, such as a comparing a six furlong sprint against a seven furlong sprint or a comparing a mile and a sixteenth route against a mile and an eighth (or a mile and seventy yards, or a mile and three eighths or any other varying distance).

But before we tackle the problem of making comparisons between different distances, let us first establish standards for the comparison races that were run at the same class and the same distance. Remember, the races to be compared are the horse's two most recent races, provided that they fall within the necessary 28 day time frames.

Comparing Races at the Same Distance

Once again, we are going to rely on the stretch call as the key indicator. First, we compare lengths behind at the stretch calls of the two comparison races. If the stretch call in the last race shows that the horse was one length or more nearer to the lead at that call than in the previous race, we go to the next step to measure improvement or decline. If the last race stretch call shows that the horse was one length or more *farther* from the lead than in the previous race, we take the next step also. If the horse was neither a length or more closer to the lead or farther from it at the stretch call of its last race, there is no next step—we can put down the neutral or non-applicable N and move ahead.

The second and final step is to compare the winning times of the winning horses in the two comparison races. It does not matter whether they are faster or slower at this point. We then compare the final times of the horse under consideration. They will be compared in tandem with the winning times. If the winning time of the victorious horse in the last race was two-fifths of a second, or what many racetrackers call two "ticks," better than the winner's time in the semi-final race, to have held even the horse under consideration must also have run two-fifths of a second faster in its last effort than in its next to last race. To show the improvement necessary for a + rating, the horse must have run yet an additional two ticks faster, for a total of four-fifths faster. This "extra two ticks" rule for measuring improvement applies no matter how much faster the last winning time was compared to the winner's time in the next to last race. For example, if the last race winning time at the same class was one second (or five-fifths) faster, then the horse under consideration must have run five-fifths plus two, or seven ticks faster in its last race than in the prior race to show an improvement.

The same formula works in reverse to show a decline. Whatever the comparative winning times of the last two comparison races show, the final comparison times of the horse under consideration must be compared in the same vein, faster or slower. If the last race winner's time was two-fifths of a second faster than the winning time in the next to last race, our potential declining horse must at least have kept up the pace, or else he is in decline. The measuring rod is still two-fifths of a second slower. In other words, if in this example our "declining" horse ran in the same time as he turned in previously he is falling off by two-fifths, since the winning time of the last race was two-fifths faster than the previous race.

It works the same way if the winning time of the last race was slower. Use one second slower as an example. If our horse that was farther behind at the stretch by one length or more wound up with a final time that was also one second slower than his final time in his next to last race, he would neither be declining or improving. But if this horse's final time in his last race was only three-fifths of a second slower than the previous race, he would have performed two ticks better than the comparison of winning times, and thus he would get a + for improvement. But if, in this comparison of two races where the winner's time in the last effort was one second slower, our horse ran seven-fifths slower, he would not be keeping up with the comparative times of the two races, and would show a decline. A declining horse is a very poor betting proposition and gets the O rating.

This is extremely effective, as you will see when you put it into practice. And with practice, the time comparisons will not be too difficult for you to do. As a quick glance test, even without any effort at computation, note how many winning horses were closer to the lead at the stretch call in their last race than they were in their previous effort. You can also, just by looking at any collection of past performances in the *Daily Racing Form*, quickly note how many losers were farther behind at the stretch call in their last race than they were in the previous one. But for serious application, you still have to do the tandem comparison of times.

There is but one major exception to this new, highly effective declining horse test. When a horse scores a gain of three, either in lengths or horses passed, from the stretch call to the finish, he is not really declining. He is coming on strongly enough to overcome the evidence of a decline, even if his final times fail to match up. Therefore, despite his comparative times, if a horse shows a gain of three in the stretch, he should be given an N rating. I will show you a good example of this later on, but for now, let us do a few hypothetical exercises merely to show how the method works.

	Str.	Fin.	Win Time	Horse's Time
Last Race	2^2	3^2	1:11.2	1:11.4
2nd Last Race	2^3	2^3	1:11.4	1:12.2

Since our horse was one length nearer the lead at the stretch call in his last race, we must now check comparative times. The winning time was two-fifths of a second faster, which means that if an improvement factor is to be found, our horse will have to run two-fifths faster than he did in his semi-final race, plus an additional two ticks faster to show improvement, for a total of four-fifths of a second faster. Unless he can achieve that, there will be no improvement, and an N rating will be given. In the above example our horse ran three-fifths faster, not four, and thus falls short of a plus rating for improvement. He gets a neutral.

	Str.	Fin.	Win Time	Horse's Time
Last Race	3^3	2^1	1:12.4	1:13.0
2nd Last Race	5^6	4^3	1:12.0	1:12.3

Once again, with our horse nearer to the lead in his last race, we take the next step to check for improvement, and compare winning times. The winning time was four-fifths of a second slower. If our horse also ran four ticks slower, he would be running even. But he ran only two-fifths slower, 1:13 as compared to 1:12.3, and thus improved by two in comparison to the winning times, earning this horse a + for improvement.

	Str.	Fin.	Win Time	Horse's Time
Last Race	3^4	4^4	1:49.0	1:49.4
2nd Last Race	1^3	1^3	1:46.2	1:46.2

This one was lifted from *Daily Racing Form* past performances for an actual favorite in a distance race, whose form ratings fully qualified him in all respects. The winning time in the last race was two and three-fifths seconds slower than the previous race time. While based on the times and the number of lengths behind you may think the horse was declining, we cannot know until we calculate it out. His last race time was three and two-fifths seconds slower, which meets the additional two ticks slower. Thus, we have established the decline. This favorite not only failed to win, but his declining form showed him trailing back out of the money.

What have we done here and what have we accomplished?

This is a major effort to solve some of the complications of our previous improvement-decline factors. First of all, it is the most facile way to solve the troublesome track variant problem. We are in effect letting the winning horses make a true variant of their own for us. Since we are comparing races at the same distance and same class, the winning times ought to be comparatively the same. If they are not, they may be due to varying track conditions. But since we are comparing our horse under the same conditions as those of the winning horse, comparative times can tell us a great deal. We require two-fifths of a second as a margin of error to establish either improvement or decline.

Second of all, despite the kind of calculation you saw in the three examples set forth, there is not nearly as much arithmetic required as you may think. The reason for this is that many comparisons are so obvious at a glance that nothing more is required. Many races will be out of time sequence and cannot be used. Others will not show a sufficient number of lengths closer or farther behind at the stretch call. There will be class drops which cannot be calculated. And if a horse is non-qualified by not being sufficiently close at the stretch call to earn an up close rating, you can omit the computation for improvement and decline because the horse would already have a O in his running line. With that demonstration of how often you will not have to do this calculation, our concessions to laziness end.

This is an important factor. A declining horse is poison. If you play a declining horse and lose because you were too careless to do the necessary calculation, then you are not too serious about being a topnotch winning player.

A horse showing improvement, as you will surely find out, is a good prospect for today, and that is what we are looking for.

Now that we have dealt only with horses where we can compare the past two races at the same class and same distance, how do we approach the other problems of distance shifts from sprint to route and changes in distance within the same type of races, all at the same level of competition?

Comparing Races at Different Distances

If the two comparison races consist of one sprint and one distance race, we will still first check the stretch positions. If our horse was one length or more nearer to or farther from the lead, we then use the comparative six furlong times to calculate the additional two-fifths measurement for improvement or decline—two ticks better or worse than the difference in the six furlong leader's time. You will see how this works as we approach the examples from the *Daily Racing Form* that we will be setting forth shortly.

When we have varying sprint distances, such as a shift from six to seven furlongs, we have a slightly different problem. We will have to use a comparative time chart to convert either one of the races so we may evaluate comparable times. This is not as precise as we would like, because comparative time charts are only projected figures and may not reveal the actual times at all. But the chart is all we have, so it is necessary to use it. When we have route races at diverse distances, such as a mile and seventy yards compared to a mile and a sixteenth, which is very common, we have to do the same comparisons.

We provided an excellent comparison table in *Investing at the Racetrack* for sprint races only, which we will reproduce here.

Comparative Time Chart for Sprint Races Only

5 f	5½ f	6 f	6½ f	7 f
:57.1	1:03.2	1:09.2	1:15.3	1:21.4
:57.2	1:03.3	1:09.3	1:15.4	1:22.0
:57.2	1:03.4	1:09.4	1:16.0	1:22.1
:57.3	1:04.0	1:10.0	1:16.1	1:22.2
:57.3	1:04.0	1:10.1	1:16.2	1:22.3
:57.4	1:04.1	1:10.2	1:16.3	1:22.4
:57.4	1:04.1	1:10.2	1:16.4	1:23.0
:58.0	1:04.2	1:10.3	1:17.0	1:23.1
:58.1	1:04.3	1:10.4	1:17.0	1:23.2
:58.1	1:04.3	1:10.4	1:17.1	1:23.3
:58.2	1:04.4	1:11.0	1:17.2	1:23.4
:58.2	1:04.4	1:11.0	1:17.3	1:24.0
:58.3	1:05.0	1:11.1	1:17.4	1:24.1
:58.4	1:05.1	1:11.2	1:18.0	1:24.2
:59.0	1:05.2	1:11.3	1:18.1	1:24.3
:59.1	1:05.3	1:11.4	1:18.2	1:24.4
:59.1	1:05.3	1:12.0	1:18.3	1:25.0
:59.2	1:05.4	1:12.1	1:18.4	1:25.1
:59.3	1:06.0	1:12.2	1:19.0	1:25.2
:59.3	1:06.0	1:12.2	1:19.0	1:25.3
:59.4	1:06.1	1:12.3	1:19.1	1:25.4
1:00.0	1:06.2	1:12.4	1:19.2	1:26.0
1:00.0	1:06.2	1:12.4	1:19.2	1:26.1
1:00.1	1:06.3	1:13.0	1:19.3	1:26.2
1:00.2	1:06.4	1:13.1	1:19.4	1:26.3
1:00.2	1:06.4	1:13.2	1:20.0	1:26.4
1:00.3	1:07.0	1:13.3	1:20.1	1:27.0
1:00.4	1:07.1	1:13.4	1:20.2	1:27.1
1:00.4	1:07.2	1:14.0	1:20.3	1:27.2
1:01.0	1:07.3	1:14.1	1:20.4	1:27.3
1:01.1	1:07.4	1:14.2	1:21.0	1:27.4
1:01.1	1:07.4	1:14.2	1:21.0	1:28.0
1:01.2	1:08.0	1:14.3	1:21.1	1:28.1
1:01.3	1:08.1	1:14.4	1:21.2	1:28.2
1:01.3	1:08.1	1:14.4	1:21.3	1:28.3
1:01.4	1:08.2	1:15.0	1:21.4	1:28.4
1:02.0	1:08.3	1:15.1	1:22.0	1:29.0
1:02.1	1:08.4	1:15.2	1:22.1	1:29.1
1:02.1	1:09.0	1:15.3	1:22.2	1:29.2
1:02.2	1:09.1	1:15.4	1:22.3	1:29.3

Such a table is reasonably workable, because sprint races are ordinarily quite uniform in character. They are run around one turn and the length of the backstretch, based upon the distance of the race, is the major divergent factor. But when we come to distance races, we have much more variety and consequently, much more difficulty in comparing times at different distances.

In New York, for example, the main track at Aqueduct is a mile and an eighth. The inner track, used in the winter months, is one mile. At Belmont, where the oval is a mile and a half, distance races up to a mile and an eighth are run around one turn. You can readily recognize some of the problems in comparing different distances in the longer races.

Workable Time Differences Between Distances

Equally important in the longer races is the different running styles that may greatly influence times. What we are warning against is any situation where you have to use comparative times in distance races. They are estimates, and from these estimates, we can try to produce something that is "workable."

To try for comparison times, however, we will divide races into fast, medium, and slow, based upon the track, class of horse, and the final times that are turned in. We shall make our attempt by using times between a mile and a·mile and an eighth.

Track Type	Mile to 1^{40}	Mile to 1^{70}	1^{70} to $1\frac{1}{16}$	Mile to $1\frac{1}{16}$	$1\frac{1}{16}$ to $1\frac{1}{8}$
Fast	:02.1	:04.1	:02.2	:06.3	:06.3
Medium	:02.2	:04.2	:02.3	:06.4	:06.4
Slow	:02.3	:04.3	:02.4	:07.0	:07.0

You can add or subtract in particular situations, as necessity requires. These time spans can give you rough, approximate ideas for comparison purposes.

We will next go to the specific examples from past performances, and work enough exercises out of them so that you will soon have a quick, efficient method to find out whether a horse is improving, declining, or neither, as we continue our search for the answer to how our horse will run today.

We will begin with an easy one, but we will also use other pairs of running lines besides the past two contained within this past performance to do additional examples. Lady Gambol is running in the seventh race at Golden Gate on June 18, and we are able to compare her last two races because they are at the same class and distance and within our necessary time frames.

Lady Gambol — B. f. 4, by Petrone—Lady in Orbit, by Royal Orbit

Own.—Aleo H J — **114** — Br.—Jellen J (Cal) — Tr.—Gilchrist Greg — $12,500

1982	8	1	1	0	$9,820
1981	14	2	2	3	$15,193
Lifetime	31	4	3	4	$26,034

4Jun82-7GG	$1\frac{1}{16}$	:47^{4}	1:13^{1}	1:48	ft	14	110^{5}	$5^{8\frac12}$	$6^{5\frac12}$	$5^{2\frac14}$	$4^{2\frac12}$	SchvnvldtCP^{2}	Ⓕ 12500	60	DriftingDun,Brb'sOut,Plnum'sChick	9
14May82-9GG	$1\frac{1}{16}$	:47^{4}	1:12^{3}	1:46^{2}	ft	$6\frac14$	114	$6^{8\frac12}$	8^{10}	8^{14}	8^{18}	Chapman TM^{1}	Ⓕ 12500	53	Blessed Bicker,Barb'sOut,EsterFast	8
5May82-7GG	$1\frac{1}{16}$	:47	1:12^{1}	1:47^{1}	ft	4	114	7^{13}	6^{10}	6^{9}	6^{11}	Schacht R^{1}	Ⓕ 16000	56	She's a Gal, Stingy Lady, EsterFast	7
9Apr82-5GG	1	:47^{2}	1:12^{1}	1:39	ft	$3\frac12$	114	7^{11}	8^{14}	7^{12}	$7^{9\frac12}$	Schacht R^{2}	Ⓕ 25000	63	My DearTam,QuarterLea,Let'sParty	8
25Mar82-7GG	1	:46	1:11^{3}	1:39	ft	13	114	7^{18}	7^{10}	6^{6}	$4^{3\frac12}$	Schacht R^{5}	Ⓕ 32000	69	CurrentLine,FstTrcie,OhHowSweet	8
26Feb82-6GG	$1\frac{1}{16}$	:48^{1}	1:13^{3}	1:46^{2}	ft	*$3\frac12$	114	5^{5}	$4^{2\frac12}$	$3^{2\frac12}$	$7^{4\frac34}$	AndersonJR^{6}	Ⓕ c25000	66	FoxholeHustlr,BgofChrm,CurrntLin	8
26Feb82—Placed sixth through disqualification																
15Feb82-4GG	$1\frac{1}{16}$	:48^{1}	1:13^{1}	1:47^{3}	sy	$7\frac12$	114	4^{10}	5^{7}	$3^{2\frac12}$	$2^{\frac12}$	Anderson JR^{1}	Ⓕ 25000	64	Current Line,LadyGambol,MinneOh	6
7Jan82-7BM	$1\frac{1}{16}$	:48^{2}	1:14^{1}	1:48^{1}	gd	$4\frac12$	114	5^{9}	$5^{5\frac14}$	1^{hd}	$1^{\frac34}$	Anderson JR^{6}	Ⓕ 16000	58	LdyGmbol,GoldnPolicy,WhispringSl	7
23Dec81-7BM	6f	:23^{1}	:46^{4}	1:12^{4}	gd	11	112	7^{11}	7^{10}	7^{9}	5^{7}	Anderson JR^{5}	Ⓕ 16000	69	MyShnngLdy,WllsPrcos,BronzBobb	8
29Oct81-4BM	1	:46^{3}	1:12^{4}	1:39^{3}	gd	*2	115	4^{8}	$3^{4\frac12}$	$2^{2\frac12}$	$2^{3\frac12}$	Baze D^{2}	Ⓕ 16000	67	OurGlmor,LdyGmbol,LovngThoght	5

Jun 13 GG 5f ft 1:01^{3} h **May 31 GG 5f ft 1:01^{1} h** **Apr 27 GG 6f ft 1:13^{4} h** **Apr 20 GG 5f ft 1:03^{2} h**

At an obvious glance, she was much closer at the stretch call in the last race than in her next to last race. But immediately you should notice that the last race was run in much slower time than the preceding event on May 1, which again was likely due to a wide track variant. When you have precisely the same distances involved, you can shortcut your calculations by relying on speed ratings, since these numbers are taken off final times. But we must caution again that speed ratings can be used only when the distance of the two races is precisely the same and the two races were run at the same track. Otherwise, never use them and instead, fall back on your calculations.

The winning time in the last race was one and three-fifths seconds (eight ticks) slower than the winning time on May 1. Therefore, if Lady Gambol also ran eight ticks slower, she would have been equalling her time, comparatively speaking. But she ran seven-fifths *faster*, as you can see from the speed rating of 60 she earned in her last race compared to the 53 from the previous effort. With speed ratings, one number difference equals one-fifth of a second difference. If she had run only six ticks slower, she would have had the necessary improvement standard of two ticks better than the comparison time. Because she was faster she easily meets the test, and thus gets a + for improvement.

Lady Gambol's past performances can be used to do another exercise. Look down to the races of January 7, 1982, and December 23, 1981, near the bottom, both at the same class, but one at a sprint and the other at a distance. In the mile and a sixteenth race on January 7, Lady Gambol was much nearer to the lead than in the six furlong sprint on December 23. Now, we take the next step of comparing the six furlong times of the two races.

In the January 7 race, the lead time at six furlongs was 1:14.1. We compare it with the final six furlong time on December 23, which was 1:12.4. Thus, the second race was one and two-fifths seconds slower. Lady Gambol's December 23 time at the finish was 1:14.1, adding on seven-fifths for the seven lengths she finished off the lead. If her six furlong time at the second call of the January 7 race was seven ticks slower, she would have been holding her own. It would have to be one second (five ticks, or two ticks better than seven-fifths) or less slower to show the necessary improvement that appears on the surface of the two races.

Her six furlong time on January 7 was 1:15.1, which was one second slower. Thus, comparatively speaking, she improved her running line by the requisite two-fifths to warrant a + for improvement. In her following race, however, she was rising in class off a victory, and also after a layoff. Her more than 7-1 odds reflected her chances, although she did surprisingly well to place.

A quick glance at the other races in her past performances shows how infrequently you would hvae to do this comparative calculating. The numerous drops in class do not require much analysis, and in races where the same distance and class were involved, such as those on April 9 and March 25, the second race in the pair was so obviously weaker at a glance that you would hardly have to go further, especially since there would be a zero for the last race running line.

Let us do another obvious one, not only to show how easy it is, but to further make the point that an improving horse is a substantial contender in today's race. We resurrect Cliff Hanger from an earlier chapter to now demonstrate his improvement in his last race.

Cliff Hanger — Dk. b. or br. c. 4, by Mr Prospector—Nana Blanch, by Sherluck
Own.—Sommer Viola — 117 — Br.—Heinen P & Patricia (Fla) — 1982 7 2 0 0 $12,600
Tr.—Martin Frank — $12,500 — 1981 10 1 0 2 $15,480
Lifetime 17 3 0 2 $28,080

12Jun82-9Bel	6f	:22^{3}	:45^{4}	1:10^{4}ft	7¾	117	1^{1}	$2^{\frac{1}{2}}$	3^{3}	$5^{5\frac{1}{2}}$	Miranda J^{2}	16000	82	Truce, Soudan, Greene Go	9
26May82-3Bel	6f	:23	:46^{2}	1:10^{4}ft	3e	117	$1^{1\frac{1}{2}}$	$3^{1\frac{1}{2}}$	6^{4}	$8^{9\frac{3}{4}}$	Rivera M A^{1}	16000	78	Whambang, Clodion,RajaTheGreat	11
14May82-9Aqu	6f	:22^{1}	:45^{3}	1:11^{2}ft	*6-5	119	$2^{2\frac{1}{2}}$	$2^{\frac{1}{2}}$	1^{3}	1^{nk}	Vasquez J^{9}	c12500	84	CliffHanger,PowerMster,PokieJoe	10
8May82-9Aqu	1	:47	1:12	1:38 ft	6¾	115	$1^{1\frac{1}{2}}$	$2^{1\frac{1}{2}}$	7^{11}	8^{15}	Vasquez J^{4}	19000	61	Sprink, Click Off, Marlago	10
30Apr82-2Aqu	6f	:22^{3}	:46^{2}	1:11^{1}ft	*3-2	117	$2^{2\frac{1}{2}}$	$1^{\frac{1}{2}}$	1^{3}	$1^{5\frac{1}{2}}$	Russ M L^{1}	c10000	85	Cliff Hanger, Born Great, I'm Vital	7
21Apr82-7Aqu	6f	:22^{2}	:45^{3}	1:10^{4}ft	*8-5e	117	2^{1}	2^{5}	$3^{7\frac{1}{2}}$	6^{11}	Velasquez J^{5}	25000	76	WstgtBrnswck,MstrMgcn,Whmbng	8
3Apr82-4Aqu	6f	:22^{3}	:45^{1}	1:11 ft	7	117	$3^{1\frac{1}{2}}$	5^{6}	6^{11}	6^{13}	Vergara O^{6}	35000	73	El Bombay, Assension, Royal Jove	6
28Dec81-7Aqu	6f	⊡:23	:46^{1}	1:11^{3}gd	8-5e	115	6^{4}	$7^{3\frac{3}{4}}$	$6^{2\frac{1}{2}}$	6^{4}	Migliore R^{5}	Aw16000	82	Grand Felice, FountainofGold,Rigid	8

Note that his last two races were at the same class and distance, so we can use them for comparison purposes. At the stretch call of his last race, Cliff Hanger was the required one length nearer to the lead than he was at the same point in the prior race. The final times of the two races were both 1:10.4 at the same class, which is the ideal situation. By looking at the Belmont speed ratings, you can see that Cliff Hanger ran four-fifths better, going from a 78 speed rating to an 82, which is plenty for the + rating. As you already know, he was a solid winner in his race.

The next example is not quite as simple. Let us examine the past performances on Raise the Tempo out of the fifth race at Golden Gate on June 18.

Raise the Tempo — B. c. 3, by Native Royalty—Fur Boots, by Northern Dancer
Own.—Phipps R W — 113 — Br.—Warner M L (Ohio) — 1982 4 1 1 1 $10,750
Tr.—Martin R L — 1981 11 1 1 2 $14,970
Lifetime 15 2 2 3 $25,720

5Jun82-2GG	6f	:22	:45^{2}	1:12 ft	5½	114	$6^{3\frac{1}{4}}$	6^{6}	5^{4}	2^{2}	Anderson J R^{3}	25000	77	GoldenGroom,RisthTmpo,Worhwhil	8
21May82-2GG	6f	:22	:45^{2}	1:11^{2}ft	4½	117	1^{hd}	1^{hd}	1^{hd}	$3^{5\frac{1}{2}}$	Lamance C^{1}	25000	76	Michi'sSlor,GoldnGroom,RsthTmpo	7
1May82-6GG	6f	:22	:45	1:11^{1}ft	3½	113	$7^{2\frac{3}{4}}$	$6^{4\frac{3}{4}}$	$6^{5\frac{3}{4}}$	$5^{8\frac{3}{4}}$	GonzalezRM^{7}	Aw13000	74	CyneWho,PrimePrformnc,WhitFlg	11
29Apr82-6GG	6f	:22	:45	1:10^{3}ft	8	114	4^{3}	$4^{5\frac{1}{2}}$	3^{2}	$1^{\frac{1}{2}}$	Anderson J R^{1}	25000	86	RisetheTempo,SoGos,ProprProcdur	7
26Nov81-4BM	6f	:22^{4}	:46^{3}	1:13 m	2½	114	$6^{2\frac{3}{4}}$	5^{4}	$6^{6\frac{1}{4}}$	$6^{9\frac{1}{4}}$	Mahorney W^{7}	25000	66	Two Buddys, Kin Folk, Hoot Fire	7
12Nov81-2BM	6f	:22^{1}	:45	1:10^{1}sy	4½	114	1^{2}	1^{1}	3^{2}	$4^{9\frac{1}{2}}$	Mahorney W^{7}	40000	79	Ali Kato, Sail'n Easy, Scheib	8
3Nov81-6BM	6f	:22^{4}	:45^{4}	1:10^{4}ft	6¾	117	$3^{1\frac{1}{2}}$	4^{2}	$4^{3\frac{1}{2}}$	4^{5}	Mahorney W^{1}	Aw11000	81	ThBrginHuntr,WindySturdy,Adstrin	9
20Oct81-7BM	6f	:22^{3}	:45^{4}	1:11^{1}ft	13	117	$7^{7\frac{1}{2}}$	$7^{9\frac{1}{4}}$	$6^{9\frac{3}{4}}$	$3^{7\frac{1}{2}}$	Mahorney W^{5}	Aw10000	76	HeyRob,DustyTrader,RisetheTempo	8
8Oct81-6BM	6f	:22^{2}	:45^{3}	1:11 ft	2½	120	4^{3}	$4^{4\frac{1}{2}}$	$4^{5\frac{1}{2}}$	$5^{8\frac{1}{2}}$	Burkes T^{1}	Aw10000	76	Little Tis, Sunday Addition, Scheib	8
6Sep81-4Dmr	6f	:23	:46^{2}	1:10^{4}ft	*2¼	118	1^{hd}	$1^{1\frac{1}{2}}$	$1^{2\frac{1}{2}}$	1^{3}	Hawley S^{4}	Mdn	84	Raise the Tempo,Tular,LateSleeper	9

A first glance raises the declining horse question, since he was considerably farther from the lead at the stretch call in his last race than in the previous race on May 21. The winning times show the June 5 race as three-fifths of a second slower. This means that Raise the Tempo would have had to run one second slower to be labeled a declining horse. Without calculating, the same speed ratings tell us that he actually ran one-fifth faster, a comparative improvement of four, but we cannot do more than an N here, since the horse was farther behind at the stretch call of his last race, not nearer, as is necessary for the + rating. Again, you might note that there is not another brace of comparison races under comparable conditions anywhere else in the past performances.

Another interesting series of circumstances is shown in the record of Power Brigade, entered in the first race at Golden Gate on June 19.

Power Brigade ∗

B. g. 5, by Power Ruler—Harry's Sister, by Curragh King
Br.—Weaver Dr D E (Cal)

Own.—Hagopian Erika   **117**   Tr.—Kiesner James

								1982	11 6 4 1	$37,635
								$8,500	1981 19 2 3 1	$35,746
Lifetime	56 13 12 6 $117,485							Turf	6 0 1 0	$6,270
6Jun82-7GG	1¹⁄₁₆:48¹ 1:12⁴ 1:47¹ft	*2 1125	109¹⁄₂ 74³⁄₄ 64¹⁄₄ 22¹⁄₄	SchvnevldtCP¹⁰	12500 64 Cvlero,PowerBrigde,BrutlityofHop 10
16May82-2GG	1¹⁄₁₆:47² 1:12¹ 1:45³ft	*8-5 1105	68¹⁄₂ 43¹⁄₂ 2¹ 1¹⁄₂	SchvneveldtCP⁵	11000 75 PowerBrigde,O'LuckyPt,TodysSpcil 8
8May82-1GG	1¹⁄₁₆:46³ 1:12 1:46 ft	2 120	45¹⁄₂ 33¹⁄₂ 22 2²	Anderson J R⁷	c8500 71 Tom Daly, PowerBrigade,MakeWay 7
24Apr82-7GG	1¹⁄₁₆:47² 1:11³ 1:43⁴ft	*9-5 117	2² 2¹ 2hd 1¹	Anderson J R⁹	8500 84 PowerBrigade,TomDaly,NobleHeir 10
13Apr82-4GG	1¹⁄₁₆:48² 1:13 1:45³ft	*9-5 117	65¹⁄₂ 3² 3² 1hd	Anderson J R⁴	8500 75 PowerBrigade,PortVelt,EglsFlyHigh 7
27Mar82-1GG	1 :46² 1:12 1:39 ft	*4-5 120	3³ 4³ 4¹⁄₂ 3¹⁄₂	Anderson J R²	11000 72 CptinBionic,Bendique,PowerBrigde 7
20Mar82-9GG	1¹⁄₁₆:48⁴ 1:14¹ 1:47³gd	*9-5 120	31¹⁄₂ 3³ 2² 2¹	Anderson J R²	12500 64 Ruffaway, Power Brigade, DealsOn 8
6Mar82-9GG	1¹⁄₁₆:47 1:11³ 1:45 ft	*8-5 117	1¹⁄₂ 1¹⁄₂ 1¹⁄₂ 1¹⁄₂	Anderson J R¹	12500 78 PowrBrigd,ComonKvn,EglsFlyHgh 11
27Feb82-5GG	1¹⁄₁₆:48 1:12⁴ 1:45⁴m	*8-5 115	41³⁄₄ 1¹ 1¹ 1³⁄₄	Anderson J R⁴	16000 74 PowerBrigade,TopFool,BanjoCreek 8
30Jan82-9BM	1¹⁄₁₆:47¹ 1:12⁴ 1:46 gd	*1 118	21¹⁄₂ 1hd 1hd 2nk	Wilburn J⁴	16000 69 TightShp,PowrBrgd,VctorousRunnr 6

Here is another example of a horse being much farther back at every call of his last race on June 6, than he was in his previous race on May 16. A declining horse? What do you think?

The winning time of the last race was 1:47.1, one and three-fifths seconds slower than Power Brigade ran on May 16, when he scored a victory in 1:45.3. If you are concerned about the class price differential, this concern is hardly warranted, since the $1,500 difference in claiming price simply is not enough to form a separate level of competition. Thus, if Power Brigade ran the same eight ticks slower on June 6, he would be holding his own. But the speed ratings show he ran two and one-fifth seconds slower, which you can see from the eleven point difference between the ratings of 64 and 75. This establishes the declining horse, but wait. Remember, I told you there was one major exception. When a horse gains three in either lengths or horses, or both, between the stretch and the finish in his last race, he is overcoming the decline that was earlier shown in his running line. You can see that Power Brigade gained two lengths and passed four horses, a gain of six.

This is not inserted here merely as an excuse for Power Brigade. This steady old gelding won the June 19 race. I have seen this same pattern emerge in dozens of races that I have checked. If a horse is up close at the stretch call, as Power Brigade was, and keeps coming on to the finish, even though he may be passing tired horses, he may not safely be put into the declining horse bin in his next race. Too many victories emerge and they are not surprises. So, you will continually have to watch for this gain of three rule as an important exception to the sound standards we use here to mark a declining horse.

There is more we can learn from looking through other races in Power Brigade's past performances. Look at the two races of May 8, and April 24, 1982. With a two length poorer showing at the stretch call of the May 8 race, you have to investigate to see if you have a declining horse on your hands. Again, we see a rather enormous divergence in final times at the same class and distance. The last race winning time was two and one-fifth seconds slower than the April 24 winning time of Power Brigade. Yet he finished two and three-fifths slower, and that barely meets the requirement for a declining horse. Power Brigade was claimed and raised in class to score a victory on May 16. While the declining horse factor is extremely powerful, it, too, is not infallible, as you see an example of a steady old campaigner overcoming both it and a rise in class (even though there was strong back class showing).

Let us now try one where there was a distance switch down from a mile and a sixteenth to seven furlongs. We have Lil' Miss Goody out of the ninth race at Hollywood on June 16.

Lil' Miss Goody ✷				B. f. 3, by Bold Joey—Little Bigjo, by War Emperor										
				Br.—Dante T C (Cal)					1982 9 1 2 0					$12,325
Own.—Dante Janet & T C			**116**	Tr.—Scarvace Philip				$32,000	1981 0 M 0 0					
				Lifetime 9 1 2 0 $12,325										
28May82-1Hol	7f :21³ :45¹ 1:23 ft	23 119	2¹½ 2hd 2hd 2nk	Olivares F¹	ⒻⓈ 32000 82	Figurehed,Lil'MissGoody,Agittetrss 8
14May82-9Hol	1¹⁄₁₆:46³ 1:11⁴ 1:45²ft	18 116	4³¹ 42½ 47 48	Olivares F⁶	Ⓕ 32000 60	Sh'sSplndd,MssnglnActn,AThOdds 7
7May82-9Hol	6f :22¹ :45² 1:10³ft	62 119	3¹ 4² 22 65½	Olivares F³	Ⓕ 32000 78	DuchssTin,CollnMri,BrkOutThWin 11
21Apr82-1SA	6f :21⁴ :45 1:10¹ft	45 120	6⁴ 89½ 99 99½	Pierce D⁶	ⒻⓈ 32000 77	ModestyBlise,MielHost,Duchss Tin 10
8Apr82-1SA	6f :21⁴ :44³ 1:09⁴ft	51 115	118¾ 91¹ 81⁴ 99¾	Pierce D⁸	Ⓕ 40000 79	Miss Swiss, Brandy's Reb,Rameda 12
1Apr82-3SA	6¹⁄₂f:22² :46¹ 1:19³sy	*3 117	2¹½ 22 2hd 1¹	DlhossyE⁹	ⒻⓈM32000 72	Ll'MssGody,GldCnty,RylWndstrm 10
12Mar82-3SA	6¹⁄₂f:22³ :46³ 1:20²sl	4¹ 117	4² 32½ 23 26½	DlhossyE¹⁰ⒻⓈM25000 61	Brndy'sReb,Lil'MissGoody,AliMrie 11
4Mar82-2SA	6¹⁄₂f:22 :44⁴ 1:17²ft	17 114	4¹½ 43 32½ 53½	Olivares F¹ⒻⓈM28000 79	Agittetress,PstMmoris,Lord'sLssi 12
17Feb82-3SA	6f :22 :45³ 1:12¹ft	31 117	108¾ 712 88½ 68½	PedrozMC¹¹ⒻM32000 69	Native Rae, Agitatetress,IrmaOlga 11
Jun 6 Hol 3f ft :37 h		May 26 Hol 3f ft :36 h		May 21 Hol 6f ft 1:14¹ h		May 2 Hol 6f ft 1:16³ h

Again, we compare the stretch calls of the last two races and see immediately that there is a substantial difference. But we still have to compare the times, and since we are dealing with a seven furlong race, we have to convert the final time to six furlongs to be able to weigh it against the six furlong time registered in the May 14 race at a mile and a sixteenth. We check the conversion table and see that 1:23 for seven furlongs is equivalent to 1:10.2 at six furlongs. We now compare the 1:10.2 with the 1:11.4 lead time at the six furlong call in the previous race, noting that it is one and two-fifth seconds faster. Lil' Miss Goody's six furlong time in the mile and a sixteenth race was 1:12.2 because she was two and a half lengths behind the leader (we add a full fifth of a second for the half length, thus adding three ticks to the 1:11.4 lead time). She was only a neck off the 1:10.2 six furlong time in the May 28 race, thus making her time also 1:10.2 (for margins less than half a length we do not add any ticks). So you can see that she picked up two seconds, a splendid improved showing. This was an easy one, but the purpose was to put you through the exercise of converting seven furlong to six furlong times.

We can next try another easy one where we have to deal with different sprint distances. Here is J.O. Mason from the first race at Hollywood on June 18.

J. O. Mason ∗ — Ch. g. 4, by Senor Lucky—Barz an Stars, by Barzan
Br.—Mason Mr-Mrs V (Cal) — 1982 6 0 0 0 $1,425
Own.—Coffee & Milligan — **116** — Tr.—Coffee John — $16,000 — 1981 8 0 2 0 $8,950
Lifetime 18 1 2 0 $15,875

5Jun82-3Hol	6½f	$:21^4$	$:44^3$	$1{:}16^3$ft	15	115	1^1	2^{hd}	$5^{4½}$	7^{13}	Valenzuela P A[1]	20000	74	Varga, Bold Khal, Embermatic	7
22May82-2Hol	6f	$:21^3$	$:44^3$	$1{:}10^1$ft	52	115	2½	2^{hd}	2^{hd}	$4^{2½}$	Valenzuela P A[2]	20000	83	Pat's Pet,BoldKhal,Parkinthedark	11
4Mar82-1SA	6f	$:21^3$	$:44^1$	$1{:}09^1$ft	5¾	116	$3^{½}$	$5^{2¼}$	$7^{4¾}$	$6^{5¾}$	ValenzuelaPA[7]	c12500	86	Tulsea,RisingEcho,ImmanentIssue	11
27Feb82-1SA	6½f	$:21^4$	$:44^4$	$1{:}16^1$ft	5½	115	1^{hd}	1^{hd}	2½	6^7	McCarron C J[2]	16000	82	TurningWheels,FncyGuy,Prdilction	9
16Jan82-1SA	6f	$:21^4$	$:44^1$	$1{:}09^2$ft	7	115	12^{11}	12^{20}	12^{18}	12^{27}	Sibille R[9]	c20000	64	Ggntc,Truxton'sDobl,Trrsto'sSrgr	12
9Jan82-2SA	6f	$:21^3$	$:44^3$	$1{:}08^3$ft	17	115	2½	$3^{3½}$	4^9	5^{12}	Sibille R[1]	25000	83	SuperStrVincent,StblPt,KingGonzo	7
25May81-1Hol	6f	$:22^1$	$:45^2$	$1{:}10^1$ft	17	116	1^{hd}	2^2	6^7	12^{12}	Valdivieso H A[3]	32000	74	TopGaelic,TomMck,GrfieldCounty	12
17Apr81-2SA	6f	$:21^3$	$:44^4$	1:10 ft	7¼	116	$2^{1½}$	$4^{5½}$	3½	$4^{2¼}$	DelahoussayeE[8]	32000	87	GrfieldCounty,Princeo'Dncrs,Morr	11
3Apr81-7SA	6f	$:21^4$	:45	$1{:}10^2$ft	5¼	116	2^{hd}	2^{hd}	3½	7^8	Shoemaker W[6]	40000	79	ProudDuk,It'sGoodOn,MyWindyMl	8
19Mar81-1SA	6f	$:21^1$	$:43^4$	$1{:}09^3$ft	5¼	116	3½	$4^{2½}$	4^2	$7^{2¾}$	Valenzuela P A[1]	40000	88	WarHouse,Embermtic,HighErnings	9

Jun 15 Hol 4f ft $:47^3$ h — May 30 Hol 5f ft $1{:}01^1$ h — May 18 Hol 5f ft $1{:}01^1$ h — May 13 Hol 6f ft $1{:}14^4$ h

You might not even want to bother to calculate one that appears this obvious. As it is, J.O. Mason is a declining horse, without much doubt. But you should still check to make sure, and that requires converting the six and a half furlong time to six furlongs, or vice versa. Since six furlong times are the most familiar ones, we look at the chart and move the 1:16.3 final time of the six and a half furlong race down to a converted 1:10.2, which is only one tick slower than the time we have for the winning horse on May 22. J.O. Mason was more than two seconds slower as you can see from the fact that he was 13 lengths off the leader, and that is hardly arguable. Yet off this declining performance this horse was reasonably well bet down to fourth choice, no doubt because of the drop in class and the good early speed he was accustomed to producing.

When horses that show a decline at the same class in which they previously ran do register their rare triumphs next time out, these victories are usually attributable to well-defined drops to lower levels of competition. Despite his drop in class, however, J.O. Mason struggled to finish second, better than we would have expected. But the important thing is that he did not win.

Let us now do a conversion problem within varying distance at the same class in a route race.

Princely Verdict — B. c. 4, by Prince John—Just Judgement, by Hail to Reason
Br.—Hillbrook Farm (Ky) — 1982 7 1 2 1 $27,950
Own.—Blum Maribel G — 116 — Tr.—Winick Randy — $65,000 — 1981 10 1 3 2 $33,325
Lifetime 19 2 5 4 $63,315 — Turf 6 0 2 1 $16,500

27May82-7Hol	$1\frac{1}{16}$ Ⓣ $:47^3$ $1{:}11^1$ $1{:}41$ fm	3	117	$5^{4\frac{1}{2}}$	$5^{5\frac{1}{2}}$	$7^{8\frac{1}{2}}$	$7^{5\frac{1}{2}}$	Pincay L Jr[1]	Aw24000	88	Essenbee,Fager'sBid,Parson'sLeder	7
16May82-9Hol	$1\frac{1}{8}$ Ⓣ $:46^2$ $1{:}10^2$ $1{:}47^1$ fm	11	117	$5^{5\frac{1}{2}}$	5^5	3^4	2^2	Pincay L Jr[4]	Aw24000	92	PetrJons,PrinclyVrdict,MdlofHonor	9
21Mar82-5SA	$1\frac{1}{8}$ $:46^1$ $1{:}10^2$ $1{:}48^1$ ft	$9\frac{1}{4}$	120	4^6	6^8	$4^{4\frac{1}{2}}$	$4^{7\frac{1}{2}}$	Sibille R[7]	Aw27000	80	DurbanDeep,Rostropovich,Disclaim	7
7Mar82-7SA	$1\frac{1}{8}$ Ⓣ $:45^4$ $1{:}10^4$ $1{:}47^4$ fm	$2\frac{1}{2}$	120	$6^{3\frac{3}{4}}$	$6^{3\frac{1}{2}}$	$4^{8\frac{1}{2}}$	5^8	Pincay L Jr[5]	Aw27000	80	RasPenng,Essenbee,FbulousReson	10
7Feb82-5SA	$1\frac{1}{4}$ Ⓣ $:47$ $1{:}36^2$ $2{:}00^4$ fm	$3\frac{1}{2}$	120	3^2	$3^{\frac{1}{2}}$	2^1	3^1	Sibille R[2]	Aw27000	82	Jurisconsult,CptnGnrl,PrnclyVrdct	11
16Jan82-5SA	$1\frac{1}{4}$ Ⓣ $:47^3$ $1{:}36^4$ $2{:}02$ fm	27	120	2^1	2^{hd}	2^{hd}	2^1	Sibille R[2]	Aw27000	76	SunshnSwg,PrnclyVrdct,FllPymnt	11
8Jan82-9SA	$1\frac{1}{8}$ $:48^3$ $1{:}13$ $1{:}50^3$ ft	$3\frac{1}{2}$	114	$2^{\frac{1}{2}}$	2^{hd}	2^{hd}	$1^{\frac{3}{4}}$	CastanedaM[6]	Aw20000	76	Princely Verdict, Ram Boldly, Pelin	8
26Dec81-9SA	$1\frac{1}{16}$ $:46^1$ $1{:}10^4$ $1{:}42^2$ ft	*8-5	117	$3^{1\frac{1}{2}}$	$3^{1\frac{1}{2}}$	$4^{4\frac{1}{2}}$	$3^{4\frac{1}{2}}$	Pincay L Jr[5]	Aw20000	84	Zmperini,It'sShm,PrincelyVerdict	11
8Nov81-9SA	1 $:45^4$ $1{:}10^3$ $1{:}35^4$ ft	7	115	$5^{4\frac{1}{2}}$	4^3	$4^{4\frac{1}{2}}$	3^6	Rivera M A[8]	Aw21000	84	It'sthOn,SpringDiggr,PrinclyVrdict	9

Princely Verdict ran in the ninth at Hollywood on June 18, 1982. In his last race at a mile and a sixteenth he was farther from the lead at the stretch call than he was in the previous run at a mile and an eighth. Again, we can convert the final times to either distance. It is usually easier to convert the last race into the distance of the preceding race, and we will do it that way by running the mile and a sixteenth time to a comparable figure for a mile and an eighth. We add :06.3 to the mile and a sixteenth winning time of 1:41 and obtain 1:47.3, which is two-fifths of a second slower than the time of the May 16 race. Princely Verdict's time on May 16 was 1:47.3 and his converted time on May 27 would be 1:48.4, some six ticks slower. This puts him over the line and turns him into the declining horse that we expected.

The factor assessing the impact of performance within the form cycle with regard to improvement or decline will be measurable less frequently than the other form factors. But the occasions when it does turn up, as we have indicated, are extremely important. Again, the ultimate thrust is more negative than positive. An improving horse, while showing good credentials for victory, might not make it for any number of reasons. But a declining horse, except for rare exceptions, is almost sure to lose. On the infrequent occasions when you do see a winner that shows a decline in its last performance, you will likely see a horse with a class advantage or one whose rating is only a shade off the dividing line, or a horse with vastly superior ability times. Declining horses are still very poor prospects.

In the 433-race study at the four eastern tracks, there were 29 favorites that turned up with a declining rating. Of this group, four managed to win, which is more than I would expect from other studies and observations. Horses that were declining and backed as second favorites showed five winners out of 47.

Moving to the positive side, there were 65 favorites with the + rating for improvement, and here we had 32 winners and 48 places. This was a sparkling win percentage of 49.2 and a place percentage of 73.8, which is perhaps even more remarkable. Here, these strong horses were undoubtedly aided by other plus factors, which many of them had. But it is still a powerful showing.

While strongly played horses sometimes carry enough class with them to threaten the failure status of the declining horse, animals with lesser credentials rarely do. Among the longer-priced winners in the study, the declining horse was only seldom in evidence. At Belmont, for example, there were 40 such longer-priced winners, and only three of them overcame the declining pattern. At Meadowlands, the declining horse was nearly dead. Among 68 longer priced winners, only one with a O rating in performance within the form cycle managed to win.

Declining horses among longer priced winners fared almost as poorly at Keystone and Bowie. Among the 55 longshots at Keystone, there were but two that carried the declining horse rating. At Bowie, among 28, there was a single winner. Overall, out of 191 longer priced winners, there were only seven declining horses that came home in front.

If you are looking for a good longshot play, you are not likely to find it among declining horses.

Taking another look at the positive side among longshot winners, you will see an entirely different picture. Ten of the 40 Belmont winners, or 25%, showed a plus for improvement. At Meadowlands, there were 15 out of the 68, at Keystone seven of the 55, and at Bowie, five out of 28. There were 37 longer priced winners with a + rating as compared to seven with a O rating— seven times as many. Does this tell you something?

It must be reiterated that these figures are derived with no handicapping whatsoever, except for the form factors. There was no attempt to weed out horses rising in class or horses returning off a victory, no matter what the level of competition they were entered against.

When improving or declining performance within the form cycle is blended with other form factors and sound handicapping techniques, it should be apparent that it is a vitally important part of your inquiry into how your horse will run today.

7 The Fourth Form Factor: Stretch Performance

THE FOURTH FORM FACTOR is how the horse performed in the stretch in its last measurable race. This factor takes its place along with the recency rules as very easy to rate. Its greatest impact is also in identifying a negative factor, since it centers upon horses that are very likely to lose today. But weeding out losing horses is one of the most vital aspects of predicting the outcome of races. It is when I become very sure that a particular competitor will lose that I build up healthy confidence in the horse that I have selected to win. If you are able to get rid of the losers, the winning horses will ordinarily take care of themselves in your handicapping regimen. I especially enjoy seeing well-played losers, because they help reinforce the odds on the horses I do like. And you will find a great many favorites and second choices in the betting carrying the fourth form defect that contributes so heavily to their losing.

The great disability here is when a horse suffers a significant loss in the stretch. When we define what we mean by "significant," you will be able to award the O rating with substantial confidence and expect the horse very likely to lose. On the other hand, I do not award a + for a stretch gain. Sure, I prefer to see my horse gain in the stretch rather than lose ground, but far too often a horse that seems to be coming on in the stretch is passing tired horses. While we can be pleased about it, there is not nearly enough impact to justify the + rating, which we try to save for substantial and meaningful factors.

The only + area for stretch performance, as has been indicated earlier, is when a horse scores a Big Win. To register a Big Win a horse does not actually have to gain in the stretch, but he must not lose ground. If a horse is out in front by a substantial margin when it hits the stretch, and maintains that lead to the wire, this adequately demonstrates the horse's splendid form. In my studies for writing *Investing at the Racetrack*, I was so impressed with the power of the Big Win that I awarded it four points in my point evaluations. Interestingly enough, the 1981 and 1982 research continued to support what I had found in 1979 and 1980—the Big Win is always a potent force. Since one of the thrusts of this book is to proceed on form ratings without a point structure, leaving that to other methods of rating horses (such as ability times, with appropriate points which I have found to be so effective), I have not continued the practice in this book of giving any form points at all. The plus for the Big Win is in itself a strong recognition of its strength.

Thus, we return to the emphasis on the elimination factor that is the vital part of the fourth form line. When does a loss in the stretch disable a horse from winning in his next race and why? Once we identify the kind of stretch loss that concerns us, since many kinds of stretch losses have little impact at all, we will recognize that a horse that falters in the stretch is entering a kind of decline (and thus there is some interrelationship with the declining horse). Another reason horses that lose ground in the stretch do poorly next time out may be due to the possibility that the horse's equine will-to-win, whatever that may be, is sufficiently bruised to weaken his desire to try as hard the next time. This is somewhat akin to the old look-'em-right-in-the-eye confrontation that many horsemen speak about.

But whatever the inbred reasons, what we need to know is how it works in the real world. You may readily assume that a horse that falls back in the stretch when he is far back in the crowd and has no chance of finishing in the money is not hampered in his next race by the previous poor showing. We will readily discount that kind of stretch loss, and give this horse an N for this factor. And as we move forward, there will be precise lines drawn that make execution of this form rating quite easy.

At the outset, you will examine how your horse performed in the stretch of his last race run within the past 28 days. If he has not run within 28 days, this form factor becomes inapplicable and you can write in the N for irrelevant. Likewise, if the horse's last race was not useable for running line rating purposes, it may not be applied to this form factor either.

While evaluating running lines, we frequently are able to use the next-to-last race under prescribed conditions, but we will not do so in dealing with stretch performance. Too much can happen in the last race, whether or not it is useable for rating a running line, that might influence future stretch behavior. Accordingly, at any time we are unable to use the last race, for whatever reason, we put down an N and proceed onward.

As for defining what is a "significant" stretch loss, we can quickly eliminate losses of less than a length as not significant. A horse battling hard enough down the stretch to keep alongside his opponent, who may be superior that day, is worth looking at again. Thus, any stretch loss, to be considered significant, must be of at least one length or more.

Extended research has also demonstrated that a stretch loss is only significant when a horse is within striking distance of the lead at the stretch call. And what is striking distance? This one is easy—our old friend, "up close." In a sprint race of a distance less than seven furlongs, if a horse is within less than three lengths of the lead at the stretch, and loses one length or more to the finish, this is a significant loss. In races of seven furlongs and one mile the up close standard is less than four lengths, and at races longer than a mile, it is less than five lengths.

Now, we can begin to formulate a rule before we come to the exceptions that make it workable. Any loss in the stretch of one length or more when a horse is up close as measured by the distance of the race at the stretch call, is a significant stretch loss. Such a stretch loss will be a form defect with a O rating, unless the horse fits within one of the critical exceptions.

Here are these critical exceptions:

1. If a horse is dropping in class from his last race, then the stretch loss will not be held against him or counted as a form defect. The lowering of the level of competition is the offsetting factor which may allow the horse to carry his speed to

the wire when he was unable to do so previously against horses of a higher caliber.

2. If a horse's last race, the one where he lost ground in the stretch, was the first race after a layoff of 28 days or more, the stretch loss will not be counted as significant and will not be held against the horse. He may simply have "come up short." The effort in the last race, after a return, may be all that was needed to crank up the horse for a good effort today.

3. If a horse is running a shorter distance today by one furlong or more, a stretch loss in his last race will not be determinative and will not be counted as a form defect. The reason seems rather obvious: since he would not have as far to run today, his last furlong fall-off may not happen again. For example, if a horse ran last out at seven furlongs and lost ground in the stretch, you would not count the stretch loss against him if he is running six furlongs today.

4. If a horse is running a *longer* distance today by *more* than one furlong, a stretch loss last out in the shorter race will not be held against him. If the distance is that much longer, running patterns may be sufficiently different so that we cannot presume the horse will run the same style of race today.

As distinguished from a horse shortening distances, where a one furlong change is enough, the critical line here is at *more* than one furlong. Thus a change in distance from six furlongs last out to seven furlongs today, or from a mile or a mile and seventy yards to a mile and an eighth is not sufficient to bring about a major shift in running styles. But a horse moving from seven furlongs to a mile and a sixteenth, for example, which is quite common, is now running eight and one-half furlongs, which exceeds the necessary one furlong or more extension. This makes the race an entirely new ball game. Horses will surely be conserving more energy in the early part of the race, saving more for the end. This alone may cause such an adjustment in a horse's energy output that the last race stretch loss at a shorter distance may not matter at all.

Correspondingly, a horse than last raced at a mile and a sixteenth and is stretching out to a mile and a quarter is altering its running style sufficiently so that a stretch loss at a mile and a sixteenth begins to take on far less significance.
As long as you are careful when evaluating increases in distance to stick to the requirement that the added distance exceed one furlong, you are on the right road.

Let us get to some examples to show how this vitally important form factor of significant stretch loss works.

In the fifth race at Golden Gate on June 18, 1982, a six furlong allowance sprint, the favorite was Top Pole. This is a classic case of a horse that was in contention in his last race but lost ground in the stretch. The fact that he was the favorite today would be additional icing on the cake for those of us who would be serene in our belief that, because of this last race significant stretch loss at the same distance as today's race, this favorite was going down the tube as an almost certain loser.

Top Pole		B. c. 3, by Peleax—Speedy Wave, by Ahoy			
		Br.—Hawn W R (Cal)		1982 5 1 3 0	$13,690
Own.—Hawn W R	113	Tr.—Comiskey C A		1981 2 M 0 0	
		Lifetime 7 1 3 0 $13,690			
4Jun82-6GG	6f :22⁴ :46 1:11²ft	*2¾ 114	5³ 2ʰᵈ 2ʰᵈ 2²	Baze R A⁶ Aw12000	80 De Wan I Love,TopPole,ManyMore 8
27May82-6GG	6f :22² :46 1:11¹ft	4½ 110⁵	66 65¾ 55¼ 24½	DillenbckBD¹ Aw12000	78 Delta Gambler,TopPole,SeetheKing 7
7Apr82-8GG	6f :22² :45⁴ 1:11³ft	*1 117	79½ 61² 511 45¼	Baze R A⁴ Aw13000	76 Mich'sSlor,RoomEnough,CoolItJms 7
5Mar82-8GG	6f :22¹ :45³ 1:11²ft	11 120	89 811 87¼ 2ⁿᵏ	Baze R A⁵ Aw12000	82 Cousin Josh, Top Pole, Kissin'Jon 10
20Feb82-2GG	6f :22⁴ :46³ 1:12¹ft	27 118	32 31 11 1ⁿᵒ	Baze R A⁹ Mdn	78 TpPl,Shrly'sStvR.,NmHmAnythng 11
4Sep81-6Dmr	6f :22¹ :45³ 1:11 ft	44 113⁵	3¹ 10⁹½10¹³10¹⁵	Winland W M⁷ ⑤Mdn	68 PrinceSpellbound,CrystlStr,Shntin 12
19Aug81-6Dmr	6f :22² :45¹ 1:11 ft	16 118	9¹⁴ 9¹⁵ 7¹⁵ 6¹¹	DelahoussyeE⁶ ⑤Mdn	72 GenerlJimmy,Glic'sSport,CrystlStr 10
Jun 17 GG 3f ft :36² h	Jun 13 GG 4f ft :49¹ h	Jun 3 GG 3f ft :36 h	May 26 GG 3f ft :37² h		

In his last race on June 4, he was battling for the lead as he reached the eighth pole in a race that he was also favored to win. Although as you can see, his running line on May 27 shows a form defect because he was not up close at the stretch call. But here, it is the last race that concerns us. Top Pole faltered in the stretch at the same class and the same distance as today. Unless every other horse in the race is hampered by some serious defect, Top Pole was almost sure to lose. He did.

Let us study another example where this form factor again shows its real value. Any time you can safely eliminate the favored horse as a highly likely loser, you can concentrate on the more probable winners, horses that will be paying the higher odds that you seek. Any time you see two well played horses vying in the betting for the role of favorite, and one of them carries this form defect of a significant stretch loss in his last race, you can play the other with great confidence.

In this case, Axe the Odds was entered in the ninth race at Hollywood Park on June 16, a mile sixteenth claimer for fillies running with a price tag of $32,000.

Axe The Odds — **Ch. f. 3, by Twist The Axe—Smother Dots, by Dotted Swiss**
Br.—Old English Rancho (Ky) — **1982 8 1 1 3 $15,705**
Own.—Cowan I & Marge — **116** — **Tr.—Winick Randy** — **$32,000** — **1981 13 2 1 1 $8,883**
Lifetime 21 3 2 4 $24,588 — **Turf 3 1 0 0 $7,150**

3Jun82-4Hol	1 1/16	$:46^1$	1:11	$1:44^4$ft	10	112	$1^{2\frac{1}{2}}$	$1^{1\frac{1}{2}}$	2^{hd}	3^4	Guerra W A^5	Ⓕ 35000	67	QuietFlight,SunnyRidge,AxThOdds	6
14May82-9Hol	1 1/16	$:46^3$	$1:11^4$	$1:45^2$ft	6	116	$2^{\frac{1}{2}}$	$3^{\frac{1}{2}}$	$3^{4\frac{1}{2}}$	$3^{5\frac{1}{2}}$	Guerra W A^7	Ⓕ 32000	62	Sh'sSplndd,MssngInActn,AThOdds	7
13Apr82-5GP	a1 Ⓣ			$1:37^2$fm	3¾	116	$2^{\frac{1}{2}}$	$2^{\frac{1}{2}}$	$7^{6\frac{1}{4}}$	$7^{8\frac{1}{4}}$	Perret C^8	Ⓕ 40000	86	DevineDiver,ThirdndTn,NtstQustion	8
2Apr82-8GP	a1 Ⓣ			$1:40^1$fm	3	116	$9^{7\frac{1}{4}}$	$7^{7\frac{1}{4}}$	7^9	5^9	Perret C^7	Ⓕ 50000	71	Accptr'sSong,LovTHp,NtvNwYrkr	10
1Mar82-5Hia	1 1/16	$:47^3$	$1:12^2$	$1:45^3$ft	3	108^3	$7^{4\frac{1}{4}}$	$3^{4\frac{1}{2}}$	2^5	3^9	Migliore R^7	c40000	66	Yunque, Be A Flipper, AxeTheOdds	8
27Jan82-10Hia	a1 1/16 Ⓣ			$1:43^4$fm	5¼	106^3	$7^{4\frac{3}{4}}$	5^7	3^5	1^{nk}	Migliore R^{11}	30000	80	AxeTheOdds,PriceRng,GorgMorris	12
21Jan82-4Hia	7f	$:23^1$	$:46^2$	$1:26^2$ft	9	113^3	$5^{4\frac{1}{2}}$	4^4	2^2	2^1	Migliore R^8	Ⓕ 20000	70	GbbieRuner,AxeThOdds,RibotO'Rl	12
12Jan82-4Hia	7f	$:23^2$	$:46^4$	$1:25^3$ft	8½	113^3	5^2	1^1	3^3	8^{15}	Migliore R^{10}	Ⓕ 25000	60	Rb'sGlory,Evnng'sFool,I'mAGodn	12
31Dec81-7Crc	1	:48	$1:13^3$	1:41 ft	42	113	$4^{2\frac{1}{2}}$	5^4	4^8	5^{13}	Lee M A^4	ⒻAw11000	70	BdDncnRt,ChrgMyAccont,PrclssHr	8
26Nov81-7CD	7f	:23	$:46^1$	$1:26^4$ft	28f	115	$12^{6\frac{1}{2}}$	14^{13}	14^{13}	14^{18}	SpsEJ^{11}	ⒻPocahontas	55	MjesticGold,ISeeSpring,GoldnTry	15

●Jun 12 Hol 4f ft $:46^1$ h — May 28 Hol 4f ft $:47^4$ h — May 9 Hol 5f ft 1:01 h — May 3 Hol 5f ft 1:01 h

Today's race is at the same distance as the previous race. There is a small differential in the claiming prices, as she is entered today for $3,000 less than the $35,000 tag she carried in the last race. Is this slight lowering of claiming price sufficient to drop Axe the Odds into a lower bracket of competition? You may readily conclude that it is too slight—there is hardly any difference at all between horses at this level. However, it is possible that her claiming price of $35,000 in her last race could have resulted in a weight-off allowance in a race with a top claiming price of $40,000. We can not know this without having the conditions of the race of May 1, 1982 before us. If this were the case, a drop from a $40,000 claiming race to a $32,000 event would present a bit of a problem, since we would have the full 20% that so often indicates a different level of competition. However, as we approach these higher priced claiming races, the 20% begins to assume less and less significance, and you might even be justified in requiring a little more before you adopt a lower level of competition.

At any time you have cause for concern about whether weight off affected the claiming price value of the last race, you can compare the weights to help your search. And in this case, there is the possibility that the last race may have been at a higher claiming price than the $35,000 shown. Axe The Odds carried 112 in her last race, down from 116 in the previous contest, and is back up to 116 today. While I am not ready to give any handicapping significance as such to these weight changes, they do have to be carefully watched for trainer intentions and as clues to possible different claiming prices of races when you do not have the conditions of the race available.

With that doubt in mind, we look at the stretch loss of Axe The Odds. Because it was a sliding drop-off, as she steadily yielded her front running position to finish four lengths behind, I would not hesitate to resolve any doubt about the class drop and would readily award the O rating.

At this point, you may see a conflict between form factors. In her last race, Axe The Odds improved her running line and comparative times over her semi-final race on May 1, 1982 sufficient to pick up a + for improvement in her form cycle. While the improvement is solidly positive, the negative impact of a loss in the stretch while in contention may not be denied. This is one of the strongest negative factors in form analysis, deadly enough to overcome the signs of improvement most of the time. Axe The Odds was another loser.

We can next look at a mixed bag of some differences in class and distance as we view the favorite in the third race at Hollywood on June 19, to see how Miel's Magic impresses us.

3rd Hollywood

1 MILE. (1.33⅕) CLAIMING. Purse $13,000. 3-year-olds. Weight, 121 lbs. Non-winners of two races since April 18 allowed 3 lbs.; a race since then, 6 lbs. Claiming price $20,000; if for $18,000 allowed 2 lbs. (Races when entered for $16,000 or less not considered.)

Miel's Magic — B. c. 3, by Decidedly—Mon Miel, by Montparnasse II

Own.—168 Stable — 118 — Br.—Pope G A Jr (Cal) — Tr.—Vienna Darrell — $20,000

1982	9	2	1	1	$22,240
1981	2	M	0	0	
Turf	1	0	0	0	
Lifetime	11	2	1	1	$22,240

9Jun82-9Hol	$1\frac{1}{16}$	$:47^{2}$	1:12	$1:44^{3}$ft	*3-2	117	1^{hd}	2^{hd}	2^{1}	$3^{2\frac{3}{4}}$	Pincay L Jr[7]	25000	69	ForwrdCourt,RoscotorGrn,Ml'sMgc	8
20May82-3Hol	$1\frac{1}{16}$	$:46^{4}$	$1:12^{2}$	$1:45^{1}$ft	*1	118	$5^{5\frac{3}{4}}$	$2^{\frac{1}{2}}$	2^{1}	1^{hd}	DelahoussayeE[3]	20000	69	Miel'sMgic,JusticeForAll,PrincPlfc	7
8May82-2Hol	$1\frac{1}{16}$	$:46^{3}$	$1:11^{3}$	$1:44^{4}$ft	19	115	1^{hd}	1^{hd}	$4^{2\frac{1}{2}}$	8^{5}	Valenzuela P A[3]	35000	66	Kings Dawn,StreamSide,LimoJohn	11
1May82-1Hol	1	$:45^{4}$	$1:10^{4}$	$1:36^{4}$ft	$7\frac{3}{4}$	119	5^{6}	5^{6}	6^{9}	5^{9}	Hawley S[5]	32000	73	Chckr'sOrphn,ClubFlsh,Ed'sDynsty	9
8Apr82-9SA	1	:46	$1:10^{3}$	1:36 ft	$4\frac{1}{4}$	120	$6^{3\frac{3}{4}}$	$7^{8\frac{3}{4}}$	9^{11}	8^{12}	McCarron C J[5]	50000	77	BisonBy,FortyEightFcts,Rconfirm	10
26Mar82-6SA	1	$:46^{1}$	1:11	$1:36^{2}$ft	$6\frac{1}{2}$	118	$3^{2\frac{1}{2}}$	2^{hd}	2^{hd}	1no	McCarron C J[4]	[S]Mdn	87	Ml'sMgc,EnvoysIntrg,BroksN'Brc	10
27Feb82-2GG	$1\frac{1}{16}$	:48	$1:13^{2}$	$1:46^{1}$m	*9-5	118	$3^{1\frac{1}{2}}$	$6^{2\frac{1}{4}}$	4^{6}	$4^{4\frac{1}{2}}$	Pierce D[5]	Mdn	67	Hasty Work, Mucha Risa, Lured	8
7Feb82-3SA	$1\frac{1}{16}$	:47	$1:11^{3}$	$1:43^{3}$ft	15	118	$5^{1\frac{3}{4}}$	$5^{4\frac{1}{2}}$	$8^{6\frac{3}{4}}$	$6^{9\frac{3}{4}}$	Delahoussaye E[7]	Mdn	73	WterBnk,ConsciousEffort,NtivBllo	9
16Jan82-1BM	$1\frac{1}{16}$	:48	$1:13^{2}$	$1:47^{1}$ft	$8\frac{1}{2}$	118	2^{hd}	2^{hd}	2^{hd}	$2^{\frac{1}{2}}$	Meza R Q[3]	Mdn	62	SeniorCitizn,Mil'sMgic,CountyNtiv	8
6Aug81-4Sar	1	[T]$:48^{3}$	$1:14^{3}$	1:39 gd	33	118	9^{6}	$8^{8\frac{3}{4}}$	7^{13}	7^{18}	Hernandez R[3]	Mdn	63	Mjsty'sPrnc,ClssHro,Who'sFrDnnr	10

Jun 7 Hol 3f ft $:37^{2}$ h — Jun 2 Hol 6f ft 1:14 h — May 28 Hol 3f ft $:37^{4}$ h — May 18 Hol 3f ft $:36^{4}$ h

We can dispose of the distance issue quickly, since the shorter mile race today is only half a furlong less than the mile and a sixteenth distance of the previous race of June 9, 1982. Miel's Magic, up close at the stretch in his last race, fell back significantly, since he lost one-and-three-quarters lengths. The only remaining question is whether the drop from $25,000 in the last race to $20,000 today wipes out the defect.

While we were not certain in discussing Axe The Odds whether her lowered claiming price did reflect a move to a lower level of competition, the problem is not nearly so difficult here. From $25,000 down to $20,000 is a full 20%, no doubt about that. As horses descend lower in claiming price value, the 20% line takes on a much greater force than it does at higher claiming levels. We also see the up-and-down dropper pattern with Miel's Magic, since he was raised from a $20,000 race where he won, up to a $25,000 race where he ran strongly until fading in the stretch.

You should have no hesitation here. Miel's Magic does not warrant a O rating. We can give him an N, and note that he has a + for his last race running line, since he was up close at every call. Because he has no form defect, we can play this favorite with renewed confidence. He was the winner that his record demonstrated he should be.

The pure example of a horse losing ground in the stretch in his last race and shortening the distance of his next race by a full furlong is often found in sprints when a horse shortens up from seven to six furlongs. On the same June 19, 1982 card at Hollywood that we have so frequently used, we can look at Incorporator in the fourth race.

4th Hollywood

6 FURLONGS. (1.07⅘) CLAIMING. Purse $21,000. 4-year-olds and upward. Weight, 125 lbs. Non-winners of two races since April 18 allowed 3 lbs.; a race since then, 6 lbs. Claiming price $40,000; for each $2,500 to $35,000 allowed 2 lbs. (Races when entered for $32,000 or less not considered.)

Incorporator ✻ — Dk. b. or br. g. 7, by Verbatim—Sultan's Lady, by Bagdad
Br.—Runnymede Farm (Ky) — 1982 8 0 4 2 $26,300
Own.—Brown R — **116** — Tr.—Vienna Darrell — $40,000 — 1981 14 3 2 1 $60,330
Lifetime 54 13 15 6 $186,875 — Turf 1 0 1 0 $5,200

31May82-5Hol	7f	$:21^4$	$:44^2$	$1{:}22^1$ft	*4-5	117	1^{hd}	1^{hd}	2^{hd}	2^1	Pincay L Jr^8	40000	85	Sam'sComet,Incorportor,HrdtoLee	8
13May82-5Hol	6½f	:22	$:44^3$	$1{:}15^1$ft	2¼	117	1^{hd}	1^{hd}	1^{hd}	2no	Pincay L Jr^2	40000	94	RoughRidr.Incorportor,GritsndFritz	6
18Apr82-3SA	6½f	$:21^2$	$:44^1$	$1{:}14^2$ft	*7-5	116	$3^{1\frac{1}{2}}$	$3^{2\frac{1}{2}}$	$3^{3\frac{1}{2}}$	$3^{6\frac{1}{2}}$	McCarron C J^1	50000	91	NaynoBay,BeachWalk,Incorporator	6
21Mar82-1SA	6f	$:21^4$	$:44^4$	$1{:}09^1$ft	5½	116	1^{hd}	1^{hd}	1^2	2^1	McCarron C J^1	50000	91	Fingal, Incorporator, Beach Walk	8
21Feb82-5SA	a6½f Ⓣ	$:21^2$	$:43^1$	1:13 fm	33	114	$4^{1\frac{3}{4}}$	$4^{2\frac{1}{2}}$	2^3	2^3	Valenzuela P A^2	57500	91	FrndlyUncAln,Incorprtr,AmnBrthr	11
23Jan82-9SA	1$\frac{1}{16}$	$:46^2$	1:11	$1{:}43^1$ft	11	116	7^{11}	8^9	$8^{8\frac{1}{4}}$	8^9	Shoemaker W^5	62500	76	HrdtoLee,TheArgylKid,AlwysAChnc	9
17Jan82-9SA	6½f	$:22^1$	$:44^2$	$1{:}15^1$ft	4¼	116	6^4	5^7	6^{12}	$7^{9\frac{1}{2}}$	DelahoussyeE^9	c50000	84	MrblCourt,ThArgylKid,AmnBrothr	12
6Jan82-7SA	6f	:22	:46	$1{:}12^3$hy	7	116	$4^{2\frac{1}{2}}$	$5^{2\frac{1}{4}}$	4^4	$3^{2\frac{1}{4}}$	DelahoussayeE^3	62500	73	GrayDandy,HardtoLee,Incorporator	6
23Aug81-8Lga	1	$:45^3$	$1{:}10^1$	$1{:}36^3$ft	*3	122	3^5	4^5	7^{13}	7^{12}	Pierce L^7	Aw15000	74	BigCougar,HedHwk,BigDddy'sDrem	8
25Jly81-9EP	6½f	$:22^2$	:46	$1{:}17^3$ft	*6-5	122	2^1	2^{hd}	3^{nk}	2^1	Wales H^2	Speed H	89	No Vices, Incorporator, Pilot Lea	10

Jun 13 Hol 5f ft 1:00^2 h — Jun 8 Hol 4f ft :49^1 h — May 26 Hol 5f ft :59^4 h — May 21 Hol 5f ft 1:01^4 h

He fits this well-known pattern precisely. He is running back at the same $40,000 claiming price today, down to six furlongs after losing one length in the stretch in his seven furlong effort. This would not be a form defect and we would inscribe an N for this factor. Incorporator won nicely, thank you.

The important exception that we have referred to for a horse that is stretching out today to run a distance longer by more than one furlong is shown when we look at Victoria Pearl. She was the second choice in the wagering in the ninth at Hollywood on June 16, the race in which Axe the Odds was the losing favorite.

Victoria Pearl — B. f. 3, by Cerf Volant—Pearl Pistol, by Gunflint
Br.—Stevens S E (Tex) — 1982 3 0 1 0 $3,820
Own.—Amen Donna & J — **116** — Tr.—Mitchell Mike — $32,000 — 1981 6 1 0 0 $1,548
Lifetime 9 1 1 0 $5,368

4Jun82-3Hol	6½f	:22	:45	$1{:}17^2$ft	2½	117	2^1	$4^{2\frac{1}{2}}$	4^1	$2^{3\frac{1}{2}}$	Pincay L Jr^6 Ⓕ	c25000	79	Comman'Dear,VictoriaPerl,EweWin	7
13May82-3Hol	7f	$:22^1$	$:44^2$	1:23 ft	9	117	$4^{1\frac{1}{2}}$	4^2	$6^{6\frac{1}{4}}$	6^6	Pincay L Jr^6 Ⓕ	50000	76	RoyaCurie,SartogRoxie,SonnetAglo	8
21Apr82-7SA	6f	$:21^2$	$:44^1$	1:10 ft	25	114	$6^{5\frac{1}{2}}$	$6^{4\frac{1}{2}}$	5^6	4^5	ShoemkrW^4 Ⓕ	Aw19000	83	HawiinShke,FirstClss,JoJoDimggio	8
17Jly81-10Rui	5½f	$:23^2$	$:49^1$	$1{:}09^4$ft	27	112	$7^{7\frac{3}{4}}$	$8^{4\frac{1}{2}}$	8^{10}	8^{16}	Gomez L N^5	Aw5000	61	TenGllonHt,Luckluster,Dunc'sMiss	8
25Jun81-6Rui	4f		:23	$:48^3$gd	13	117	8	$8^{4\frac{3}{4}}$	$7^{8\frac{1}{2}}$	$6^{7\frac{3}{4}}$	Gomez L N^6	Fut Trl	72	SunnyMama,Pocketpurse,Bgdd'ble	8
10May81-6Rui	4f		$:21^2$	:49 ft	6¼	117	8	4^2	4^1	$1^{2\frac{1}{4}}$	Gomez L N^1	Mdn	78	VictoriPerl,Lucklustr,BitofSovrign	10
24Apr81-12Sun	5f	$:22^3$	$:46^4$	$:59^3$m	50	118	$8^{8\frac{1}{2}}$	8^{11}	8^{10}	7^{11}	Gomez L N^1	Fut Trl	73	PluckyHussy,PrdofLoom,Pocktpurs	9
12Apr81-11Sun	4½f	:23	$:46^4$	:53 ft	27	115	2	$5^{1\frac{1}{4}}$	5^3	$4^{5\frac{1}{4}}$	Gomez L N^6	Mdn	82	T. Dykes, Dunce's Miss,AzILetcho	10
7Mar81-8Sun	4f		:23	$:46^4$ft	24	115	6	$8^{6\frac{1}{2}}$	6^9	7^{11}	Meaux M^8	Mdn	79	BugBopper,Indi'sPcific,PersinQuen	9

Jun 2 Hol 3f ft :39^4 h — May 26 Hol 5f ft 1:00 h — May 20 Hol 5f ft 1:02^2 h — May 4 Hol 5f ft 1:01^4 h

In her last race, she lost ground in the stretch at six-and-one-half furlongs. But today, she is running at the longer distance of a mile and a sixteenth, which we learned when we talked about Axe The Odds. But before we come to that, a look at her line raises another question—even though she lost ground in the stretch, she passed two horses, moving from fourth to second. When this occurs, is   sufficient to overcome the stretch loss itself? This one has to be faced frequently.

This is not too difficult. Victoria Pearl was likely passing tired horses. It is loss in lengths that counts, and even though a horse that is not in the lead may pass others that are falling back more rapidly, there is still a significant stretch loss in lengths that would merit a O rating unless proper exceptions are involved. Thus, if Victoria Pearl were not stepping up to a longer distance, we would give her a zero.

But, because of the extended distance today around two turns, Victoria Pearl's stretch loss in her last race would not be held against her. A mile and a sixteenth is definitely more than one furlong longer than six and a half furlongs—to be exact, it is two furlongs greater. She will be embarking upon a different running style today, which she has never done before, since all her nine lifetime races show that she has never toured around two turns. In addition to that, she carries the handicap of rising in class off a claim. But who won the race? Go to the head of the class if you guessed Victoria Pearl.

This bears one further passing comment, since we have stressed the serious defect of a class rise without important + factors, of which Victoria Pearl has none. She is a young three-year-old filly who has run but nine times, and six of these races were at minor tracks. She was brought to Santa Anita for her new season, ran first against allowance animals, then tried high priced claimers, and was dropped in class. Sharp horseman Mike Mitchell thought enough of her to put down the $25,000 it cost to buy her. The handicapping reality is that we know very little about her class ability, since under her record, there is not a great deal on which to focus. But it is this kind of an aberrant outcome that makes our game so tough and likewise fills in the statistical holes to show that some horses do win when they rise in class without visible support.

As was said earlier, another important exception that will prevent a horse from earning the stretch loss form defect is a stretch loss in the first race following a layoff. This is the typical situation of "coming up short." When you become attuned to looking for the stretch loss, and when you see it, it is easy enough to overlook the dates of the last two races. But these must always be checked to determine if the horse's last race was off a layoff of 28 days or more. Here again, drawing a line to show form cycles is the best way to avoid overlooking this critical point. Here we have I'm In Time out of the sixth race at Belmont on June 17, a seven furlong maiden special event.

I'm In Time — Dk. b. or br. f. 3, by Isgala—In Tempo, by Amerigo
Br.—Isaacs H Z (Fla) — 1982 1 M 0 1 $2,040
Own.—Brookfield Farm — **114** — Tr.—Kelly Edward I — 1981 7 M 1 3 $8,960
Lifetime 8 0 1 4 $11,000 — Turf 2 0 0 0

7Jun82-6Bel	6f	:23	:46	1:10^{4}gd	9½	114	6$^{2\frac{3}{4}}$	1^{hd}	3^{nk}	3^{2}	MacBeth D^{9}	ⒻMdn	86	Grldn'sStor,AllMyMmors,I'mInTm	10
26Dec81-6Aqu	6f	⊡:23^{1}	:47^{2}	1:12^{4}ft	6½	117	11^{7}	7$^{3\frac{1}{2}}$	4$^{\frac{3}{4}}$	2^{1}	Saumell L^{7}	ⒻMdn	79	Adept, I'm In Time, Splendidly	14
19Nov81-4Aqu	6f	:22^{3}	:46	1:11^{2}ft	5	117	8^{5}	5$^{6\frac{1}{2}}$	3^{8}	3$^{6\frac{3}{4}}$	Santiago A^{5}	ⒻMdn	77	Sssy'nBright,RomnticOn,I'mInTim	13
12Oct81-9Bel	1	Ⓣ:46	1:11	1:36 fm	9	117	3$^{6\frac{1}{2}}$	2^{hd}	5$^{2\frac{1}{4}}$	5$^{5\frac{1}{2}}$	Santiago A^{4}	ⒻMdn	79	Bedside, Palace Gate, Captivating	12
3Oct81-3Bel	7f	:23^{2}	:47^{1}	1:24^{3}ft	11	117	6$^{4\frac{1}{4}}$	3$^{2\frac{1}{2}}$	4^{4}	3$^{7\frac{1}{2}}$	Santiago A^{9}	ⒻMdn	71	SnowPlow,SvedGround,I'mInTime	12
25Sep81-1Bel	1	:47^{2}	1:13	1:40 ft	12	117	4$^{3\frac{1}{2}}$	3$^{1\frac{1}{2}}$	2$^{1\frac{1}{2}}$	3$^{3\frac{1}{2}}$	Santiago A^{6}	ⒻMdn	64	Suspicious, Astorian, I'm In Time	7
29Aug81-9Bel	1$\frac{1}{16}$	Ⓣ:47^{4}	1:13^{2}	1:45^{4}fm	9½	117	5$^{2\frac{3}{4}}$	3$^{1\frac{1}{2}}$	5^{12}	5^{16}	Santiago A^{8}	ⒻMdn	51	Gulf, Mattan, Belles Girl	10
23Aug81-4Sar	6f	:22^{1}	:45^{2}	1:11^{1}ft	8¾	117	8$^{7\frac{1}{2}}$	9^{12}	10^{12}	9^{14}	Lovato F Jr^{1}	ⒻMdn	70	SmpthtcMss,RmblnPt,ChrMAccnt	14

In her last race on June 7, at six furlongs, this filly faded in the stretch, losing two lengths in the last furlong. The fact that she is extending out to a seven furlong race today may not inspire most handicappers, but when you are able to fully evaluate stretch performance factors, you will be sure that it does not make very much difference in these circumstances, especially when you note that her previous race was back in December, 1981. She truly "came up short" last out when she lost ground in the stretch, but it was her first outing after a long vacation. Her form rating for this factor would be a neutral. She was the second choice in the wagering, and returned home a winner.

Note that I'm In Time gets her N rating because of the layoff, and not because of the increased distance rule. I'm In Time would not have qualified on distance, since her longer race was only an additional furlong, from six to seven. There must always be more than one furlong before the exception comes into play.

In considering the effect of the last race insofar as stretch loss is concerned, you will often be confronted with that old handicapping difficulty of switches from turf to dirt and vice versa. If a horse ran on the grass in his last race and lost ground in the stretch and is entered on the dirt today, the safest guide is to omit the last grass race and rate the horse off the next-to-last race, as long as the semifinal race was not also on the grass. By the same approach, if a horse ran on the dirt in his last race and lost ground in the stretch, and is going on the grass today, you may ignore the last race stretch loss, provided both the last two races were not on the dirt. The profound difference between grass form and dirt form requires this separation of the two surfaces when they are being switched back and forth.

But if there are two successive races on a particular surface, whether it be dirt or grass, and today's run is on a different surface, you can make your stretch performance evaluation off the last race. The reason is that two races in a row on a particular surface tend to establish form. A good demonstration of this is found in the second race at Belmont on June 20, 1982, at a mile and a sixteenth on the grass, where Bedside was a strong favorite. I had the winner in that race, who was only the third favorite, which made it the start of a most profitable afternoon, as I eliminated Bedside with a great deal of confidence.

Bedside

Dk. b. or br. f. 3, by Le Fabuleux—On Duty, by Sea–Bird
Br.—Tartan Farms (Fla)

Own.—Tartan Stable **109** Tr.—Nerud Jan H

Lifetime 6 1 1 3 $21,580

				1982	2 0 1 1	$6,580
				1981	4 1 0 2	$15,000
				Turf	2 1 0 1	$12,960

5Jun82-4Bel	1¹⁄₁₆:463 1:103 1:423gd	3½ 112	1hd 1hd 1½ 31½	CordroAJr¹	⑤Aw20000	88	Fabled Morn, Alzabella, Bedside 10
22May82-2Bel	6f :222 :454 1:104ft	5½ 113	43½ 63½ 52	22¾ CordroAJr³	⑤Aw19000	85	Syrian Sands, Bedside, Noranda 7
12Oct81-9Bel	1 ⑦:46 1:11 1:36 fm*8-5 117		25 1hd 1½	12½ Cordero A Jr¹	⑤Mdn	85	Bedside, Palace Gate, Captivating 12
30Sep81-7Bel	1¹⁄₁₆⑦:491 1:133 1:444fm*9-5 117		52 33 33	24 † Cordero A Jr⁸	⑤Mdn	73	Syrian Circle, ‡Bedside, Harp 8
13Sep81—Disqualified and placed third							
9Aug81-5Sar	6f :224 :462 1:114ft	3½ 117	2½ 32½ 33½ 36½	Cordero A Jr¹	⑤Mdn	74	Finality, DecemberSeventh,Bedside 8
17Jly81-5Bel	6f :224 :462 1:113ft	6½ 1125	78½ 710 89½ 67½	Foley D⁴	⑤Mdn	76	LittleBullet,UnexpectedTurn,Pmir 11

Jun 14 Bel 4f sy :52 b (d)   May 31 Bel 4f gd :493 b   May 16 Bel 5f ft 1:02 b   May 10 Bel 4f ft :474 h

Her last race was at the same mile and a sixteenth distance of today's grass event. She carries over her significant stretch loss on the dirt as a detriment in today's turf run. The stretch loss factor is to be fully applied, and she gets a O rating. That judgment was verified as she failed to cope with her rivals in the last furlong, and was the loser that I had so heavily counted on her to be.

Like all our other handicapping rules, this one, too, is not infallible, although it works so often that your confidence in it will grow and grow. But what about those infrequent occasions when it does not work? Is there some way we can spot the exceptions and protect ourselves against them?

The most common situation when a stretch loser manages to overcome the defect and win the next time out concerns a horse with exceptional early speed, facing no other speed in the race. Yet even this is a gamble. But the horse that beats this defect will often fit this pattern. If all his rivals are laggards, the early speedster may get so far out in front that even when he begins to crawl in the stretch, the others may not be able to catch him.

I watched one of this kind recently at Keystone in a mile and a sixteenth race. While I could see that the horse with a stretch loss in its last race had a real chance to win, I am too ingrained with the weakness of these kinds of horses to want to take the risk. I could not bet on him and I certainly was not ready to bet against him, so I passed the race to watch and see what happened. Our early speed friend did just what he was expected to do. When he hit the far turn, he was 12 lengths ahead of the nearest horse in a bunched pack, and coasting. By the time he rounded the last turn, there had been a noticeable slippage in his margin.

By the time he hit the eighth pole, his lead had melted to seven lengths, still an enormous gap. Out of the pack, one horse emerged to make a run, gaining in stride after stride. Had I bet the race, I would have had the figurative heart attack. At the wire, our early speedster had only a shaky nose in front, just barely. But he was the winning horse. Thanks, but no thanks.

The other occasional deviation from this powerful rule of elimination comes when a horse has so much inherent class over his rivals that he can prevail despite his last race weakness. This is usually shown by superior ability times, such as the Double Advantage Horse that was identified in *Investing at the Racetrack* whose two rated ability times are superior to the best of any of his competitors. This kind of horse can occasionally win despite the stretch loss defect, but like the early speedster, he becomes a risky proposition. If all the other horses are burdened down with defects of their own, plus weaker ability, then the strong horse can be played, even with a significant stretch loss in his last race.

And, of course, there is the common exception for maiden races. This really fits in with the second exception of superior ability. I have seen several maiden winners whose last race showed a stretch loss—almost universally, their foes are weak indeed. This is the only kind of situation where the maiden stretch loser can prevail—otherwise, he, too, must be eliminated.

In making these ratings for the fourth form factor of stretch loss performance, you will find that the great majority of all horses will get neither a + nor a O for this factor. Since we limit the + to a Big Win, there will obviously be a limited number of these ratings. The O for significant stretch loss is more common, as you will see, and is potent enough to take its place alongside the declining horse as a prime elimination factor (carefully evaluating the exceptions that are possible). Everything else falls in between, and you can use the N rating, if you wish. Often, when writing down the form ratings, to save an overburdening of N's, I will insert a short dash (–) for this factor, which indicates that it has been checked and there is nothing there. Since there is absolutely no significance whatever to assigning an N for stretch performance, in distinction to the role of the N rating for the factors of recency or last race running line, where an N means the horse is qualified on form, the use of some other brief symbol to let you know that you have paid attention to the factor is enough, whether it be the – that I prefer, or an X, or even a check mark (and the use of an N works just as well.)

With our ratings in hand, how did horses in the 433-race study fare when they exhibited significant stretch loss as a form defect? At each of the four tracks, first and second favorites were first compiled. At Belmont, there were but six favorites out of the 97 that showed this form defect. No winners. Among second choices in the betting, 12 turned up out of the 97 horses involved. Not one winner. **This is a powerful reality!**

The percentages were a little better at the other tracks, but with some variance as levels of competition began to descend. At Meadowlands, there were 15 favorites out of the 130 encountered. Only one of them managed to win. Read it again—one favorite out of 15—impressive again. As for second favorites, there were 18 among the 130 showing this form defect. Two of them managed to get home first.

This form factor is so powerful, I repeat, that whenever any horse wins that has it, I am surprised. My surprise even extends to the early speedsters, the class horses, and to a somewhat lesser extent, the strong maidens. Before we come to some of the whys, let us complete our recapitulations for Keystone and Bowie, where the stretch loss horses did manage to do somewhat better.

At Keystone, there were 13 such favorites out of 108, and there were four winners. As for second choices, there were 20 with the defect out of 108, and only two of them came home in front. The Bowie figures were somewhat similar, with ten of 98 favorites showing a significant stretch loss, with three of them managing to win. Among second favorites, only one of 12 turned up a winner.

All told, out of the 433 favorites we encountered, 44, or roughly ten percent, had this form defect. Eight of them won, which was surprisingly high, and much higher than in other studies I have done. Among second choices, there were 62 with only five winners, and even that is more than I would ordinarily expect.

Looking at all winners, where we dipped into the long shot categories, among the 40 winners at Belmont that were not among the well played choices, only two managed to win with the handicap of a significant stretch loss. At Meadowlands, of 68 winners in the longer priced group, only three showed this form defect. At Keystone, there were five out of 55 winners who survived this handicap, and at Bowie, there were four in 28. But even here, you see a very small percentage of winners emerging. There were some 191 winning horses in the longer priced ranges, with only 14 winning with the stretch loss handicap, roughly seven percent of the whole. Not very promising, especially when you are looking at all kinds of winners in all kinds of races.

Now to review some "whys," since I am always surprised when

any horse manages to win carrying a defect that my research in the past year and a half has taught me is crucially important in any scheme of sound handicapping. Among the 433 races, I looked at long shot winners as well as low priced winners to always search for why any horse could win with this defect.

I have already given you the example of the strong early speed horse that can hold on to win when there is no other speed in the race. You will recall a few pages earlier, I pointed out that horses with strong class advantages might overcome this handicap and also, strong maiden plays could circumvent it. Among the three winners at Meadowlands who were first or second favorites, two of them were strong in the class department (with one of them having an additional early speed advantage), and the third was a maiden. At Keystone, two of the tabulated winners had blazing early speed, one was a very strong maiden, and the other had a positive running line against weak opponents. These occasional explainable winners make the figures run up as much as they do in final tabulations.

One other question might occur to you at this point: does an intervening five furlong workout aid the stretch loss horse? I have pursued that one a great deal, and the answer is no, it does not. The stretch loser, even with the good five furlong work, will still likely turn out to be a loser.

Why is this trait so effective? Why do these horses lose so frequently, especially when so many of them are well played?

Earlier I speculated that part of the reason could be a kind of decline in the form cycle. But that is only one element. It seems more likely that a horse that loses in the stretch may be slightly out of his class company, running against a level of competition that is just a bit too stiff for him. This is demonstrated by the occurrences when horses drop in class after a stretch loss and score a victory. However, as this factor relates to form, it may be also that the horse's training has not induced sufficient stamina, and when pressed in the last furlong, the horse does not have sufficient working muscle and breathing power, or energy, to triumph over a better tuned rival.

There may be even better reasons for all I know, and perhaps a keen and observant horseman could enlighten us somewhat. But what counts for the handicapper is the bottom line. This discovery of the appalling weakness of the horse that shows a significant stretch loss is one of my better research findings in the last two years, and since I began to use it with the confidence that I have in it, my own predictions of the outcome of a race have progressed immeasurably. We can cast aside the occasional surprise that throws us off, because over any reasonable period of time, this factor will serve you richly. You will learn to stay away from favored horses that are going to lose, and in those races, you can look at some other animal with our strong form factors that will most likely win. That is how we get better at this game.

8 Using Form Factors on an Entire Racing Card

ALMOST ANY DAY AT THE TRACK will present most of the various situations that you will find in unraveling the form factors discussed in this book. Let us pick out a day and work our way through an entire racing card. This does two things: it reveals the effectiveness of these form factors; and it gives us added practice and experience in trying them.

I selected a particular day at Golden Gate before I knew what the final outcome would be, for that was not nearly as important as going through a careful run on form, win, lose, or draw. Golden Gate serves our purpose well, because it is a high quality track across the bay from San Francisco. It does not rank with the prime southern California circuit, but it does have good purses and good horses, and certainly rates with most of the eastern and midwestern tracks outside the New York circuit. There is enough up and down variety to allow trainers a wide range of maneuverability within form cycles, which is often such a big part of racing strategy. The final reason for selecting Golden Gate was the very necessary one of having west coast editions of *Daily Racing Form* available for the dates in and around Thursday, June 17, 1982, the day to be used for our test run.

As we approach working through the racing card for June 17, 1982, it must be stressed once more that we are dealing only with the form factors that are set forth in this book. There will be no handicapping for speed, ability times, or even essential class levels, other than those which are vitally necessary to give reliability to our form ratings within the true context of the big question—how will your horse run today?

As we enter into card, we will use a few simple selection rules to make only win and place bets on qualified horses. First, we will confine our selections to either the first or second favorite (with the right to use the third betting choice also if his odds are reasonably close to those of the second favorite.) The reason for this, aside from the essential one of statistical likelihood, is that we can better test well played horses because we can compare the results to long range expectancies.

Also, we want to see how heavily bet horses hold up under both positive and negative form factors—again leading us to a perception of horses that can be eliminated and horses that can be played with some degree of confidence. While you might not get all that in one racing card, we hope for enough to give you a good running start towards practical application.

We will obviously not play any horse with a form defect. And the final rule we will follow is that we will not play any horse that won his last race, unless he meets the exacting standards earlier set forth by showing a Big Win or having positive form factors and back class. These guidelines are enough for our test run, since they are based primarily on what has been said earlier.

If the favorite passes these simple qualifications, without any form defects, he will be our play, no matter what else we may think of his chances. If the first betting choice fails to qualify, we will then turn to the second betting favorite, and if he passes, that is our play. If both the first and second choices are eliminated on the selection rules set forth (and all of this takes into account the third betting choice as well if his odds are very close to those of the second choice), then we will pass the race altogether.

In the next chapter, I will have much more to say about selection methods, including the one we are going to use here. But let us get on with it, as we turn to the first race.

The absolute first thing that must be done in every race, and I repeat—every race—is to look at the conditions of the race. They are shown at the outset, under the listing of the event. Looking down at the past performances printed below, we can see that the first race is a six furlong sprint, an $8,500 maiden claiming race for three and four-year-olds, bred in California. Already you can see the importance of the conditions, even in a cheap maiden claiming race, for now we know we are dealing with a state bred race. This is a weaker level of competition than an open maiden event for horses at the same claiming price.

We can start with the favorite, Sapience.

1st Golden Gate

6 FURLONGS. (1.07%) MAIDEN CLAIMING. Purse $4,500. 3- and 4-year-olds. Bred in California. Weights, 3-year-olds, 112 lbs.; 4-year-olds, 120 lbs. Claiming price $8,500.

Sapience

B. g. 3, by Tree of Knowledge—Farewell Patrice, by Turn-to or Candy Spots

Br.—Klussman Mr-Mrs W (Cal)   1982 6 M 0 0 $1,604

Own.—Round Tree Farms   **112**   Tr.—Griffin Joseph A $8,500   1981 0 M 0 0

Lifetime 6 0 0 0 $1,604

28May82-4GG	6f :222 :46 1:122ft	*3 112	2½	2hd 22	45	Anderson J R5	M10000	72 Flippin Bill, Unagloshi,Brainstorm	12
5May82-4GG	1¼:462 1:131 1:471ft	4½ 118	2¼	22 46½	613	Winland W M3	M25000	54 In the Rye, Bold Jacinto,FlyDancer	6
18May82-2GG	6f :22 :453 1:113ft	4½ 112	1hd 2hd 44½	611	Winland W M7	SMdn	70 PrmPrformnc,DollrCotton,MnyBth	9
18Apr82-4SA	1 :461 1:103 1:36 ft	4½ 118	21½ 46	412 523	Black K8	SMdn	65 EnvoysIntrg,BroksN'Brc,IndcDncr	10
7Apr82-2SA	6f :214 :444 1:103ft	22 1135	3nk 42½ 65½ 65¾	Steiner J J3	SM32000	79 Twib, Gravitas, Shirley's Steve R.	11
25Mar82-3SA	6f :214 :45 1:102ft	27 1135	46 44½ 43½ 43½	Steiner J J3	SM25000	83 Haukea, I Love Company, Listr	12

May 25 GG 4f ft :483 h   Apr 29 GG 3f ft :36 h

RECENCY, being the first factor we encounter as we study past performances, is the first one to be rated. We must always bear in mind the date of today's race—June 17. Quickly, we observe that Sapience has not run or worked since May 28, which is 20 days ago. While he is close to a form defect for recency, he is still within the 21 days that entitles him to an N rating.

RUNNING LINE: We are following the form factors, of course, in the sequence in which they are set forth in the *Racing Form*. We sweep across the last race running line and see that in his last six furlong race Sapience was within two lengths of the lead, and thus up close at three successive calls, including the important stretch call. This was followed by a pronounced stretch loss. But since all we are rating at this point is the running line, the stretch call position warrants another neutral. Remember, Sapience would have had to be up close at all four calls to merit a +, and his failure at the finish call wipes this out.

FORM CYCLE PERFORMANCE: Here we have our first analytical problem, as we search for improvement or decline or neither. We first check the next to the last race to see if it is within a useable time frame of 28 days. Since it was 23 days prior to the last race, we can compare the two. Our next look is at the stretch calls, where Sapience was much nearer the lead at the stretch in his last race than he was in the effort of May 5, 1982. The only reason that a dividing form cycle line is drawn between the May 5 and May 28 races is because of the decline to a lower level of competition on May 28 after higher class races of close to the same value. Ordinarily, this separation would not affect our comparisons unless there are some other dominant factors, as there are here. However, this considerable drop in class does affect how we treat the third form factor, and when you see a fall to such a pronounced lower level of competition, we are unable to tell whether what looks like a good improvement in the last race is due to the class drop or is a genuine improvement as such.

Accordingly, we award a third N for neutral, or non-applicable.

STRETCH PERFORMANCE: We come to another decision-making point. Sapience suffered a bad stretch loss in his last race, and although we have not yet begun to compare his opposition, we must evaluate what the stretch loss means. The key, of course, is whether there is another drop to a lower level of competition. In his last race, Sapience ran in open maiden company for $10,000. Today, he is entered in a state bred race for a price of $8,500. While the $1,500 in money is less than the 20% line we like to follow, the fall from an open maiden to a state bred race indicates an additional lowering of the level of competition. Sapience thus meets our standard for a drop in class. The stretch loss would not be held against him, and another N gets recorded. We write the form factors like this:

Sapience: N N N N

It is now time to look at the competition. Two horses were at 4-1 as the bell rang. We can begin with an analysis of Persecution.

Persecution

B. g. 3, by Bunny Dancer—Khaleas Jane, by Khalea

Own.—Curd & Dominguez

Br.—Dyer & Bennett Ann E (Cal)   1982   3 M   1   0 $1,052
Tr.—Dominguez Roger $8,500   1981   0 M   0   0

1075

Lifetime   3   0   1   0 $1,052

28May82-1GG	1⅟₁₆ :48² 1:13² 1:47²ft	12	1105	1¹	11½	1²	2³	CapitaineNM² Ⓢ M8500	63	Spectculrly,Persecution,BookRviw 11
21May82-7GG	1⅟₁₆ :46¹ 1:11³ 1:46 ft	26	114	5⁷	8¹³	8¹⁷	9¹⁹	McGurn C⁷	12500	54 Carimetovegas,SeniorCitizen,AlaNt 9
7May82-4GG	6f :22¹ :46¹ 1:12 ft	26	118	8⁸½	8⁹	6⁸½	5⁹½	McGurn C³	Ⓢ M16000	69 Rise 'am, Credit Worthy,KingCarm 9

Jun 8 GG 3f ft :35³ h   May 20 GG 3f ft :36³ h   May 13 GG 7f ft 1:31⁴ h   May 4 GG 3f ft :36³ h

RECENCY: This one ran on the same May 28 as Sapience ran, so the N rating is rather quickly and easily applied, since that race was 20 days ago.

RUNNING LINE: This horse was up close in a mile and a sixteenth race at all four calls, and accordingly, gets a + here.

FORM CYCLE PERFORMANCE: We have another example of a much better showing in the last race, but again, you can see a rather substantial class drop between the May 21 event and the last race on May 28. Accordingly, we can do no more with this factor than the common non-applicable.

STRETCH PERFORMANCE: While there was a stretch loss in the last race, it was at a mile and a sixteenth. Accordingly, Persecution is entitled to an N since today's distance is shorter by at least one furlong (and more). Thus the stretch loss in the last race does not count against him.

The other 4-1 horse is Hock a Day, a four-year-old colt who has not run in two years, but who shows good workouts.

Hock a Day

Dk. b. or br. c. 4, by Pelegrin—Atajane, by Atalayero

Own.—Hockaday C R

Br.—Utley D (Cal)   1980   2 M   0   0 $1,395
Tr.—Utley Doug $8,500   1979   0 M   0   0

120

Lifetime   2   0   0   0 $1,395

5Jly80-6Pln	5½f :21⁴ :45³ 1:04³ft	26	114	65¾	78½	59½	4¹²	StllsWE⁵ Ⓢ AlamedFut	77	BoldndGold,BlowngSnow,RndfPlsr 7
¹⁷Jun80-3Pln	5½f :21⁴ :45⁴ 1:04⁴ft	28	118	99½	9¹¹	5⁹	46½	Stallings W E⁶ M16000	81	Vinchnzo,Lnty'sMik,BudgtYourslf 10

Jun 8 GG 5f ft 1:00⁴ h   Jun 3 GG 5f ft 1:02 h   May 26 GG 5f ft 1:03² h   May 19 GG 4f ft :50 h

RECENCY: Off the last five furlong workout alone, we would award an N for recency, because it was within 14 days of today's race. But every other factor cannot be evaluated because of the two-year layoff. Thus, we must assign ratings of unknown for Hock a Day's running line, improvement, and stretch loss. We could either string out a series of U's representing unknown, or write in the easier − − − −.

In a situation of this kind, we would be required to handicap the horse off his 1980 performances to get some idea of what kind of ability he may possess. Since we are dealing solely with form at this point, we can pass for now, although you would surely agree with me that his previous efforts are not exactly overwhelming.

We might lay out our form ratings for the three like this:

Sapience:	N N N N
Persecution:	N + N N
Hock a Day:	N – – –

Because we are not taking the second step of doing any handicapping of the two horses with no form defects beyond assigning form factor ratings, our play will be Sapience, the favorite. The result chart gives us much pleasure, as the favorite won and Persecution finished second.

FIRST RACE
Golden Gate
JUNE 17, 1982

6 FURLONGS. (1.07$\frac{4}{5}$) MAIDEN CLAIMING. Purse $4,500. 3- and 4-year-olds. Bred in California. Weights, 3-year-olds, 112 lbs.; 4-year-olds, 120 lbs. Claiming price $8,500. 27th DAY. WEATHER CLEAR. TEMPERATRUE 66 DEGREES.

Value of race $4,500, value to winner $2,475, second $878, third $630, fourth $404, fifth $113. Mutuel pool $46,954.

Last Raced	Horse	Eqt.A.Wt	PP	St	¼	½	Str	Fin	Jockey	Cl'g Pr	Odds $1
28May82 $^{4}GG^{4}$	Sapience	b 3 112	4	4	1^{2}	1^{4}	1^{4}	1^{3}	Anderson J R	8500	1.90
28May82 $^{1}GG^{2}$	Persecution	b 3 110	8	5	7^{3}	6^{2}	$4^{1\frac{1}{2}}$	2^{nk}	Capitaine N M^{5}	8500	4.20
28May82 $^{1}GG^{6}$	Harold Topp	b 3 112	10	2	4^{2}	$3^{\frac{1}{2}}$	$2^{1\frac{1}{2}}$	3^{1}	Campbell B C	8500	18.00
28May82 $^{4}GG^{6}$	Daga's Boy	b 3 112	11	1	3^{1}	4^{2}	3^{1}	4^{2}	SchvaneveldtCP	8500	6.00
12Feb82 $^{1}GG^{7}$	Hedidit	b 4 120	9	8	6^{hd}	5^{hd}	5^{4}	5^{5}	Montiel R G	8500	40.90
14May82 $^{1}GG^{7}$	Coley's Pride	b 3 112	3	12	12	11^{2}	$8^{\frac{1}{2}}$	6^{1}	Caballero R	8500	29.90
28May82 $^{4}GG^{7}$	First Shadow	4 120	5	10	9^{1}	8^{4}	7^{1}	$7^{2\frac{1}{2}}$	Sanchez E	8500	14.30
	The B. G. Comet	3 114	1	9	8^{hd}	9^{2}	9^{5}	8^{3}	Stallings W E	8500	24.30
28May82 $^{1}GG^{11}$	New American	3 110	2	11	11^{3}	12	10^{2}	$9^{\frac{1}{2}}$	Dillenbeck B D^{5}	8500	94.60
30May82 $^{1}GG^{10}$	Reb's Empire	3 112	12	3	$2^{\frac{1}{2}}$	$2^{\frac{1}{2}}$	6^{2}	10^{3}	Lamance C	8500	14.00
21May82 $^{1}GG^{10}$	Bold Vengeance	3 114	7	6	10^{3}	$10^{\frac{1}{2}}$	11	11	Hummel C R	8500	54.10
5Jly80 $^{6}Pln^{4}$	Hock a Day	4 120	6	7	$5^{\frac{1}{2}}$	$7^{1\frac{1}{2}}$	—	—	Gonzalez R M	8500	4.20

Hock a Day, Lame.

OFF AT 1:02. Start good for all but COLEY'S PRIDE. Won handily. Time, :22$\frac{1}{5}$, :45$\frac{4}{5}$, :59$\frac{4}{5}$, 1:12$\frac{3}{5}$ Track fast.

Official Program Numbers↘

$2 Mutuel Prices:

4-SAPIENCE	5.80	3.20	2.60
8-PERSECUTION		4.20	3.00
10-HAROLD TOPP			6.00

B. g, by Tree of Knowledge—Farewell Patrice, by Turn-to or Candy Spots . Trainer Griffin Joseph A. Bred by Klussman Mr-Mrs W (Cal).

SAPIENCE took command quickly, opened a long lead on the turn and was not seriously threatened. PERSECUTION, reserved early, came inside for the drive and closed gamely for the place. HAROLD TOPP, just off the early leaders, loomed a threat into the stretch but could not sustain his bid. DAGA'S BOY, well-placed to the stretch, finished evenly. HEDIDIT raced wide and lacked the needed response in the drive. COLEY'S PRIDE broke in a tangle and found his best stride too late. FIRST SHADOW showed little. REB'S EMPIRE attended the pace to the stretch and faltered. HOCK A DAY had brief speed, gave way and went lame in the stretch run.

Owners— 1, Round Tree Farms; 2, Curd & Dominguez; 3, Frankfurt Stable; 4, Boyajian & Mims; 5, Heigh F H; 6, Brower-Dimitt et al; 7, Dohgel Stables; 8, Yolando Stable & Bills; 9, Cal Rose Farm; 10, 4-Fun Stb-McPeak-Murphy; 11, Djernes Patricia; 12, Myers & Utley.

Sapience was much the best horse, and with lack of form defects, was a very solid play. Even the price, as short as it was, could hardly be tossed aside. Persecution's previous race, in which he had shown good early speed for six furlongs, had placed him in good tune for his sprint effort. Hock a Day, perhaps demonstrating why he had not raced in two years, pulled up lame.

The second race, as the conditions printed below show, is a mile and a sixteenth claimer at a $16,000 claiming price. The conditions also show the weight off allowances for decreases in claiming price. We will start with the favorite, Tank's First.

2nd Golden Gate

1 1-16 MILES
GOLDEN GATE
START ▲   FINISH

1 ⅟₁₆ MILES. (1.40%) CLAIMING. Purse $9,000. 3-year-olds. Weight, 120 lbs. Non-winners of two races at one mile or over since May 1 allowed 3 lbs.; one such race since then, 6 lbs. Claiming price $16,000; for each $1,000 to $14,000 allowed 1 lb. (Maiden, starter and claiming races for $12,500 or less not considered.)

Tank's First

B. g. 3, by Cathy's Reject—Our Trudy, by Grounded II
Br.—Manzi & Lee (Cal)

Own.—Lee-Manzi-Ozer   **117**   Tr.—Retherford N J $16,000

									1982	9 4 0 0		$22,025
									1981	1 M 0 0		

Lifetime   10 4 0 0 $22,025

31May82-1GG	1⅟₁₆ :46 1:11⁴ 1:46¹ft	*2½ 114	3³ 2¹½ 2¹½ 1½	Meza R Q⁷	16000	72	Tank'sFirst,ShastFleet,BoldEncing 8
13May82-7GG	1⅟₁₆ :47⁴ 1:12² 1:46³ft	3½ 117	78½ 7¹² 8¹⁴ 8²¹	Baze R A⁵	25000	49	MuchaRis,CombtEcho,Michi'sSilor 8
22Apr82-4GG	1⅟₁₆ :47 1:11² 1:45²ft	*8-5 114	44½ 43 31 1½	Baze R A⁴	25000	76	Tnk'sFirst,SeniorCitizn,CombtEcho 5
26Mar82-5GG	1⅟₁₆ :46⁴ 1:12 1:45³gd	*8-5 114	46½ 33 2½ 1¹½	Baze R A¹	16000	75	Tank's First, Michi's Sailor, Scheib 9
5Mar82-1SA	6f :21⁴ :44⁴ 1:10³ft	21 120	96½ 89 9¹¹ 96¾	Guerra W A¹²	20000	78	Mchll'sDrm,Prt'sOvr,Chcr'sOrphn 12
18Feb82-2SA	6½f :21⁴ :44⁴ 1:16²ft	29 120	107½ 89½ 58½ 5¹⁰	Guerra W A¹	20000	78	SndsofVegs,BrightIsle,Prty'sOver 10
3Feb82-1SA	6½f :22¹ :45⁴ 1:17⁴ft	13 120	108½109 77½ 69¾	McHargue D G²	20000	71	ImaSizzler,SandsofVegs,Bright'sle 10
21Jan82-9SA	1 :46⁴ 1:12² 1:38³m	7¾ 115	3⁴ 6¹⁰ 6¹⁶ 6²⁰	Castaneda M⁵	32000	56	Subdivide,Nancy'sHoney,GloveMan 8
8Jan82-3SA	6½f :21⁴ :45¹ 1:19¹gd	*2½ 118	66 44½ 22 11½	CastanedM⁴ ⑤M25000	74	Tnk'sFirst,ILovCompny,JustGoofin 8
2Sep81-4Dmr	6f :22³ :46 1:11³ft	12 118	121511¹⁴ 7¹¹ 78¾	McHargue DG³ M32000	71	Rise'nFly,Vnquish,RememberJckL. 12

May 29 GG 4f ft :49¹ h   May 6 GG 5f ft 1:02 h   Apr 17 GG 5f ft 1:03³ h

As we look at this horse, we encounter our first problem of having a winner returning at the same class. Nonetheless, we will go through the form factors to see what is revealed.

RECENCY: With 17 days from the last race, we have an N for neutral.

RUNNING LINE: This shows an excellent +, as Tank's First was up close at every call in his fine winning effort.

FORM CYCLE: Here we have our last race winner, which we would show as a W within a circle: Ⓦ. The substantial drop in class between the last two races gives us a wash as far as evaluating improvement is concerned.

STRETCH PERFORMANCE: If there had been a Big Win, which there was not, because he won by only three-quarters of a length, only an N is appropriate here.

If Tank's First had shown two + factors instead of one, we would have looked for back class to evaluate his chances of scoring a second successive victory. You can see that he won at $25,000 on April 22, 1982, which makes you wonder, with that ability, why his handlers keep him at $16,000. But without the two + form factors, we will have to pass this horse.

When we come to the second choice in the wagering, Hot Tracks, we see another last race winner, this time off a Big Win. You can now begin to appreciate the frequency with which this factor shows up, and how important it is to evaluate it when you undertake to predict how your horse will run today.

Hot Tracks

									Ch. g. 3, by Earls Erma—Tina Lina, by The Shoe				
									Br.—Ellsworth R C & Kim (Ariz)		1982 10 2 0 0		$10,875
Own.—Martin-Patterson-Wright					**114**		Tr.—Schvaneveldt Phil		$16,000		1981 5 M 0 0		$100
						Lifetime	15 2 0 0	$10,975					

4Jun82-3GG	6f :221 :454 1:122ft	*2½ 1105	7¹⁰ 66½ 2³ 1⁴	Schvneveldt CP⁷	10000	77	Hot Tracks, Zinger B., J.Pedroncelli 9
20May82-3Hol	1¹⁄₁₆:464 1:122 1:451ft	5¹ 113	6¹² 64½ 66½ 77¼	Ortega L E⁶	18000	61	Miel'sMgic,JusticeForAll,PrincPlfc 7
29Apr82-5Hol	6f :22 :443 1:094ft	5⁹ 115	96¾ 8¹¹ 9¹⁰ 8¹⁰	Ortega L E⁸	20000	78	ExtrQuick,OleKingTuck,Jo'sTribut 10
16Apr82-1SA	6f :213 :444 1:104ft	2⁸ 120	88½ 9¹² 79 77½	Cruz J B¹⁰	20000	76	ILoveCompny,FltBttr,OlKingTuck 10
24Mar82-1SA	6½f :221 :451 1:163ft	2⁴ 120	72½ 86¾ 7¹² 69½	Cruz J B⁴	20000	77	Bright Isle, Joe'sTribute,ElTrapito 11
3Mar82-1SA	6½f :213 :442 1:172ft	2⁴ 120	6⁶ 77½ 96¾ 9¹⁰	Cruz J B⁵	32000	73	IndinO.,SndsofVegs,ClonmelArms 10
15Feb82-7SA	1¹⁄₁₆:47 1:113 1:431ft	2⁹ 116	2½ 75¼ 7¹³ 7¹⁹	Cruz J B⁴	50000	66	BisonBy,CourtComplinc,ClubFlush 7
4Feb82-2SA	6½f :221 :45 1:164ft	4⁵ 116	7² 53½ 53¾ 55½	Cruz J B⁷	50000	81	CptrthSprt,DlwrExprss,Mr.Enthssm 8
22Jan82-3SA	6½f :222 :454 1:203gd	3⁰ 115	52½ 56½ 32½ 1⁴	Cruz J B⁶	M28000	67	HotTrcks,Ed'sDynsty,HllljhBrothr 11
7Jan82-6SA	6f :221 :47 1:141sl	3³ 115	31½ 5² 42¾ 5⁵	ValenzuelaPA⁴	M28000	62	Mr.Enthusism,MuchRis,Rb'sOutlw 11
Jun 16 GG 3f ft :38¹ h		May 29 GG 3f ft :37⁴ h		May 19 Hol 3f ft :39³ h		May 15 Hol 6f ft 1:16² h	

RECENCY: With a race 13 days ago, we have an N rating here for non-applicable.

RUNNING LINE: This one gets an N also because of the victory in the last race. But he was not up close at any call except the finish, and thus cannot get a plus.

FORM CYCLE: We have the last race victory of course, with a rise in class, and we can insert an R inside the circle: ®. Again, because of the big drop in class between the two most recent races, there is no improvement rating.

STRETCH PERFORMANCE: The Big Win dominates this factor here, and Hot Tracks gets his first + rating.

Because of the last race victory off a Big Win, we have to look again to see if this horse can remain as a contender. There is no other + form factor to go with the Big Win. We search next for back class and find it wanting. While the horse ran earlier in the year for a claiming price of $50,000 at Santa Anita, it is obvious from his poor performances at high levels that his owners became overly impressed after his maiden claiming triumph. Since any maiden claiming price is not commensurate with claiming prices against established winners, we cannot give him appropriate credit for that victory. None of his races at higher claiming prices against winners showed anything at all until he was dropped all the way down to $10,000. Without sufficient back class, I would not want to bet on this horse—no way.

We are thus in a position to pass both the top betting choices and since the third selection is almost a long shot at 5-1, we shall pass the race altogether. Look at the chart, and we will make further comments thereafter.

SECOND RACE
Golden Gate
JUNE 17, 1982

$1\frac{1}{16}$ MILES. (1.40⅘) CLAIMING. Purse $9,000. 3–year–olds. Weight, 120 lbs. Non–winners of two races at one mile or over since May 1 allowed 3 lbs.; one such race since then, 6 lbs. Claiming price $16,000; for each $1,000 to $14,000 allowed 1 lb. (Maiden, starter and claiming races for $12,500 or less not considered.)

Value of race $9,000, value to winner $4,950, second $1,755, third $1,260, fourth $810, fifth $225. Mutuel pool $89,890.

Last Raced	Horse	Eqt.	A.	Wt	PP	St	¼	½	¾	Str	Fin	Jockey	Cl'g Pr	Odds $1
31May82 ^{1}GG^{5}	Hasty Work	b	3	114	7	2	$1\frac{1}{2}$	2^{1}	1^{2}	$1^{1\frac{1}{2}}$	1^{2}	Munoz E	16000	9.10
31May82 ^{1}GG^{1}	Tank's First	b	3	117	3	4	3^{1}	3^{1}	2^{hd}	2^{3}	2^{4}	Baze R A	16000	1.70
31May82 ^{3}Fno^{2}	Nearly Bucked	b	3	116	8	5	2^{1}	1^{hd}	$3\frac{1}{2}$	3^{hd}	3^{1}	StubblefieldDP	16000	15.10
27May82 ^{9}GG^{6}	Charles Michael	b	3	117	1	3	6^{2}	5^{3}	$4^{1\frac{1}{2}}$	$4\frac{1}{2}$	$4^{1\frac{1}{2}}$	Anderson J R	16000	9.40
4Jun82 ^{3}GG^{1}	Hot Tracks		3	114	4	1	5^{2}	6^{3}	6^{5}	$5\frac{1}{2}$	5no	SchvneveldtCP	16000	3.10
28May82 ^{3}GG^{1}	Ala Nat	b	3	115	5	6	$4\frac{1}{2}$	$4^{1\frac{1}{2}}$	5^{2}	6^{6}	6^{5}	Burkes T	16000	9.60
4May82 ^{2}GG^{4}	Count Elite		3	114	2	7	8	$7^{1\frac{1}{2}}$	$7^{1\frac{1}{2}}$	7^{3}	7^{5}	Mills J W	16000	15.50
28May82 ^{3}GG^{2}	Jolly Kanuck	b	3	113	6	8	$7^{1\frac{1}{2}}$	8	8	8	8	Winland W M	14000	5.20

OFF AT 1:33. Start good. Won driving. Time, :24, :48, 1:12⅕, 1:38⅗, 1:45⅗ Track fast.

$2 Mutuel Prices:			
7–HASTY WORK	20.20	7.40	4.60
3–TANK'S FIRST		3.40	3.00
8–NEARLY BUCKED			6.00

Dk. b. or br. g, by Hard Work—Gilliflower, by Advocator. Trainer Greenman Walter. Bred by Conrad J A (Ky).

HASTY WORK dueled with NEARLY BUCKED for the early lead, drew clear on the second turn and responded to strong pressure in the drive to turn back the bid of TANK'S FIRST. The latter, never far back, moved to attend the pace on the second turn but could not sustain his bid. HOT TRACKS showed little. ALA NAT, well-placed early, had no rally. COUNT ELITE was outrun. JOLLY KANUCK gave a dull effort.

Owners— 1, Cronin-McClure-Raney; 2, Lee-Manzi-Ozer; 3, Kershen R; 4, Manyak J N; 5, Martin-Patterson-Wright; 6, Zelkoski D; 7, Battles Mr or Mrs O; 8, Salamoni B F.

Overweight: Nearly Bucked 2 pounds; Ala Nat 1; Jolly Kanuck 1.

Neither of the last race winners could prevail. Tank's First did run a good race and wound up second. Hot Tracks, over his head in class, was never a threat. The point we make here, however, is that last race winners are seriously compromised and usually always face imposing difficulties, which can be overcome ordinarily only under ideal conditions. Tank's First was very close to the line and was indeed a threat. But finishing second is not winning a race, and when you see what the winner showed at a payoff of $20.20, you can appreciate even more the burden on this well played favorite that did manage to finish second.

Hasty Work — Dk. b. or br. g. 3, by Hard Work—Gilliflower, by Advocator

Own.—Cronin-McClure-Raney — 114 — Br.—Conrad J A (Ky) — Tr.—Greenman Walter — $16,000

1982 9 1 1 0 $10,268

1981 6 M 0 2 $2,660

Lifetime 15 1 1 2 $12,928

31May82-1GG	1$\frac{1}{16}$	:46	1:11^{4}	1:46^{1}ft	6	114	8^{11}	$5^{7\frac{1}{2}}$	5^{4}	$5^{3\frac{1}{4}}$	Munoz E[4]	16000	69	Tank'sFirst,ShastFleet,BoldEnding	8
14May82-4GG	1$\frac{1}{16}$	:47^{4}	1:12^{4}	1:47^{1}ft	5$\frac{1}{2}$	114	5^{5}	$5^{2\frac{3}{4}}$	$3^{1\frac{1}{2}}$	$4^{2\frac{1}{4}}$	Munoz E[1]	16000	65	SniorCitizn,Amrigoknt,RndomWind	7
4May82-2GG	1$\frac{1}{16}$	:47^{1}	1:13	1:49^{2}ft	3$\frac{1}{2}$	114	4^{8}	5^{3}	$5^{6\frac{1}{2}}$	$5^{5\frac{1}{4}}$	Winland W M[4]	16000	51	ChrlesMichl,IndmniFir,BoldEnding	8
22Apr82-4GG	1$\frac{1}{16}$	:47	1:11^{2}	1:45^{2}ft	5$\frac{1}{2}$	114	$5^{9\frac{1}{2}}$	5^{6}	$5^{3\frac{1}{2}}$	$5^{4\frac{1}{2}}$	Lamance C[3]	25000	71	Tnk'sFirst,SeniorCitizn,CombtEcho	5
6Apr82-7GG	1	:48	1:13^{3}	1:40^{1}gd	11	114	6^{10}	6^{11}	$5^{6\frac{1}{2}}$	$5^{7\frac{1}{2}}$	Munoz E[4]	32000	59	WindySaturdy,MuchRis,BronzeGod	7
11Mar82-8GG	1$\frac{1}{16}$	:47^{4}	1:13	1:46^{3}sy	8	120	$5^{4\frac{1}{2}}$	$5^{1\frac{3}{4}}$	4^{3}	$5^{5\frac{1}{2}}$	Munoz E[3]	Aw13000	64	FishinFleet,BronzeGod,ChinaPuzzle	6
27Feb82-2GG	1$\frac{1}{16}$	:48	1:13^{2}	1:46^{1}m	7	118	7^{11}	$5^{2\frac{1}{4}}$	1^{1}	1^{hd}	Munoz E[4]	Mdn	72	Hasty Work, Mucha Risa, Lured	8
27Jan82-4BM	1$\frac{1}{16}$	:47^{2}	1:13^{1}	1:46^{2}m	3$\frac{1}{2}$	117	$6^{5\frac{1}{2}}$	$4^{2\frac{1}{2}}$	2^{3}	$2^{3\frac{1}{2}}$	Howell W C[7]	M25000	63	Bronze God,HastyWork,FlagsAhead	9
20Jan82-5BM	6f	:22^{4}	:46^{4}	1:13^{3}sy	21	118	$9^{9\frac{3}{4}}$	$8^{8\frac{3}{4}}$	$8^{6\frac{1}{2}}$	4^{5}	Howell W C[2]	M25000	67	JustIntrvwd,NmHmAnythng,Tunnl	11
30Dec81-3BM	6f	:22^{4}	:46^{2}	1:12 sy	11	118	8^{8}	8^{11}	7^{13}	7^{12}	Baze R A[4]	M25000	68	First Count, So Goes, Tunnel	11

Jun 14 GG 5f ft 1:03^{1} h — May 12 GG 3f ft :38 hg — May 2 GG 3f ft :39^{2} b

It must be noted that here is a horse with no form defects at all, and any horse with no form defects that is able to run within his level of competition is always a threat to win a race. There can be no better example than here, and when you view the $20.20 price, it is nearly incredible that this horse would be so lightly backed.

RECENCY: His last race 17 days ago merits the neutral.

RUNNING LINE: The horse gets another N for being within less than five lengths at the stretch call at the same class.

FORM CYCLE: Hasty Work was farther behind at the stretch call in his last race than he was in the previous event at the same class. Next, you compare the final times of the two races and see that the last race winning time was one second faster than in the race of May 14, 1982. Hasty Work ran his last race four-fifths of a second faster than in his previous event, which you can see from the 69 speed rating, compared to the prior race's speed rating of 65.

(This is another example of how the much-maligned speed ratings prove somewhat useful.) Thus, he maintained a relatively even keel, and gets an N again.

STRETCH PERFORMANCE: With no loss nor a Big Win, he gets an N rating here.

Now note the five furlong workout three days before the race. This is but one more very positive sign. And while I want to re-emphasize again that we are not using any other handicapping factors here except the form rules developed in this book, when I applied my own revised ability times for comparing Tank's First, the favorite, and Hasty Work, the latter was a shade ahead.

Sure, Tank's First might have won the race, as we can purvey in any "woulda, coulda, shoulda" situation. But against a strong foe like Hasty Work, despite the unreasonable odds, the favorite was laboring in very speculative circumstances, and the result proved it. This demonstrates again the wisdom of passing this kind of well played horse.

Let us take a look at the third race, a six furlong claiming event for three-year-old fillies, with a claiming price of $10,000. In this contest the form players did not like anyone much at all. The two top choices were unenthusiastically backed at 7-2. We can start first with Paula Mason.

3rd Golden Gate

6 FURLONGS. (1.07⅘) CLAIMING. Purse $7,500. Fillies. 3-year-olds. Weight, 120 lbs. Non-winners of two races since May 1 allowed 3 lbs.; a race since then, 6 lbs. Claiming price $10,000; if for $9,000 allowed 2 lbs. (Maiden and claiming races for $8,500 or less not considered.)

Paula Mason — **B. f. 3, by Port Wine—Countess Candy, by Ali's Gem**
Br.—Weir Mr-Mrs N (Idaho) — 1982 7 1 0 2 $4,707
Own.—Bolinske L **114** **Tr.—Dutton Jerry** **$10,000** — 1981 0 M 0 0
Lifetime 7 1 0 2 $4,707

13May82-1GG	6f	$:22^2$	$:46^2$	$1{:}12^4$ft	$*2\frac{1}{4}$	113	$5^{5\frac{1}{2}}$	$4^{2\frac{1}{2}}$	3^1	$1^{1\frac{1}{2}}$	Munoz E^6	ⒻM8500	75	Paula Mason,DebsDu,TootSaBella	10
28Apr82-1GG	6f	$:22^3$	$:46^3$	$1{:}12^4$ft	41	117	$10^{9\frac{3}{4}}$	9^9	6^7	$3^{2\frac{1}{2}}$	Munoz E^9	ⒻM12500	72	FrnDeesDrem,SolidEffct,PulMson	11
1Apr82-4GG	$1\frac{1}{16}$	$:49^1$	1:16	1:53 sy	$3\frac{1}{4}$	117	1^{hd}	$3^{\frac{1}{2}}$	7^{12}	8^{17}	Gonzalez RM^3	ⒻM8500	—	Shy Blusher, Aprildust,RightOnMal	8
11Mar82-1GG	$1\frac{1}{16}$	$:47^3$	$1{:}14^1$	$1{:}50^2$sy	12	117	8^{12}	5^6	$4^{3\frac{1}{2}}$	3^5	Pyfer R^{10}	ⒻM10000	46	TraceO'Music,Aprildust,PaulMson	12
19Feb82-3GG	6f	$:23^1$	:48	$1{:}15^1$gd	$4\frac{3}{4}$	117	$7^{7\frac{1}{4}}$	$6^{5\frac{1}{2}}$	$4^{4\frac{1}{2}}$	$4^{5\frac{1}{2}}$	GonzlezRM⁶	ⒻM10000	57	FrnsVcton,GongCrookd,RlThCcrt	12
15Jan82-1BM	6f	:23	$:47^4$	$1{:}14^1$ft	$7\frac{1}{2}$	117	$6^{3\frac{1}{2}}$	$7^{4\frac{3}{4}}$	$8^{4\frac{1}{4}}$	$7^{6\frac{1}{4}}$	GonzlezRM⁸	ⒻM12500	63	FinlJudgment,BoleroBrz,BootyBg	12
1Jan82-1BM	6f	:23	$:47^1$	$1{:}13^1$m	11	117	$4^{3\frac{1}{2}}$	$3^{3\frac{1}{2}}$	3^3	$4^{6\frac{3}{4}}$♦	GonzlezRM⁹	ⒻM12500	67	Star of Ali, Booty Bag, June Gale	12

♦ 1Jan82—Dead heat

Jun 12 GG 4f ft :51 h **May 22 GG 6f ft $1{:}14^4$ h** **Apr 24 Pln 7f ft $1{:}31^2$ h** **Apr 17 Pln 5f ft $1{:}04^4$ b**

RECENCY: We begin with a 34-day layoff between races. There is a four furlong workout five days earlier, which is not sufficient to overcome the layoff problem. Then you see a six furlong work on May 22, which was 21 days before the four furlong workout. This long workout is not recent enough to help Paula Mason qualify for recent action. We have a form defect and a zero.

RUNNING LINE: Where there is a O in the recency department, I will rate a horse's last running line if the horse ran within four weeks, even though the race is outside the three-weeks' period which picks up the form defect. But when a horse such as Paula Mason has not run within four weeks, there is little need to evaluate the running line, since the layoff form defect eliminates the horse from further serious consideration. Thus, with Running Line, Form Cycle, and Stretch Performance all being non-rated, we can write Paula Mason this way:

Paula Mason: O — — —

Also at 7-2, with a few dollars less in the win pool, is Oui Farrah, who has just recently come down from Portland Meadows to take on the California horses. While we may have some difficulty with the Oregon races, we have a very rateable last race here.

Oui Farrah

Dk. b. or br. f. 3, by Porky Pine—Qui Mamzell, by My Host
Br.—Schmidli Mr–Mrs T M (Ore)   1982 10 2 2 2 $6,190
Own.—Schmidli W M   **109⁵**   Tr.—Merrill Doris $10,000   1981 12 2 3 1 $4,537
Lifetime   22   4   5   3 $10,727

28May82-2GG	6f :23	:46² 1:12¹ft	8¾ 1105	1ʰᵈ 1ʰᵈ 33¼ 49	CapitaineNM⁵ ⓕ 11000	69	DwnBeQuick,BouncingNtiv,‡ShWin 8
28May82—Placed third through disqualification
24Apr82-9PM	6f :22²	:46³ 1:13³ft	45 111	8¹¹ 7¹¹10¹⁹10¹³	Garcia R Jr⁹	ⓕHcpO	66	GreyPulus,FetureFntsy,SummrPlc 11
14Apr82-7PM	6f :22²	:46² 1:13 gd	2½ 1155	2½ 1ʰᵈ 1ʰᵈ 32¼	Glenn J W⁴	ⓕ 12500	79	Coburgs Nudge, Cigale, Oui Farrah 7
4Apr82-7PM	6f :22³	:46⁴ 1:13 sy	*6-5 1145	2ʰᵈ 1ʰᵈ 1½ 2ⁿᵒ	Knapp S L³	ⓕ 12500	82	Carrie'sStar,OuiFrrh,StrofDuntreth 6
28Mar82-9PM	6f :22	:45² 1:12 sy	9½ 114	3ⁿᵏ 31 44 47¼	Garcia R Jr⁷	ⓕAw3000	79	FetureFntsy,Rosie'sNightie,RvlSpy 7
14Mar82-7PM	6f :22⁴	:47 1:13²gd	*3-2 1105	33½ 24 1ʰᵈ 2ⁿᵏ	Knapp S L²	12500	80	Beau Brad, Oui Farrah, Eraser Too 6
7Mar82-8PM	6f :22⁴	:47¹ 1:12⁴ft	2½ 1145	2¹ 2½ 1½ 12	Knapp S L³	ⓕ 16000	83	OuiFarrah,Rosie'sNightie,Crrie'sStr 6
20Feb82-9PM	1 :48¹	1:15² 1:43¹gd	33 108	2ʰᵈ 76¾ 9¹⁸ 9¹⁷	GrcRJr⁶ ⓕMtStHelens	48	‡Writin'Mm,RiSlm,Doc'sLittleMiss 10
30Jan82-7PM	1 :48²	1:14³ 1:42 gd	8 1075	11 32½ 62¹ 7¹⁸	Knapp K R¹	Aw3100	53	CtIsleDon,VegsJeff,LighthouseJim 8
22Jan82-5PM	6f :22¹	:45⁴ 1:13⁴sy	12 1115	1½ 1½ 14 14	Knapp S L⁴	12500	78	OuiFarrah,‡TimelyRequest,Csey'sPl 8

Jun 11 GG 4f ft :50² h   May 24 GG 3f ft :36² h

RECENCY: The last race was 20 days ago—an N for non-applicable.

RUNNING LINE: This filly was short of qualifying in the stretch since she was not less than three lengths behind in a six furlong race. Her last race showed a claiming price of $11,000 and the fleeting thought might pass that there could be a drop in class level. Not at all, since the $1,000 difference is far from enough to signify any different level of competition. We award the O for running line.

FORM CYCLE AND STRETCH PERFORMANCE: There are no comparison races within a time frame to check for either improvement or decline. The severe stretch loss is not essential since this factor applies only when a horse is up close at the stretch call. Although we disregard it here, you may note in passing that the May 28 race was the first one after a layoff and had Oui Farrah been up close at the stretch call, the exception for a first race after a return would have nullified the stretch loss factor.

Oui Farrah: N O – –

And we pass this race, since neither of the two top betting choices was without form defects. Here is the outcome:

THIRD RACE
Golden Gate
JUNE 17, 1982

6 FURLONGS. (1.07⅘) CLAIMING. Purse $7,500. Fillies. 3-year-olds. Weight, 120 lbs. Non-winners of two races since May 1 allowed 3 lbs.; a race since then, 6 lbs. Claiming price $10,000; if for $9,000 allowed 2 lbs. (Maiden and claiming races for $8,500 or less not considered.)

Value of race $7,500, value to winner $4,125, second $1,463, third $1,050, fourth $675, fifth $187. Mutuel pool $58,324. Exacta Pool $107,293.

Last Raced	Horse	Eqt.	A.	Wt	PP	St	¼	½	Str	Fin	Jockey	Cl'g Pr	Odds $1
28May82 ^{2}GG^{5}	Saturdays Child		3	114	9	4	4^{1}	$4\frac{1}{2}$	2^{hd}	1^{hd}	SchvneveldtCP	10000	6.10
28May82 ^{2}GG^{3}	Oui Farrah		3	110	4	3	1^{hd}	$1^{1\frac{1}{2}}$	$1^{1\frac{1}{2}}$	2^{hd}	Capitaine N M^{5}	10000	3.80
13May82 ^{1}GG^{1}	Paula Mason	b	3	114	8	11	11^{5}	$7^{1\frac{1}{2}}$	5^{2}	3^{1}	Munoz E	10000	3.60
2Jun82 ^{3}GG^{1}	Debs Du		3	114	11	5	6^{2}	5^{3}	$3^{1\frac{1}{2}}$	$4^{2\frac{1}{2}}$	Baze R A	10000	7.80
28May82 ^{2}GG^{7}	All the Reasons		3	114	2	6	$5\frac{1}{2}$	6^{2}	6^{5}	5^{4}	Schacht R	10000	8.20
28May82 ^{2}GG^{4}	She Win	b	3	110	6	1	$2^{1\frac{1}{2}}$	2^{3}	4^{1}	6^{2}	Dillenbeck BD^{5}	10000	4.00
3Jun82 ^{3}GG^{6}	Carrie Paper		3	114	12	10	9^{hd}	9^{hd}	$7\frac{1}{2}$	7^{nk}	Sorenson D	10000	28.40
3Jun82 ^{3}GG^{8}	Lew's Cutie		3	114	10	9	10^{2}	10^{2}	$9\frac{1}{2}$	$8\frac{1}{2}$	Hamilton M	9000	74.90
3Jun82 ^{3}GG^{5}	Dainty Dottie		3	114	1	12	7^{hd}	$8^{1\frac{1}{2}}$	8^{1}	$9\frac{1}{2}$	Gonzalez R M	10000	24.40
28May82 ^{2}GG^{6}	Tickle Baby		3	112	3	7	8^{hd}	11^{8}	10^{3}	10^{6}	Mills J W	9000	49.80
26May82 ^{2}GG^{6}	Ruler's Pride		3	114	7	2	3^{2}	3^{hd}	11^{6}	11^{4}	Lamance C	10000	11.60
28May82 ^{2}GG^{8}	Welch Bokay	b	3	114	5	8	12	12	12	12	Stallings W E	10000	103.50

OFF AT 2:07 Start good. Won driving. Time, :22⅖, :46, :59⅘, 1:12⅗ Track fast.

$2 Mutuel Prices:

9-SATURDAYS CHILD	14.20	6.20	3.80
4-OUI FARRAH		6.20	5.00
8-PAULA MASON			3.40

$5 EXACTA 9-4 PAID $211.00

Dk. b. or br. f, by First Saturday—Shirley G, by Catchpenny II. Trainer Steele Roy. Bred by Gavazza Shirley C (Cal).

SATURDAYS CHILD, just off the leaders to the stretch, responded to steady left-handed pressure in the drive and edged OUI FARRAH. The latter dueled for the early lead, drew clear in midstretch and held on gamely in a long drive. PAULA MASON, far back to the stretch, rallied well wide in the drive and closed willingly. DEBS DU, reserved early, moved up wide on the turn and finished gamely in the drive. ALL THE REASONS lacked the needed rally. SHE WIN pressed the pace to the stretch and weakened. CARRIE PAPER showed little. DAINTY DOTTIE broke slowly and could not menace. RULER'S PRIDE had speed for a half-mile and stopped.

Owners— 1, Gavazza Shirley C; 2, Schmidli W M; 3, Bolinske L; 4, Kidd Mardee; 5, Harris Farm, Inc & Marley; 6, Arterburn & Madden; 7, Egan-Gonzlz-Hrmn-Toll; 8, Walnut View Fm & Web Stable; 9, Duffel J & W; 10, McMeans Connie; 11, Blumer D G; 12, McVicker R L.

The fact that the top two betting choices, even with their form defects, ran second and third, tells you something about the weakness of the field. I might also add that the third choice, She Win, whose past performances were not reproduced here, had a severe stretch loss in her last race and would not have qualified either. While Oui Farrah ran a strong race, she suffered greatly in the stretch again and was passed by the outsider, Saturday's Child. Good avoidance, once more.

4th Golden Gate

5 ½ FURLONGS. (1.02⅕) MAIDEN CLAIMING. Purse $6,000. 2-year-olds. Weight, 118 lbs. Claiming price $16,000.

The fourth race was a maiden claimer for two-year-olds at five and a half furlongs. This early in the two-year-old season, if young horses are already running for a claiming price as moderate as $16,000 you should realize that playing almost anything would be a wild gamble. If something did look exceptionally good on our form rules, we would not be compelled to pass. But here, neither the favorite, Bam's Rascal, nor the second betting choice, Pardon Me Mac, had ever raced before. Would you want to risk your money on either of these two?

Bam's Rascal

Gr. c. 2, by Shady Fellow—Misty Banner, by Green Banner
Br.—Bam Stable (Cal)   1982 0 M 0 0
Own.—Bam Stable   **118**   Tr.—Hess R B $16,000
Lifetime   0 0 0 0
Jun 11 GG 5f ft 1:02³ hg   Jun 6 GG 3f ft :36⁴ hg   Jun 1 GG 5f ft 1:07¹ b   May 26 GG 4f ft :49³ hg

Pardon Me Mac

B. g. 2, by MacArthur Park—Pardon Me Miss, by Tulyar
Br.—Johnson & Rancho Paraiso (Cal)   1982 0 M 0 0
Own.—Johnson R C   **118**   Tr.—Murphy Chuck $16,000
Lifetime   0 0 0 0
Jun 14 Pln 4f ft :49³ h   Jun 3 GG 5f ft 1:04³ b   May 29 GG Tr. 5f ft 1:01⁴ hg   May 22 Pln 4f ft :48¹ h

While both of these colts show five furlong workouts, which is to their credit, the fact that their owners have placed a very modest price tag on them in their initial start tells you all you need to know. In *Investing at the Racetrack*, the critical nature of the unknown factor was stressed, and advice there was not to play any horse whose form was unknown. While that harsh rule has been softened because of the shining value of the five furlong workout, a first-time maiden claimer starter is so unknown, even with the good workout, that you might as well try to pin the tail on the donkey as to fathom the winner. If a young, unraced horse showed a really impressive five furlong workout, he would not be running for a price tag. It is as simple as that.

While no one likes to pass three races in a row, this is still a key discipline factor in making money at the racetrack. You have to keep away from the dubious gambling propositions. While you may be able to make an argument for playing the second or third races on this card, which would be foolish enough, there is no way to soundly play this event. You might even expect one of the entries to romp in with the kind of big price that is shown.

FOURTH RACE **5 ½ FURLONGS. (1.02⅕) MAIDEN CLAIMING. Purse $6,000. 2-year-olds. Weight, 118 lbs. Claiming price $16,000.**

Golden Gate

JUNE 17, 1982

Value of race $6,000, value to winner $3,300, second $1,170, third $840, fourth $540, fifth $150. Mutuel pool $96,448.

Last Raced	Horse	Eqt.A.Wt	PP	St	¼	⅜	Str	Fin	Jockey	Cl'g Pr	Odds $1
16May82 ^{4}AC^{8}	Pet Me	2 118	4	7	$6^{1\frac{1}{2}}$	4^{hd}	2^{2}	1^{2}	Munoz E	16000	21.70
11Jun82 ^{4}GG^{6}	De Novo	2 118	3	1	$1^{\frac{1}{2}}$	1^{3}	1^{5}	2^{3}	Winland W M	\ 16000	3.30
	Bam's Rascal	2 118	1	5	$4^{\frac{1}{2}}$	5^{2}	5^{1}	3^{nk}	Caballero R	16000	2.60
5May82 ^{6}GG^{9}	Hazit	2 118	5	8	$7^{\frac{1}{2}}$	$7^{1\frac{1}{2}}$	$6^{1\frac{1}{2}}$	4^{2}	Campbell B C	16000	37.50
	Pardon Me Mac	2 118	10	3	$3^{1\frac{1}{2}}$	2^{hd}	3^{1}	5^{hd}	Lamance C	16000	2.90
26May82 ^{3}TuP^{4}	Kevin The Great	2 118	6	6	8^{3}	8^{3}	8^{2}	6^{hd}	Stallings W E	16000	9.00
27May82 ^{4}GG^{7}	A Faster Piaster	2 115	2	2	5^{2}	6^{hd}	7^{hd}	7^{nk}	McGurn C	16000	22.60
28May82 ^{1}Fno^{5}	King's Fleet	2 118	8	9	9^{1}	9^{2}	9^{6}	8^{2}	Troestch R	16000	8.60
21May82 ^{6}GG^{8}	Rudolph	b 2 118	9	4	2^{hd}	3^{1}	4^{hd}	9^{13}	Tohill K S	16000	15.70
28May82 ^{1}Fno^{7}	Sporty's Star	b 2 118	7	10	10	10	10	10	StubblefieldDP	16000	23.40

OFF AT 2:36. Start good. Won driving. Time, :22⅘, :47, 1:00⅗, 1:07⅖ Track fast.

$2 Mutuel Prices:				
	5-PET ME	**45.40**	**14.40**	**7.40**
	3-DE NOVO		**5.40**	**3.80**
	1-BAM'S RASCAL			**3.60**

B. c, by Petrone—Milady Grace, by Ky Pioneer. Trainer Hess R B. Bred by Marshall J (Cal).

PET ME, reserved early, rallied slightly wide into the stretch, lugged inward through the drive despite left-handed urging and was up in time. DE NOVO dueled for the early lead, drew clear on the turn, opened a long lead into the stretch but could not last. BAM'S RASCAL, never far back, finished evenly in the stretch run. HAZIT, outrun early, came out for the drive but lacked the needed response. PARDON ME MAC attended the pace from the outside to the stretch and weakened. KEVIN THE GREAT was wide and showed little. KING'S FLEET was outrun. RUDOLPH had speed to the stretch and faltered.

Owners— 1, Marshall J; 2, Blain Rebecca; 3, Bam Stable; 4, Caravelli & Tribulato; 5, Johnson R C; 6, Shindel M; 7, Hi Card Ranch; 8, Lotspeich M E; 9, Rudolph E; 10, Valov J.

Scratched—Brandon's Folly (11Jun82 ^{4}GG^{5}); Lucky People (10Jun82 ^{6}Hol); Time To Star.

So douse your grumbles and be happy that some lucky soul dabbled in numbers and came up with a winner that paid $45.40. Maybe it will turn him or her into a racing fan. But with three passes in a row, we can take a hard look at the fifth race to see if we can find a play here. This is a six furlong $6,500 claiming race for fillies and mares at least four years old.

5th Golden Gate

6 FURLONGS. (1.07⅘) CLAIMING. Purse $5,500. Fillies and mares. 4-year-olds and upward. Weight, 120 lbs. Non-winners of two races since May 1 allowed 3 lbs.; a race since then, 6 lbs. Claiming price $6,500; if for $6,250 allowed 2 lbs. (Maiden, starter and claiming races for $5,000 or less not considered.)

Escort's Joy *

Own.—Marshall J C **114**

B. f. 4, by Escort—Amber Flight, by Crazy Kid
Br.—Southard Mary (Cal) 1982 9 1 0 2 $7,022
Tr.—Marshall J T **$6,500** 1981 14 3 3 3 $15,236
Lifetime 23 4 3 5 $22,258

3Jun82-2GG	$1\frac{1}{16}$	:47^{4}	1:12^{4}	1:48^{1}ft	3	114	$1^{1\frac{1}{2}}$	1^{1}	$1^{1\frac{1}{2}}$	$3^{1\frac{1}{2}}$	Gonzalez R M^{4}	Ⓕ 6500	60	KyLoriL,MoonCountss,Escort'sJoy	7
27May82-2GG	6f	:22^{2}	:46^{2}	1:12^{3}ft	17	110^{5}	1^{hd}	2^{hd}	1^{hd}	5^{2} .	SchvnevldtCP^{1}	Ⓕ 8500	74	All View, Tiffi Dere, Myrtle A Too	7
19May82-2GG	6f	:23	:46^{2}	1:11^{4}ft	20	114	2^{hd}	4^{4}	5^{9}	5^{17}	Lamance C^{8}	Ⓕ 10000	63	ArphoeDwn,Ethelyn'sDlight,AllViw	8
11May82-3GG	6f	:22^{1}	:46	1:12^{2}ft	13	114	$5^{4\frac{1}{4}}$	6^{6}	6^{14}	6^{11}	Gonzalez RM^{5}	Ⓕ 10000	66	DintySkirts,Ethlyn'sDlight,Ros'sBrt	7
15Feb82-5GG	6f	:22^{3}	:46^{1}	1:14 sy	$7\frac{1}{4}$	117	$3^{\frac{1}{2}}$	$5^{4\frac{1}{2}}$	8^{11}	9^{12}	Mahorney W^{4}	Ⓕ 10000	57	Nikki C., Windax, Book's Miss	10
5Feb82-2BM	6f	:22^{3}	:46	1:11^{1}ft	5	120	2^{3}	$4^{4\frac{1}{2}}$	$5^{7\frac{1}{2}}$	$6^{8\frac{3}{4}}$	Johnson B G^{2}	Ⓕ 10000	75	La Chevelle, Windax, Daragaya	8
27Jan82-7BM	6f	:22^{1}	:46^{2}	1:12^{3}gd	6	114	2^{2}	$2^{\frac{1}{2}}$	1^{hd}	1^{2}	Johnson B G^{5}	Ⓕ 10000	77	Escort's Joy,AtomEyes,Marvelarie	10
21Jan82-5BM	6f	:23^{1}	:47^{2}	1:13^{1}m	22	114	$4^{2\frac{1}{4}}$	$8^{5\frac{3}{4}}$	10^{12}	9^{11}	Mahorney W^{4}	Ⓕ 12500	63	WilliesHoney,Trcy'sStl,BdBdLucy	12
7Jan82-2BM	6f	:23^{1}	:47^{2}	1:13 gd	$4\frac{1}{2}$	114	$4^{\frac{3}{4}}$	$5^{3\frac{3}{4}}$	4^{4}	$3^{4\frac{1}{2}}$	Mahorney W^{2}	Ⓕ 10000	70	EgoImage,MorePrevue,Escort'sJoy	7
16Dec81-3BM	6f	:23^{1}	:47^{1}	1:13^{2}gd	7	114	1^{hd}	$3^{\frac{1}{2}}$	1^{1}	$1^{\frac{3}{4}}$	JohnsnBG^{7}	ⒻⓈ c6500	73	Escort's Joy, Marvelarie,Daragaya	11

May 3 GG 6f ft 1:15^{3} h Apr 27 GG 5f ft 1:01^{1} h Apr 19 GG 5f ft 1:02^{3} h

This slight favorite is also backed with wavering enthusiasm, since she, too, is just short of a 7-2 price at 3.4-1. But a first glance says we may have something.

RECENCY: With 14 days since the last race, an easy N here.

RUNNING LINE: The last race was at a mile and a sixteenth. Today's run is only six furlongs. She earns a solid + for running line because she was up close at every call in the mile and a sixteenth race. By now, you should know that this is one of the most impressive of positive form factors.

FORM CYCLE: While we are thrown into races at different distances and at a different class for any possible comparison, it is simple enough here to write down an N, since Escort's Joy was not farther behind at the stretch call in her last race than she was in the previous event.

STRETCH PERFORMANCE: The stretch loss here came in a distance race, and because today's race is only six furlongs, this is not considered a form defect. Thus, we can rate the form of Escort's Joy as:

Escort's Joy: N + N N

The second choice is Here Comes Help, going off at 7-2, only a small bit behind Escort's Joy in dollars in the win pool.

Here Comes Help

Ro. m. 5, by Tollie Jester—Social Editor, by George Royal

Own.—Gatto F	**114**	Br.—Rice Tandy & Barbara (NM) 1982 7 0 1 2 $2,795
		Tr.—Christiansen Albert $6,500 1981 14 3 0 2 $12,252

Lifetime   33 4 3 7 $17,807

5Jun82-5GG	6f :22² :46¹ 1:13 ft	4½ 114	53¾ 52¾ 44½ 34½	Baze R A⁷	ⓕ 8500 69	CrispyLrk,WilliesHony,HrComs4lp 11
26May82-3GG	1 1/16:47² 1:13 1:47²ft	5½ 114	3² 3³ 6¹² 72³	Baze R A⁵	ⓕ 8500 43	Im Erica, Puddin Proof,LittleKarot 7
13May82-5GG	6f :22² :46 1:12⁴ft	*6-5 114	4¹½ 3¹½ 2² 3³	Baze R A⁶	ⓕ c6500 72	NogeroK.,Cocktrice,HereComesHlp 8
28Apr82-5GG	6f :22¹ :45⁴ 1:11⁴ft	3 114	54¾ 33½ 35 2½	Mills J W¹⁰	ⓕ c5000 79	WindyPower,HereComesHelp,Pgr 12
20Apr82-7GG	6f :22⁴ :46¹ 1:113ft	44 114	88¾10¹³ 99½ 8⁷	Mills J W³	ⓕ 8500 74	MyrtleAToo,ShronsGryDwn,Mirge 11
21Feb82-4FG	6f :23 :47² 1:13¹ft	15 108⁵	12¹⁰11¹²11²¹11²²¹	Fox T L³	ⓕ c10000 58	ShrrySnrs,SlghtlyVrnshd,ForGrns 12
28Jan82-6FG	6f :22¹ :46³ 1:13⁴ft	26 113	33 44½ 32½ 95½	Herrera C²	ⓕ 12500 71	DsGurnt,BoldMdmosll,NoMnorVcs 11
31Dec81-10FG	1 40:48¹ 1:14 1:44⁴ft	20 114	55½ 66 10¹⁶10¹⁸	Herrera C⁵	ⓕ 12500 51	Flag Miss, Borita's Best,MagicFly 10
7Dec81-1FG	6f :22⁴ :47³ 1:13³ft	15 112⁵	22½ 3² 2⁴ 56½	Patin B C⁶	ⓕ 11500 70	RadioDance,‡ShanaLce,FineEnvoy 12

RECENCY: The last race within 12 days brings an N for neutral.

RUNNING LINE: Our first look is to the stretch call position. This mare was not quite there, because she was more than two and three-quarter lengths from the lead in a six furlong race. Thus, otherwise she would not qualify. But we also quickly see a drop in class from an $8,500 claiming price in that last race to a $6,500 claiming price today. This is a true decline in level of competition. Accordingly, we can now look for an up close at some other call to qualify this mare. At the second call, Here Comes Help was two and three-quarter lengths from the lead, which is our outside qualifying point. An N can therefore be written down.

FORM CYCLE: The last two races were at the same class level, but at different distances. Here Comes Help was much closer at the stretch call in her last race. Using our distance comparisons, the six furlong time in both the last two races was 1:13. Despite the apparent improvement, Here Comes Help ran two-fifths of a second slower in her last run than she did in the distance event at the same six furlong measuring distance. You can tell this from the fact that she was three lengths from the lead at the six furlong point in the May 26 race, and was four and a half lengths away at the finish of the six furlong race on June 5. While we do not award a declining horse factor here, since Here Comes Help was closer at the stretch call in her last race, this is hardly a good sign.

STRETCH PERFORMANCE: Since Here Comes Help was not up close at the stretch call in her last race, we do not count this factor here. The previously noted class drop applies for running line qualification, however, as was stated earlier. The form line on this horse now reads:

Here Comes Help: N N N –

Under our rules of play set forth for this chapter only, we will back the favorite when the favorite has no form defects or no disqualifying rise in class or last race win. While the sounder handicapping method is to go to additional factors when there are no form defects, we will stick with our announced plan here and put our money on Escort's Joy. The + factor for running line is the best sign we have, but now you can see that this was hardly enough.

FIFTH RACE
Golden Gate
JUNE 17, 1982

6 FURLONGS. (1.07⅘) CLAIMING. Purse $5,500. Fillies and mares. 4-year-olds and upward. Weight, 120 lbs. Non-winners of two races since May 1 allowed 3 lbs.; a race since then, 6 lbs. Claiming price $6,500; if for $6,250 allowed 2 lbs. (Maiden, starter and claiming races for $5,000 or less not considered.)

Value of race $5,500, value to winner $3,025, second $1,073, third $770, fourth $495, fifth $137. Mutuel pool $67,976. Exacta Pool $122,059.

Last Raced	Horse	Eqt.A.Wt	PP	St	¼	½	Str	Fin	Jockey	Cl'g Pr	Odds $1
4Jun82 ^{2}GG^{5}	Excessiva	4 117	10	1	7^{hd}	6^{3}	1^{hd}	1no	Rosales R	6500	16.30
5Jun82 ^{5}GG^{3}	Here Comes Help	b 5 114	7	4	4^{hd}	4^{hd}	2½	$2^{1½}$	Baze R A	6500	3.60
2Jun82 ^{2}GG^{2}	Roll On Lili	4 114	5	12	12	10^{hd}	7^{hd}	3^{1}	Winland W M	6500	7.60
3Jun82 ^{2}GG^{4}	Cockatrice	b 4 114	6	10	10^{1}	9^{hd}	$9^{1½}$	4^{hd}	Sorenson D	6500	6.40
3Jun82 ^{2}GG^{3}	Escort's Joy	4 114	9	2	$3^{1½}$	$2^{1½}$	$4^{1½}$	5no	Gonzalez R M	6500	3.40
5Jun82 ^{5}GG^{7}	Fancher Dancer	b 6 114	4	11	5^{hd}	$5^{1½}$	6½	6^{1}	Rond D	6500	10.10
19May82 ^{2}GG^{7}	Safeway Pat	b 4 110	11	8	8^{2}	7½	8^{1}	7½	Dillenbeck B D^{5}	6500	16.90
5Jun82 ^{5}GG^{6}	River Loom	b 5 114	3	5	1½	1^{1}	3^{hd}	8½	Stallings W E	6500	16.00
5Jun82 ^{5}GG^{5}	Field Maid	5 114	2	6	6^{1}	$8^{1½}$	10½	9^{1}	Tohill K S	6500	7.20
5Jun82 ^{5}GG^{10}	Frau	7 114	12	3	9½	11^{1}	12	10^{hd}	Campbell B C	6500	26.20
20May82 ^{5}GG^{2}	Sunshine Beach	4 112	8	9	11½	12	11^{1}	11^{nk}	Winick D	6250	18.30
20May82 ^{5}GG^{8}	Manzana Blue	b 6 114	1	7	2½	3^{hd}	5½	12	SchvaneveldtCP	6500	65.30

OFF AT 3:10. Start good. Won driving. Time, :22⅗, :46⅕, :59⅕, 1:12⅗ Track fast.

$2 Mutuel Prices:			
10–EXCESSIVA	34.60	14.60	8.80
7–HERE COMES HELP		5.40	3.20
5–ROLL ON LILI			4.80

$5 EXACTA 10–7 PAID $489.00

Dk. b. or br. f, by Excessive II—Empress Stacy, by War Emperor. Trainer Buc Joe. Bred by Enriquez C (Cal).

EXCESSIVA, reserved early, raced wide on the turn, remainded far out for the drive and closed steadily to edge HERE COMES HELP. The latter, just off the early leaders, moved out for room into the stretch and closed gamely to just miss. ROLL ON LILI, off slowly, was far back to the stretch, came out for the drive and closed well in the final furlong. COCKATRICE, far back early, was forced far wide for room in the drive and was slowly gaining. ESCORT'S JOY prompted the pace to the stretch and weakened. FANCHER DANCER moved up on the turn, lacked room in midstretch and could not recover. SAFEWAY PAT lacked the needed rally. RIVER LOOM dueled for the lead to midstretch and gave way. FIELD MAID showed little. FRAU raced wide and was outrun. MANZANA BLUE prompted the early pace and stopped.

Owners— 1, Buc Janet; 2, Gatto F; 3, Faris G; 4, Acdy Jr-Blumkin-Gffrd-Kln; 5, Marshall J C; 6, Boles H C; 7, Dallara-Muniz-Tagliaferri-Wenzell; 8, Thrush-Thrush-Cowan; 9, Seley J H; 10, Frankfurt Stable; 11, Chommanard B; 12, McDowell Mary M.

What goes on here? In five races, we have passed three. We have one winner and one horse out of the money for our two plays. With a $34.60 price following a $45.40 ticket, the long shot players are reveling. Ordinarily, when the two top betting choices show no form defects, you can expect one of them to win. While Here Comes Help battled gamely down to the wire to lose by a nose, Escort's Joy showed almost nothing and finished back in the pack. Every experienced player knows by now that this is what happens so often at the track, despite the soundest ratings of mankind.

As we crank up for the sixth race, it would be pleasant to find a winner again. The claiming price has gone upward to $25,000, so we have a better quality of horse, as we survey the favorite, the lightly raced filly, Impeccably Yours.

6th Golden Gate

6 FURLONGS. (1.07%) CLAIMING. Purse $11,000. Fillies. 3-year-olds. Bred in California. Weight, 120 lbs. Non-winners of two races since May 1 allowed 3 lbs.; a race since then, 6 lbs. Claiming price $25,000; for each $2,500 to $20,000 allowed 1 lb. (Maiden, starter and claiming races for $18,000 or less not considered.)

Impeccably Yours

Dk. b. or br. f. 3, by Ruken—Tip's Surprise, by Everett's Bid
Br.—George B & Connie (Cal)   1982 4 1 1 0 $5,720
Own.—Carfella-Keller-Meyers-Utley **114**   Tr.—Utley Doug $25,000   1981 0 M 0 0
Lifetime   4 1 1 0 $5,720

27May82-7GG	6f :223 :454 1:114ft	4½ 114	32½ 2¹ 1½ 2³	Gonzalez RM² Ⓕ	25000	77	HppyRdr,ImpccblyYors,FrsnoC⁊yn 8
14May82-6GG	6f :221 :46 1:124ft	*2½ 114	31½ 3¹ 3½ 53¾	Gonzalez RM⁷ Ⓕ	25000	71	ColdwaterCanyon,AnnSham,Cutesy 7
6May82-7GG	6f :214 :453 1:122ft	2½ 114	41½ 44½ 58½ 71⁴	Gonzalez RM² Ⓕ	35000	63	TorchyMartini,DreamGal,SrSunrise 8
22Apr82-3GG	6f :222 :46 1:112ft	2 117	3² 2hd 1⁴ 1⁸	GonzlzRM⁷ ⒻⓈM	16000	82	ImpccblyYors,PcHstr,BlEydDchss 10

Jun 12 GG 5f ft 1:01² h   Jun 7 GG 3f ft :36¹ h   May 24 GG 5f ft 1:00 h   May 1 GG 5f ft 1:01 h

RECENCY: She is right on the line at 21 days since her last race. But ah, there is the five furlong workout only five days ago that makes us smile. We start with the necessary N for non-applicable.

RUNNING LINE: While this one is close to a +, it does not quite make it, because her finish in her prior six furlong race was a full three lengths behind. A chart call at the finish line between the first two horses is likely to be the most accurate call of all. So, we get another N here.

FORM CYCLE: The last two races were run at the same class level within appropriate time frames, so we can compare them. This filly was almost one length closer to the front in her last race than in her previous start. This allows us to go to the next step, comparing final winning times of the last two races. The last race winning time at the same $25,000 claiming price was one second faster. By merely looking at the speed ratings, since we are dealing with the same distance and the same track (the only time speed ratings are totally reliable), we can see that Impeccably Yours ran six ticks faster in her last race. This wins a + for improvement.

STRETCH PERFORMANCE: We now come to the most difficult decision. There is the obvious stretch loss which otherwise would be a O factor. You have already noted the same $25,000 claiming tag. Now look at the conditions again. Today's race is restricted to California-breds. The race on May 27 was open to any competitor at the assigned price level. We have previously said that state-bred races are at a lower level of competition than open events at the same claiming price. This is critically important here.

A horse losing ground in the stretch after being up close is often a strong play when the level of competition eases off a bit, because the horse is able to hang on and not give ground. This is sufficient here to rate Impeccably Yours with an N, because there is a true decline in level of competition. We now show the following:

Impeccably Yours: N N + N

The second choice is Coldwater Canyon, coming down from an open allowance event. Since we have already stressed the lower level of competition in state-bred races, you now know, as you apply form ratings on our four factors, that we must deal with a drop in class here.

RECENCY: This filly has not run in 22 days, just over the line we like to see. But not only is there a four furlong workout four days previously, but a week prior to that, Coldwater Canyon worked a demanding seven furlongs. These workouts eliminate the recency problem and she gets an N rating.

Coldwater Canyon — Ch. f. 3, by Sun Canyon—Guarded Lady, by Advance Guard
Br.—Mole-Richardson (Cal) — 1982 8 3 1 1 $23,360
Own.—Double M Racing Stable — 117 — Tr.—Friday Charles — $25,000 — 1981 4 1 2 0 $5,090
Lifetime 12 4 3 1 $28,450

26May82-6GG	6f	:22^3	:46	1:11^{2}ft	10	113	2½	21½	46	59¼	Mills J W^6	Ⓕ Aw12000	73	TorchyMrtini,GllntTribut,DundDncr	6
14May82-6GG	6f	:22^1	:46	1:12^{4}ft	7	117	2hd	1hd	1hd	1hd	Mills J W^3	Ⓕ 25000	75	ColdwaterCanyon,AnnSham,Cu:esy	7
23Apr82-7GG	6f	:22^3	:46	1:12 ft	3¾	117	2hd	2hd	23	45½	Mills J W^6	Ⓕ[S] 25000	73	AnnSham,SaraSunrise,BeMyBargin	7
2Apr82-6GG	6f	:23	:46^2	1:13 sy	2¼	114	1hd	2hd	2½	1hd	Nicolo P^3	Ⓕ 25000	74	ColdwterCnyon,SplendidMrk,Cutsy	6
16Mar82-7GG	6f	:22^3	:46^1	1:12^{4}m	7	114	2hd	1hd	12	21	Nicolo P^1	Ⓕ 25000	74	FnlJdgmnt,ColdwtrCnyon,NtrllyGd	6
11Feb82-2GG	6f	:22^3	:46^3	1:13^{1}ft	*8-5	114	23	22	2hd	11½	Lamance C^6	Ⓕ 16000	73	ColdwtrCnyon,AnnShm,DncN.Crck	7
3Feb82-7BM	6f	:22^4	:47	1:12^{3}ft	*2¼e	114	42½	31½	1½	32½	Lamance C^8	Ⓕ 16000	74	DrmGl,FinlJudgmnt,ColdwtrCnyon	11
8Jan82-7BM	6f	:23^1	:47^2	1:13^{4}gd	6¾e	114	21½	21	2hd	53¼	Lamance C^7	Ⓕ 20000	68	DoublHostss,LodogLl,Jdy'sWordr	11
17Dec81-5BM	6f	:23^1	:47^2	1:12^{4}gd	7	112	2½	1½	42	1011	Lamance C^{12}	Ⓕ 20000	65	CountrfitCoin,MissGlry,HobiKittn	12
25Nov81-5BM	6f	:23	:46^4	1:12^{4}gd	*2¼	114	2hd	12	12	2¾	LamnceC^7	Ⓕ[S] c16000	75	Lita'sImage,ColdwterCnyon,Sisson	9

Jun 13 GG 4f ft :48^3 h — Jun 6 GG 7f ft 1:29^2 h — May 23 GG 3f ft :35^3 h — ●May 9 GG 5f ft 1:00^3 h

RUNNING LINE: Coldwater Canyon was not up close at the stretch call in her last race, and was fading fast. But since it was at a higher class level than today's event, we only have to look for an up close at any call. That is easily found at the first two calls, and we have another N here.

FORM CYCLE: We might play a bit with this one, since the last race showed a perceptible falloff. Her last race was much weaker than the previous event, as the key element here is level of competition. Even though there is not a great difference, the allowance event, because no horse is running for a price tag, is slightly higher than the open $25,000 claiming level. We stick to our rule of an N, although a falloff of this proportion is not promising.

STRETCH PERFORMANCE: As with our previous discussion, here is another N, because she was not up close at the stretch call.

Once again, we have the first two betting choices with no form defects. Impeccably Yours carries the improvement + against a dubious N rating for Coldwater Canyon in the same department. But our rule of play for this chapter is that we back the favorite when there are no form defects. Impeccably Yours scored a convincing Big Win victory, as you can see from the chart on the following page.

Ah, this is much better. We are back to the winner's circle. Coldwater Canyon even ran a healthy second, as these two pulled away from the field. This is how we like to see our form ratings

SIXTH RACE
Golden Gate
JUNE 17, 1982

6 FURLONGS. (1.07⅘) CLAIMING. Purse $11,000. Fillies. 3-year-olds. Bred in California. Weight, 120 lbs. Non-winners of two races since May 1 allowed 3 lbs.; a race since then, 6 lbs. Claiming price $25,000; for each $2,500 to $20,000 allowed 1 lb. (Maiden, starter and claiming races for $18,000 or less not considered.)

Value of race $11,000, value to winner $6,050, second $2,145, third $1,540, fourth $990, fifth $275. Mutuel pool $131,955.

Last Raced	Horse	Eqt.A.Wt	PP	St	¼	½	Str	Fin	Jockey	Cl'g Pr	Odds $1
27May82 ^{7}GG^2	Impeccably Yours	b 3 114	4	1	4^3	3^4	1^1	1^3	Gonzalez R M	25000	2.10
26May82 ^{6}GG^5	Coldwater Canyon	3 117	1	3	1^{hd}	1½	2^5	2^5	Mills J W	25000	3.40
27May82 ^{7}GG^5	Poco Heister	b 3 110	3	2	3½	4^{hd}	4^2	3$2\frac{1}{2}$	Dillenbeck BD^5	25000	11.40
4Jun82 ^{4}GG^2	Tronds Key	b 3 112	2	4	2$1\frac{1}{2}$	2^{hd}	3$1\frac{1}{2}$	4^{hd}	Lamance C	20000	3.60
26May82 ^{4}GG^2	Be My Bargain	3 114	5	6	6$1\frac{1}{2}$	7	7	5½	Baze R A	25000	3.80
6May82 ^{7}GG^6	Lucky Jackie	3 114	6	5	5^3	5^3	5^1	6^{hd}	McGurn C	25000	24.40
27May82 ^{7}GG^6	Sara Sunrise	3 114	7	7	7	6^1	6½	7	Munoz E	25000	10.00

OFF AT 3:40. Start good. Won driving. Time, :22⅕, :45⅗, :58⅕, 1:11⅗ Track fast.

$2 Mutuel Prices:			
4-IMPECCABLY YOURS	6.20	3.80	2.80
1-COLDWATER CANYON		4.20	3.20
3-POCO HEISTER			4.40

Dk. b. or br. f, by Ruken—Tip's Surprise, by Everett's Bid. Trainer Utley Doug. Bred by George B & Connie (Cal).

IMPECCABLY YOURS, reserved just off the early leaders, moved up on the turn, gained command in midstretch and was hard ridden to prevail. COLDWATER CANYON dueled for the lead to the upper stretch, could not match the winner but held for the place. POCO HEISTER, well-placed early, finished evenly in the drive.

turn out, and now with two winners out of three plays, we can go to another six furlong sprint for fairly decent three-year-old allowance fillies.

7th Golden Gate

6 FURLONGS. (1.07⅘) ALLOWANCE. Purse $13,000. Fillies. 3-year-olds. Non-winners of $2,500 twice other than maiden or claiming. Weight, 120 lbs. Non-winners of one such race since May 1 allowed 3 lbs.; one such race since April 1, 5 lbs.; one suich race since March 1, 7 lbs.

Aunt Lin — **Own.—Frankel J** — **120**

B. f. 3, by Vitriolic—Ribot's Pride, by Ribot
Br.—Frankel J (Ky) — 1982 4 2 1 0 $14,990
Tr.—Handwerker Robert I — 1981 4 M 0 0 $2,475
Lifetime 8 2 1 0 $17,465

9Jun82-6GG	6f	:21^4	:44^4	1:10^{3}ft	*1	106	2^1	1½	1^3	1$3\frac{1}{2}$	Winick D^3	ⒻAw12000	86	Aunt Lin, Jendaya, Donna Duck	6
26Jan82-4BM	6f	:23	:47	1:13^{2}sy	*9-5	117	1^1	1^2	1^4	1^7	Meza R Q^4	ⒻMdn	73	AuntLin,SplendidMark,SwapsCme	10
19Jan82-4BM	1$\frac{1}{16}$	:47^2	1:13^2	1:48 sy	*3-2	117	1$1\frac{1}{2}$	1$1\frac{1}{2}$	1^{hd}	2^2	Nicolo P^4	ⒻMdn	57	SurelyWinnr,AuntLin,CottonCndy	10
2Jan82-6SA	6½f	:22^4	:47^4	1:21^{4}hy	7½	117	1^{hd}	1^{hd}	6$8\frac{3}{4}$	—	Sibille R^4	ⒻMdn	—	TripleMch,RgingStorm,SnowDncr	11
2Jan82—Eased															
18Nov81-6Hol	6f	:22	:45	1:10^{3}ft	9½	117	5$3\frac{1}{2}$	3^3	3^5	4^3	Castaneda M^6	ⒻMdn	81	FilomenGle,IrishBlld,Melind'sP'um	9
9Nov81-4SA	6f	:21^4	:45^1	1:11 ft	4	115	1^{hd}	1½	1^{hd}	4$4\frac{1}{4}$	Shoemaker W^2	ⒻMdn	79	Deianira, Miss Cup, Filomena Calea	9
1Nov81-3SA	6f	:22	:44^4	1:10^{1}ft	41	115	1½	2^{hd}	3½	6$4\frac{1}{4}$	Sibille R^7	ⒻMdn	83	Vihava,Marie'sFastLass,HwiinShke	8
20Oct81-4SA	6f	:21^4	:45^2	1:11^{2}ft	6¼	115	2^{hd}	1^{hd}	3^3	9^{12}	Sibille R^1	ⒻMdn	69	FlyngPrtnr,WrldfSzyWng,SnDncr	10

Jun 7 GG 3f ft :39^4 b ●May 31 GG 6f ft 1:11 hg May 25 GG 5f ft 1:03^3 h May 19 GG 4f ft :47^1 h

Here we have a very strong favorite, at 3-2 on the board. Her last race, off a long layoff, was indeed a power house.

RECENCY: The eight days off the last race is not quite enough to get the coveted +, but you can see that there is a strong desire to get this filly back into action quickly.

RUNNING LINE: This is easily a strong +, up close at every call.

FORM CYCLE: There is no comparison race to measure improvement and decline, because Aunt Lin's last race was her first since January. But we do have a horse coming off a Big Win for consideration. We will give her an N for the form cycle improvement factor. Thanks to her impressive Big Win, Aunt Lin gets a + for the stretch performance factor. In evaluating the likelihood that this filly will be a repeat winner, we can see that there is a bit of a class level problem. Aunt Lin is obviously climbing one more rung up the condition ladder, since today she is competing against non-winners of two races other than maiden or claiming. But when we look at Aunt Lin's form rating line, we have our answer.

Aunt Lin: N + N +

We have a Big Win coupled with one other plus form factor—the last race running line. Since this filly is lightly raced, she may be logically moving her way upward. If we do not throw her out because of her last victory, she is our play. Off a strong race like the last one, with the factors we have written about, she becomes our selection.

But even though we are bound by our rules as a testing device, we will look at the second choice in the betting, another lightly raced filly. Dundee Dancer is racing above her conditions, since she has only a maiden victory in four starts.

Dundee Dancer

B. f. 3, by Gaelic Dancer—Scorer's Envoy, by Envoy

Br.—Mowat D A (Wash)   1982 4 1 1 1 $12,790

Own.—Willis Virginia   **113**   Tr.—Willis Barney   1981 0 M 0 0

Lifetime   4 1 1 1 $12,790

26May82-6GG	6f :223 :46 1:112ft	8-5 117	31½ 31½ 33 31½	CmpbllBC1	⑤Aw12000 80	TorchyMrtini,GllntTribut,DundDncr 6
13May82-4GG	6f :22 :453 1:104ft	*2-3 114	56½ 42½ 22 25	CmpbllBC2	⑤Aw13000 80	UnchinMyHert,DundeeDncr,CoulBy 6
7May82-8GG	6f :214 :45 1:111ft	3½ 112	78½ 76½ 46½ 42½	Campbell B	⑤Prtla 81	GrwngRgrd,AnglNckdHr,MssPrknss 8
20Apr82-6GG	6f :222 :453 1:103ft	4½ 117	55 42½ 1hd 13½	Campbell B C8	⑥Mdn 86	DundeeDncer,Doonble,AngorBgor 10

RECENCY: There is a 22-day gap from the last race, and rules are rules, so with the absence of a qualifying workout, we have to award the unwanted O here.

RUNNING LINE: Although there is a O for recency, since the last race was run in 28 days or less, we can still rate the running line. The exact three lengths behind at the stretch call would not otherwise qualify in a six furlong race, but we have a sufficient fall back-gain pattern from the second call, to the stretch, to the finish to award the N rating.

FORM CYCLE: Since we see one length farther back at the stretch call of the last race than in the previous contest, when both were at the approximate same class, we can run through our paces to test for decline. The last race was run three-fifths of a second slower than the previous event. If Dundee Dancer had run one second slower, she would be a declining horse. But she ran in the same time in both races, and since the last race winning time was slower, you can see that she is not a declining horse. She gets an N for this factor.

STRETCH PERFORMANCE: This factor is not applicable here, because she was not up close at the stretch call.

Dundee Dancer: O N N N

The chart makes our selection of Aunt Lin look very good.

SEVENTH RACE
Golden Gate
JUNE 17, 1982

6 FURLONGS. (1.07%) ALLOWANCE. Purse $13,000. Fillies. 3-year-olds. Non-winners of $2,500 twice other than maiden or claiming. Weight, 120 lbs. Non-winners of one such race since May 1 allowed 3 lbs.; one such race since April 1, 5 lbs.; one suich race since March 1, 7 lbs.

Value of race $13,000, value to winner $7,150, second $2,535, third $1,820, fourth $1,170, fifth $325. Mutuel pool $80,991

Last Raced	Horse	Eqt.A.Wt PP St	¼	½	Str	Fin	Jockey	Odds $1
9Jun82 6GG1	Aunt Lin	3 120 3 2	3 1½	4 1½	1 hd	1 2	Winick D	1.60
3Jun82 8GG5	Pass of Gold	b 3 113 1 10	9 2	8 1½	4 1½	2 nk	Anderson J R	4.00
3Jun82 6GG1	Lita's Image	3 115 9 5	7 2	6 2	5 1	3 1	Burkes T	26.00
30May82 4GG3	Alma's Glass	b 3 113 10 1	2 1	1 hd	2 ½	4 no	Lamance C	14.90
3Jun82 8GG6	Then Play On	3 115 5 8	8 1½	7 1	7 2	5 1½	Baze R A	7.90
26May82 6GG3	Dundee Dancer	b 3 113 2 7	5 hd	5 1½	6 hd	6 1½	Chapman T M	3.60
27Dec81 10TuP11	Gusto Gal	3 113 7 6	6 2	2 ½	3 1½	7 1½	Schvaneveldt C P	8.80
30May82 4GG7	Amazing Urmanski	b 3 113 4 4	4 hd	9 4	8 3	8 9	Gonzalez R M	51.80
30May82 4GG4	Rising Love	3 113 8 3	1 1½	3 1	9 4	9 3	Tohill K S	36.10
12May82 8GG4	Sanches	3 113 6 9	10	10	10	10	Winland W M	49.00

OFF AT 4:12. Start good. Won driving. Time, :22, :45, :58⅕, 1:11 Track fast.

$2 Mutuel Prices:	3-AUNT LIN	5.20	3.20	3.00
	1-PASS OF GOLD		4.00	3.60
	9-LITA'S IMAGE			6.00

$5 EXACTA 3-1 PAID $67.00

B. f, by Vitriolic—Ribot's Pride, by Ribot. Trainer Handwerker Robert I. Bred by Frankel J (Ky).

AUNT LIN, just off the early leaders to the stretch, rallied outside horses into the stretch and responded gamely to urging to draw clear. PASS OF GOLD broke slowly and raced far back to the stretch, was forced far wide for room into the stretch and finished well for the place. LITA'S IMAGE, reserved early, moved well out into the stretch, lugged inward through the drive and was slowly gaining. ALMA'S GLASS dueled for the lead to midstretch but had little left. THEN PLAY ON, outrun early, rallied inside in the drive and was slowly gaining. DUNDEE DANCER, reserved early, lacked room in midstretch and could not recover.

Now, we are picking up some steam, with three winners out of four plays after seven races. The eighth race is a one mile allowance race on the grass for fillies who have never won a race of a mile or longer. The females dominate the card today. Two of them are almost even in the betting, both showing at 9-5 on the board. We can first study Beautiful Dawn, who has a few dollars less in the win pool than her major rival.

8th Golden Gate

1 MILE. (TURF). (1.33⅗) ALLOWANCE. Purse $15,000. Fillies and mares. 3-year-olds and upward. Non-winners of a race at one mile or over anytime. Weights, 3-year-olds, 112 lbs.; older, 120 lbs. Non-winners of two races since May 1 allowed 3 lbs.; two races since April 1, 5 lbs.; a race since May 1, 7 lbs. (Maiden, starter and claiming races not considered.)

Beautiful Dawn

Own.—V H Graber Estate   **120**

B. f. 4, by Grey Dawn II—Nevada Lark, by T V Lark
Br.—Graber V (Ky)
Tr.—Brook Joseph

		1982	4	2	1	1	$20,480
		1981	2	1	0	1	$12,350
	Lifetime	6	3	1	2	$32,830	

10Jun82-8GG	6f :22¹ :45 1:10¹ft	*6-5 115	3½	2hd. 2hd 2½	Meza R Q⁵	ⓕAw16000	87	Roz H.,BeautifulDawn,Misanthropy 6
30May82-4GG	6f :22 :45² 1:11 ft	*4-5 122	42½	2hd 12 16	Meza R Q³	ⓕAw14000	84	BeautifulDawn,Jendaya,A!ma'sGlss 7
20May82-8GG	6f :22 :45 1:11²ft	*1-2 113	3½	12 14 15	Meza R Q¹	ⓕAw14000	82	BeautifulDwn,Pnnyslstctch,Prof:ınd 6
29Apr82-7GG	6f :22¹ :45² 1:11²ft	3½ 113	96½	911 77½ 3¹	StruserCE²	ⓕAw14000	81	Gismond,ShWon'tPnic,ButifulDwn 12
17Oct81-7SA	7f :22⁴ :45³ 1:23 ft	3½ 117	1½	22 2³ 35½	McCrrnCJ³	ⓕAw20000	80	MissPeruvin,BronzeLily,ButifulDwn 7
2Oct81-2SA	6½f :22¹ :45³ 1:18²ft	*8-5 112⁵	1hd	13 15 15¼	Winland W M⁹	ⓕMdn	76	BetifulDwn,TimeforRedchcks,Jujub 9

●May 12 GG ⑦ 5f fm 1:01 h (d) ●May 7 GG ⑦ 3f fm :36 h (d)   Apr 25 GG 4f ft :48³ h   ●Apr 20 GG 6f ft 1:12 h

RECENCY: This filly ran seven days ago and thus gets a + rating.

RUNNING LINE: Another + turns up again, as this filly was up close at every call.

FORM CYCLE: While Beautiful Dawn was two lengths farther back in comparison with her last race, she ran at least three-fifths of a second faster, as we can see by comparing the 87 speed rating to the 84. And so she gets an N for neutral.

STRETCH PERFORMANCE: The slight stretch loss is less than a length and is not to be considered harmful. This well backed filly is obviously an enticing play, with three victories in six starts and a finish in the money in every outing. But there is one big rap on her. This race is on the grass and she has not competed on the turf thus far. Even with grass workouts showing, this was the kind of animal that would have received a U for unknown in *Investing at the Racetrack*, and one which experience tells us must be avoided. I am well aware that some very good turf students will go to a horse with no grass experience based upon grass breeding, but if there is something else in the race that looks formidable on the grass, then Beautiful Dawn would be a risky bet indeed.

This brings us to the veteran mare, Flying Jen. Even though she was running in claiming races back in 1981, Flying Jen has finished in the money in each of her three grass races, although she has not yet won on the turf.

Flying Jen * — **Ch. m. 6, by Leonardo III—Inventory, by Bobillard**
Own.—Santucci G — **113** — **Br.—Factor S (Cal)** — **Tr.—Pollard Damon**

1982	1	0	1	0	$2,925
1981	13	4	1	2	$32,579
Lifetime	33	8	4	7	$70,449
Turf	3	0	1	2	$5,305

30May82-6GG	1	Ⓣ$:48^4 1:13^2 1:39^1$fm	6½	114	6^6	$6^{3½}$	5^6	$2^{¾}$	Baze R A^1	ⒻAw15000	70	ForgottnRulr,FlyingJn,HltoBoldnss	8
7Sep81-7Bmf	1 1/16	$:47^1 1:12^1 1:45$ ft	*3-2	115	7^{11}	5^4	5^7	5^8	Munoz E^5	Ⓕ 20000	66	PeeWeeBarb,BagofChrm,Kitty'sBy	7
21Aug81-11Stk	1 1/16	$:46 1:10^3 1:42^3$ft	2½	113	7^{13}	$4^{7½}$	$4^{7½}$	4^{12}	MnzE^1	ⒻM Dotson H	81	RomanRockette,Legere,TorndoRed	8
6Aug81-11SR	1 1/16	$:45^3 1:09^2 1:41^4$ft	10	107	5^{10}	$6^{7½}$	5^4	$3^{1½}$	WinickD^6	ⒻL Burbk H	95	Coul Victress,Here'sHow,FlyingJen	7
25Jly81-10Sol	1	$:46^4 1:11 1:37^3$ft	*2¼	116	10^{10}	$9^{7¼}$	$4^{3½}$	$1^{¾}$	Munoz E^7	Ⓕ 20000	89	FlyingJen,Kitty'sBay,Ms.Attababe	10
26Jun81-6GG	1 1/16	Ⓣ$:47^3 1:12^3 1:44^4$fm	4½	114	4^8	3^3	3^3	3^4	Munoz E^1	Ⓕ 22500	74	Miki F., Safesilver, Flying Jen	7
21Jun81-1GG	1 1/16	$:47^2 1:11^3 1:44$ ft	3½	114	$5^{4¼}$	1^{hd}	1^1	1^3	Munoz E^2	Ⓕ 16000	83	FlyingJen,PeeWeeBrb,Slri'sOlympis	8
7Jun81-3GG	1 1/16	$:46^3 1:10^4 1:43^1$ft	*2¼	114	$6^{7¾}$	$6^{4¼}$	4^4	$4^{2½}$	Munoz E^1	Ⓕ 16000	84	NoMrEnmy,‡RpOffSkr,Slr'sOlymps	7
17May81-1GG	1	$:45^4 1:10^4 1:36^2$ft	2½	117	6^9	$3^{3½}$	$2^{1½}$	2^3	Munoz E^6	Ⓕ 18000	83	Ms. Attababe, Flying Jen, JayJ.May	7
10May81-7GG	1 1/16	$:45^3 1:10^1 1:43^4$ft	*2¼	117	9^{17}	9^{11}	5^6	4^{nk}	Mena F^8	Ⓕ 16000	84	FntsticLiz,Ms.Attbbe,NoMorEnmy	10

●Jun 10 GG 7f ft $1:26^2$ h   May 21 GG 7f ft 1:27 h   May 14 GG 6f ft 1:15 h

Recency: The last race was 18 days ago, sufficient for an N, but there was also a bullet seven furlong workout a week before today's race, and while impressive, does not elevate recency into a +, because we give credit for bullet works only at five furlongs.

Running Line: The last good effort was on the grass and can be rated. At the stretch, Flying Jen was well back, but she scored an impressive gain as she almost won the race. Once again, we see the strong fall back–gain pattern from the second call, to the stretch, to the finish. This pattern is an exception to the stretch call up close requirement, and allows us to qualify Flying Jen with an N rating.

Form Cycle and Stretch Performance: Since the last race was the first one of the season, there is no comparison event. The big stretch gain is worth no more than an N for stretch performance, and we get a contender whose form line looks like this: N N N N

The question now is whether we play Flying Jen, who is actually the favorite, or Beautiful Dawn. The latter's lack of turf form is too much of an uncertainty to make her a reliable play.

Flying Jen's last strong effort plus the good seven furlong workout, is an indication that she is ready. The only possible weakness is her 1981 claiming record, but based on the last race, at the same class of today's event, she is our choice. Flying Jen did not let us down.

EIGHTH RACE
Golden Gate
JUNE 17, 1982

1 MILE.(turf). (1.33⅗) ALLOWANCE. Purse $15,000. Fillies and mares. 3-year-olds and upward. Non-winners of a race at one mile or over anytime. Weights, 3-year-olds, 112 lbs.; older, 120 lbs. Non-winners of two races since May 1 allowed 3 lbs.; two races since April 1, 5 lbs.; a race since May 1, 7 lbs. (Maiden, starter and claiming races not considered.)

Value of race $15,000, value to winner $8,250, second $2,925, third $2,100, fourth $1,350, fifth $375. Mutuel pool $153,462.

Last Raced	Horse	Eqt.	A.	Wt	PP	St	¼	½	¾	Str	Fin	Jockey	Odds $1
30May82 6GG2	Flying Jen	b	6	114	5	9	9	8^{hd}	6^{hd}	$4^{\frac{1}{2}}$	1^{hd}	Baze R A	1.80
9Jun82 3Hol2	[D]Star Mine		4	113	3	2	$3^{1\frac{1}{2}}$	3^4	3^3	$1^{\frac{1}{2}}$	2^2	Winland W M	6.60
5Jun82 4GG5	Raise a Nan		4	113	2	5	7^1	7^{hd}	8^6	$6^{1\frac{1}{2}}$	$3^{2\frac{1}{2}}$	Rosales R	65.10
3Jun82 8GG4	Cotton Candy		3	112	9	7	$5^{\frac{1}{2}}$	$5^{\frac{1}{2}}$	4^{hd}	5^{hd}	$4^{\frac{3}{4}}$	Lamance C	10.10
22May82 4GG6	Good Equation		4	113	6	4	4^3	4^{hd}	5^2	7^3	5^1	Mills J W	22.10
27May82 8GG7	Solar Sands	b	4	113	4	1	1^2	1^2	1^{hd}	$2^{\frac{1}{2}}$	$6^{1\frac{1}{2}}$	Chapman T M	46.80
29May82 8GG5	Sleep On It		5	113	8	6	6^3	6^3	$7^{\frac{1}{2}}$	8^4	7^{hd}	Anderson J R	6.30
10Jun82 8GG2	Beautiful Dawn	b	4	120	1	3	$2^{1\frac{1}{2}}$	$2^{1\frac{1}{2}}$	$2^{1\frac{1}{2}}$	$3^{1\frac{1}{2}}$	$8^{2\frac{1}{2}}$	Ochoa A	1.90
28May82 9GG1	Sensational Kiss	b	5	113	7	8	8^2	9	9	9	9	Hummel C R	21.20

[D]-Star Mine Disqualified and placed third.

OFF AT 4:43. Start good. Won driving. Time, :23⅕, :47⅕, 1:12, 1:25⅕, 1:38⅘ Course firm.

$2 Mutuel Prices:				
	5-FLYING JEN	5.60	3.80	3.00
	2-RAISE A NAN		42.20	11.00
	3-STAR MINE			3.80

Ch. m, by Leonardo III—Inventory, by Bobillard. Trainer Pollard Damon. Bred by Factor S (Cal).

FLYING JEN, allowed to lag well back early, moved up wide on the second turn, remained far out into the stretch, lugged inward under pressure bumping SLEEP ON IT in the upper stretch and closed steadily to edge STAR MINE. The latter, just off the leaders to the stretch, rallied willingly between horses in midstretch to gain command, drifted out sharply in the deep stretch and just failed to last. Following claims of foul by RAISE A NAN and COTTON CANDY'S riders against STAR MINE, the latter was disqualified and placed third. RAISE A NAN, unhurried for six furlongs, rallied between horses in the stretch run, steadied and altered course in the deep stretch and could not recover. COTTON CANDY, reserved early while slightly wide, tired to rally between horses in midstretch, was steadied in the late stages and could not recover. GOOD EQUATION, reserved early, lacked the needed rally. SOLAR SANDS dueled for the lead to midstretch and faltered. SLEEP ON IT, reserved early, was bumped and took up sharply in the upper stretch to lose all chance. BEAUTIFUL DAWN attended the early pace, moved wide at the quarter pole to challenge and stopped suddenly in the final furlong.

We are now to the ninth race, with three winners in a row, and four in five plays. In this starter allowance at a mile and three-sixteenths the big favorite was Gypsie Sister, going off at 4-5.

9th Golden Gate

1 $\frac{3}{16}$ MILES. (1.52⅘) STARTER ALLOWANCE. Purse $6,500. 4-year-olds and upward, which have started for a claiming price of $6,500 or less in 1981–82 and since that start have not won a race other than maiden, starter or claiming, or a claiming or starter race exceeding $6,500. Weight, 122 lbs. Non-winners of two starter races since May 1 allowed 3 lbs.; two such races since April 1, 5 lbs.; one such race since May 1, 8 lbs.; one such race since April 1, 10 lbs. (Maiden, starter and claiming races for $5,000 or less not considered.)

How would you rate the two betting choices, Gypsie Sister and Mercator? Both are coming off remarkably strong Big Wins and both have another plus factor, which bodes well for their chances to be repeat winners. Mercator brings in a bullet workout at six furlongs in genuinely fast time, which is also quite impressive.

Gypsie Sister

B. m. 5, by War Helmet—Tender Trap, by Tovel
Br.—Morton Mr—Mrs H D (Cal)   1982 6 3 0 0 $12,100
Own.—Buckley-Enbom-Enbom   1075   Tr.—Jenda C J   1980 11 2 0 1 $10,929
Lifetime   17 5 0 1 $23,029

Date	Dist					Wt						Jockey		Odds	Field
3Jun82-9GG	1₁/₁₆:483 1:131 1:581ft	*3-2 1035	1¹	1hd	1⁶	1⁶	English T L⁵	A6500 72	Gypsie Sister,SilverMoney,VictorE. 7
15May82-3GG	1₁/₁₆:471 1:12 1:434ft	5¹/₂ 1045	1⁴	1²	1⁵	1⁷	English T⁸	6500 84	GypsieSister,NobleHeir,FiveofHerts 8
20Apr82-7GG	6f :224 :461 1:113ft	3 114	11¹/₂	11¹/₂	2¹	64¹/₂	Meza R Q⁶	ⓕ 8500 76	MyrtleAToo,ShronsGryDwn,Mirge 11
8Apr82-7GG	6f :224 :463 1:114ft	3 117	31¹/₂	32¹/₂	89	81²	Meza R Q⁵	ⓕ 16000 68	BdBdLucy,ShWon'tPnic,Don'sHony 8
26Mar82-8GG	6f :223 :453 1:114gd	6¹/₂ 113	3³	3³	56¹/₂	78¹/₂	Meza R Q²	ⓕAw13000 71	MrtilLdy,Olly'sFirebll,ResonbleForc 7
10Mar82-7GG	6f :224 :462 1:113ft	12 114	3nk	11¹/₂	11¹/₂	11¹/₂	Meza R Q⁷	ⓕ 16000 81	GypsieSister,BronzeBobbie,CriMry 10
6Nov80-5BM	1₁/₁₆:463 1:111 1:45 ft	2¹/₂ 114	1¹	11¹/₂	11	1²	Mahorney W⁵	ⓕ 10000 74	GypsieSister,DiMargo,ChrisRmses 11
30Oct80-3BM	6f :223 :453 1:101ft	11 114	74¹/₂	78	58¹/₂	44¹/₂	MahorneyW¹²	ⓕ 12500 84	PricetoPy,BlowingStr,MistyBushl 12
16Oct80-7BM	6f :222 :452 1:104ft	14 114	97¹/₂	87¹/₂	96¹/₂	85¹/₂	Gonzalez RM⁷	ⓕ 16000 81	CottonWings,GrdnngGrl,BrbzonJy 12
30Oct80-2BM	1₁/₁₆:462 1:111 1:44 ft	*3¹/₂ 114	1¹	2hd	2hd	54¹/₂	Hall D C²	ⓕ 12500 74	TudorBronze,ReginG.,ChoiceWord 10

Mercator

B. g. 5, by Verbatim—Farsighted II, by Salvo
Br.—Elmendorf Farm (Ky)   1982 9 2 1 1 $10,348
Own.—Diamond Head Stable   112   Tr.—Wayt Paul O   1981 19 2 1 3 $17,153
Lifetime   41 5 5 6 $39,702

Date	Dist					Wt						Jockey		Odds	Field
30May82-3GG	1₁/₁₆:47 1:113 1:44 ft	7 114	2¹/₂	1¹/₂	1³	1⁶	Gonzalez R M⁶	6500 83	Merctor,FiveofHrts,GivHimWings 10
5May82-9GG	1₁/₁₆:48 1:13 1:594ft	17 113	2¹	2hd	56	77¹/₂	Gonzalez R M⁹	A6500 56	Summit Dance, VictorE.,LetM'Roar 9
16Apr82-2GG	1₁/₁₆:474 1:122 1:443ft	4¹/₂ 114	2²	2hd	2nd	2nk	Gonzalez R M⁴	6500 80	Brioso, Mercator, Cholla	8
13Mar82-5GG	1₁/₁₆:471 1:114 1:464gd	6 114	69¹/₂	59	81²	6⁷	Gonzalez R M³	8500 62	MightyFella,TimeHolder,GoneAgin 10
6Mar82-9GG	1₁/₁₆:47 1:113 1:45 ft	11 114	2¹/₂	2¹/₂	3¹	6³	Nicolo P⁷	12500 75	PowrBrigd,ComonKvn,EglsFlyHgh 11
13Feb82-9GG	1₁/₁₆:474 1:131 1:472sy	11 115	96¹/₂	10¹⁰	712	515	Nicolo P⁵	16000 51	ShrpFddl,VctorousRnnr,Ldy'sAglo 11
30Jan82-5BM	1₁/₁₆:474 1:131 1:463gd	15 115	42¹/₂	2¹	12	1nk	Nicolo P²	11000 66	Mercator, BanjoCreek,FieldForman 8
16Jan82-3BM	1₁/₁₆:47 1:123 1:454ft	4¹/₂ 115	79¹/₂	109¹/₂	99	89¹/₂	Munoz E¹²	c8500 61	O'LckyPt,ScottyMcPhrsn,CndnBd 12
2Jan82-9BM	1₁/₁₆:471 1:133 1:481sy	15 1105	3⁵	31¹/₂	12	31¹/₂	Capitaine N M¹⁰	8500 56	Field Forman, Moonman,Mercator 10
4Dec81-9BM	1¹/₈:47 1:114 1:52 ft	9¹/₂ 113	55¹/₂	44¹/₂	911	106¹/₂	Munoz E²	A6500 64	KnghtlyAnswr,VctorE.,SummtDnc 13

● Jun 11 GG 6f ft 1:12 h   May 21 GG 5f ft 1:01 h

The form ratings on these two horses should be easy, and we might lay them out like this:

Gypsie Sister: N + N +

Mercator: N + N +

The only question you might have would pertain to Mercator's form cycle rating of an N, in view of what looks like an enormous improvement in his last race compared to the previous effort. This gives us the opportunity to make one more observation about levels of competition. The race before you is a starter allowance for horses that have started for a claiming price of $6,500 or less (this is akin to the starter handicaps in the east). Since horses of much higher grade can get into these races, provided they have one race at the designated claiming level somewhere back in the time frame set forth in the conditions, a starter allowance based on a $6,500 claiming price offers a higher level of competition than a mere claiming race with a price of $6,500.

Gypsie Sister, for example, shows only one race at a claiming price of $6,500 (in her race of May 15), and all the others at considerably higher prices. On the whole, Mercator, too, has run at higher levels, but is not quite up to Gypsie Sister in class competitive value. You can see that Gypsie Sister won at $16,000 back in March, while Mercator scored in an $11,000 claimer back in January.

Our play, of course, must go to Gypsie Sister because of her role as a favorite.

NINTH RACE
Golden Gate
JUNE 17, 1982

1 $\frac{3}{16}$ MILES. (1.52$\frac{3}{5}$) STARTER ALLOWANCE. Purse $6,500. 4-year-olds and upward, which have started for a claiming price of $6,500 or less in 1981–82 and since that start have not won a race other than maiden, starter or claiming, or a claiming or starter race exceeding $6,500. Weight, 122 lbs. Non-winners of two starter races since May 1 allowed 3 lbs.; two such races since April 1, 5 lbs.; one such race since May 1, 8 lbs.; one such race since April 1, 10 lbs. (Maiden, starter and claiming races for $5,000 or less not considered.)
Value of race $6,500, value to winner $3,575, second $1,268, third $910, fourth $585, fifth $162. Mutuel pool $55,048. Exacta Pool $130,191.

Last Raced	Horse	Eqt.	A.	Wt	PP	St	¼	½	¾	Str	Fin	Jockey	Odds $1
3Jun82 ^{9}GG^{1}	Gypsie Sister	b	5	107	6	2	2^{2}	$2^{1\frac{1}{2}}$	2^{5}	$1^{\frac{1}{2}}$	1^{nk}	English T L^{5}	.80
30May82 ^{3}GG^{1}	Mercator	b	5	113	5	1	1^{1}	1^{2}	1^{1}	2^{6}	2^{7}	Gonzalez R M	3.40
3Jun82 ^{9}GG^{2}	Silver Money	b	5	114	4	3	3^{hd}	4^{5}	4^{4}	3^{1}	3^{nk}	Anderson J R	4.30
11Jun82 ^{3}GG^{1}	Give Him Wings		4	112	1	6	7	7	7	$4^{\frac{1}{2}}$	$4^{2\frac{1}{2}}$	Tohill K S	10.30
11Jun82 ^{3}GG^{5}	Bobby Goes Astray		4	113	3	4	$4^{1\frac{1}{2}}$	3^{hd}	3^{hd}	5^{6}	5^{7}	Chapman T M	18.40
5Jun82 ^{9}GG^{7}	Emil	b	4	110	7	5	5^{3}	5^{hd}	$5^{1\frac{1}{2}}$	6^{1}	6^{2}	Dillenbeck B D^{5}	27.10
3Jun82 ^{9}GG^{4}	Lafayette Leader	b	6	112	2	7	6^{4}	6^{5}	6^{hd}	7	7	Sorenson D	19.00

OFF AT 5:26 Start good. Won driving. Time, :24, :48, 1:11$\frac{4}{5}$, 1:37$\frac{3}{5}$, 1:58 Track fast.

$2 Mutuel Prices:				
	6–GYPSIE SISTER	3.60	3.00	2.20
	5–MERCATOR		3.80	2.40
	4–SILVER MONEY			2.40

$2 EXACTA 6–5 PAID $12.80

B. m, by War Helmet—Tender Trap, by Tovel. Trainer Jenda C J. Bred by Morton Mr–Mrs H D (Cal).

GYPSIE SISTER attended the pace for six furlongs, moved to gain command into the stretch and responded to steady handling to edge MERCATOR. The latter took command early while in hand, set the pace to the stretch, came back after being headed and just missed. SILVER MONEY, just off the early leaders, lacked the needed response in the drive. GIVE HIM WINGS, far back early, could not offer the needed closing response. BOBBY GOES ASTRAY showed little. EMIL had no rally. LAFAYETTE LEADER was outrun.

Owners— 1, Buckley-Enbom-Enbom; 2, Diamond Head Stable; 3, Chibidakis J & Sharon; 4, Riley G A; 5, Olson V; 6, Peoples-Peoples-Trejos; 7, Duffel J A.

Look at how those two pulled away from the remainder of the field. Gypsie Sister had a very tough time of it, holding off Mercator to win. In a race of this kind, when you have two outstanding competitors with such impressive form, you can be as reasonably sure as anything can be in racing that one of them will win. In view of this, every person who spent a single dollar betting on any other horse in the race was throwing away money. At any time you see two very strong plays together in a race, you can concentrate on them to the exclusion of everything else—with the only real task being of deciding which one is most likely to win.

As we total up the day, we see a mighty good one for favorites.

Race	Selection	W-Bet	P-Bet	W-Return	P-Return
1	Sapience	$ 2	$ 2	$ 5.80	$ 3.20
2	NO PLAY	–	–	–	–
3	NO PLAY	–	–	–	–
4	NO PLAY	–	–	–	–
5	Escort's Joy	2	2	0	0
6	Impeccably Yours	2	2	6.20	3.80
7	Aunt Lin	2	2	5.20	3.20
8	Flying Jen	2	2	5.60	3.80
9	Gypsie Sister	2	2	3.60	3.00
	Totals	$12	$12	$26.40	$17.00

Obviously, this was a very unusual day. Five favorites scoring victories on any racing card is somewhat rare. When I selected this racing day for evaluation and analysis, there was no intention to overwhelm you with unrealistic "goodies." But several important things have been shown.

First of all, when you have strong favorites with positive form, they will usually do well, as research has shown. The Golden Gate example beautifully illustrates this point. Races studied at Hollywood Park basically turn out the same way. When a favorite shows form defects, that favorite is likely to lose, as occurred in two of the races on the card.

Second, you have to stay away from doubtful races, as every veteran player knows. Keeping away from the losers, especially when you are focusing on short-priced horses, is essential to maintain a profit level on the winners you will inevitably have.

Furthermore, a long shot play with strong form and good class rating is an excellent possibility when favored horses come up with weaknesses, as the second race on the card shows.

I would have liked to have had more variety in the Golden Gate card, but that is not always possible on a single day's format. But the major use of the total day's card, looking at every race, was to illustrate our form factors in action and take you with us through the paces to show both how easily it is done and how effective it can be.

And from all this, where do we go from here?

9 Developing Methods of Play Off Form Factors

THROUGHOUT THIS BOOK, we have sought to demonstrate the critical role played by form in relation to levels of competition, in assessing how your horse will run today. From the mass of available material, you have seen that many horses have form elements that are not particularly decisive one way or the other. Some horses are difficult to assess because of variances in their recent action or their class levels.

But from all this, we have searched for those elements of form that have a positive effect, which will show that your horse is likely to run well, and at the same time, have isolated the negatives that lead you toward concluding that a horse will not win. Quite often in this stimulating contest of handicapping horses, the negative factors are more critical than the positive. You may have two or more competitors with positive factors and may find it difficult to decide which one will win. But when there is a negative factor, or a form defect, that is likely to make a horse turn up a loser, you will have achieved a tremendous advantage. Many an old pro has come to the conclusion, "Get rid of the losers and the winners will take care of themselves."

Yet, the evidence is that horses with positive form factors of the kind defined in this book do better than horses with neutral, or non-applicable, characteristics. You might very well build an extremely solid method of play by placing your major emphasis on horses with positive form factors, supplemented by other handicapping requirements.

In discussing what has been learned from the research that went into this book, there has been a heavy emphasis on favorites and near-favorites. While *Investing at the Racetrack* was a restricted method of play for investment purposes and required one to never go beyond the first three favorites in a race, this book is designed for a different purpose. The emphasis here on playing favorites is used simply as a measuring device for that purpose only, and for no other.

First of all, favorites are easily definable. There is one in every race. A favorite is the animal that the purveyors of the greatest amount of money believe is likely to win. How these favored animals perform affects every race. When a favorite is not likely to win, for example, the chances of obtaining good prices on winning horses rises remarkably. But knowing when favorites are likely to win and when they are likely to lose is such a critical piece of information that it can literally dominate any player's handicapping approach.

You can play it from the positive or the negative. But knowledge of, or insight into, how this one animal leading in the wagering will perform can make or break any handicapper's program. You can never afford to overlook how that favorite will run today, whether or not you like the way "he looks."

The importance of the measuring device is the eternal national statistic that favorites win a third, or close to a third, of all races. This benchmark permits a student of the game to test theories, methods and ideas against that well established one-third of winning races guideline. It thus becomes enormously helpful.

With these caveats in mind, we will begin setting forth methods of play built around favorites, either from a positive, neutral, or negative stance. You may want to build upon it, add or subtract, or come up with new approaches in a game that has as many variables in it as would confront any master of the chess board. For example, I learned new things in doing this book in 1982 and into 1983 as well. I expect to learn new things about handicapping horses in 1984 and every year thereafter that I am able to participate in this fascinating game.

In the first chapter, I said there was a method of playing only favorites that would produce a flat bet profit. Now, to demonstrate that claim.

Method of Play Number One: Favorites Only

By now, you have basically seen the method of play. We will eliminate any favorite with a form defect. We will eliminate any favorite that is rising in class off a last win, unless that favorite shows a Big Win with at least one other plus form factor, and has a showing of back class in his past performances. We will eliminate any favorite that won his last race at the same class of today's race, unless there are two + form factors, with a strong preference for a Big Win. We will eliminate any favorite coming off a maiden victory unless the primary competition is in the same situation of also coming off maiden victories. Maiden claiming winners almost never win when they run again against previous winners.

Not only is this method of play reliable and profitable in itself, but it provides one of the strongest demonstrations of the effectiveness of the form factors as they are presented in this book. For that reason, we will place considerable emphasis on this method of play, as you analyze its effectiveness.

The first demonstration of the profitability of playing favorites only off these form factors comes from the 433-race study from the late 1981 season that has been a major presentation in this book.

Among these 433 races, there were 206 favorites that qualified under these rules of play. This is approximately 47.5% of playable races, just a shade better than an average of four plays per nine-race card. As we provide further studies, watch how this percentage of plays runs. It is vitally important because every player craves action—the more the better.

These 206 favorites had no form defects and passed the last race winner hurdles. Of this group, there were 99 winners. This is a remarkable 48.1% figure for winning horses! Do you know of any selection method you have ever seen or ever heard that produces that percentage of winners?

A $2 wager on those 206 horses would have cost $412, easy enough. The gross return was $602.60, a magnificent profit. Other studies may vary up and down from that strong figure, but it is extremely powerful, no matter what else one may think about it. I only have to remind you of the last chapter dealing with a single day at Golden Gate where favorites with these characteristics were absolutely dominant.

Next we come to a figure that is equally impressive. For place, there were 131 successes, or 63.6%. The traditional wisdom is that favorites, if they win 33% of the time, will place approximately 50% of the time. This is a far better return, of course. The dollar return on the place prices was $470, a reasonable profit, but not nearly as good as the winning plays. Place betting, as I have argued previously, is basically an insurance technique to bail you out on those days when your selections seem to have a bad affliction of "seconditis," or else very short noses.

You can see that the key to winning with this method is the elimination of losers, as we will discuss shortly when I give you a 1982 segment from the Saratoga meet.

These figures were so remarkable that I wanted to take a second look from the *Racing Forms* I had begun to gather in my 1982 visits to the track. Was the 1981 study a fluke? Would it hold up over other periods of time? How well would it perform with scattered racing days rather than consecutive days?

From eastern tracks in the first part of 1982, I extracted 164 races, never skipping any race on any particular racing card under study. There were 78 plays out of the 164 favorites. Dust off your pocket calculator. This is exactly the same 47.5% of plays that was uncovered in the 1981 study!

This time, the percentage of winning favorites was even better. Of the 78 plays, there were 43 winners—an amazing 55%! I continued studying this phenomenon in more than 500 races in the first seven months of the 1982 season, and without actual tabulation, the figure, while perhaps subsiding slightly, still remained in that high neighborhood.

I wanted yet another followup, this time at my favorite track of all, Saratoga, where I have been fortunate enough to spend a bit of time each August.

The "Graveyard of Favorites." Where have you heard that cry before? This old reminder comes up every year when some highly favored champion fails to win at Saratoga. But is it true? How do we test it?

I stepped into the middle of the 1982 Saratoga meet and pulled together seven consecutive days, looking at every single race on each of the seven cards, for a total of 63 races. This spanned the Travers Stakes where Conquistador Cielo, the Horse of the Year in 1982, was heavily favored.

I have set forth here the form ratings for each and every favorite in those 63 races. If any of you have back copies of *Daily Racing Forms* for August, 1982, please follow the ratings and test this yourself. After providing you the full workout, we can comment and summarize and find out what this shows us.

I consider it the most remarkable study on favorites that I have yet made.

Favorites at Saratoga
Wednesday, August 18

									Result	
Race	Horse		Rating						Win	Place
1	Click Off	N	+	N	O	ⓦ	(Pass)		–	–
	Perfect Bidder	N	+	N	O		(Pass)		–	–
	(Co-favorites; Click Off placed)									
2	Duck Call	N	+	N	+				0	3.20
3	Grand Old Flag	N	+	+	–				6.60	4.40
4	Trenchant	N	N	N	–				3.60	2.80
5	Phaedra	N	–	–	–				0	0
6	Geraldine's Store	N	+	+	–				5.20	3.20
7	Reinvested	N	+	N	–				3.80	3.20
8	Smart Style	N	N	N	+				0	3.60
9	Very Valid	N	N	O	–		(Pass)		–	–

Totals: Seven plays, win and place
Four won, returning $19.20 for $14
Six placed, returning $20.40 for $14

Thursday, August 19

									Result	
Race	Horse		Rating						Win	Place
1	Polyrule	N	N	N	–				5.40	3.40
2	Cold Shoulder	N	N	N	O	ⓦ	(Pass)		–	–
3	Astor Street	N	+	N	O		(Pass)		–	–
	(Astor Street placed)									
4	Eskimo	U	–	–	–		(Pass)		–	–
5	Bemissed	N	+	N	+				0	0
6	Larida	N	+	+	–				0	3.80
7	Fit to Fight	N	N	N	–				5.20	3.20
8	Love Sign	N	+	N	–				0	0
9	Partridgeberry	N	N	N	–				7.20	4.40

Totals: Six plays, win and place
Three won, returning $17.80 for $12.00
Four placed, returning $14.80 for $12.00

Friday, August 20

Race	Horse	Rating					Win	Place
							Result	
1	Harlem Queen	N	N	N	–		0	0
2	Campilan	N	N	N	–		0	3.80
3	Get Off My Case	N	+	N	–		0	2.60
4	Ceritano	+	+	N	–		0	0
5	Belle Borne	+	N	N	–		4.60	2.80
6	Stage Gossip	O	–	–	–	(Pass)	–	–
	(Stage Gossip won)							
7	Half Iced	N	N	N	–		4.40	3.20
8	Bottled Water	N	+	N	–		3.20	2.60
9	National Banner	N	+	N	–		3.80	3.00

Totals: Eight plays, win and place
Four won, returning $16.00 for $16.00
Six placed, returning $18.00 for $16.00

Saturday, August 21

Race	Horse	Rating						Win	Place
								Result	
1	Spring Fire	N	O	O	–		(Pass)	–	–
2	Mad Rush	N	O	N	–		(Pass)	–	–
	(Mad Rush won)								
3	Middle Stage	N	O	N	–		(Pass)	–	–
	(Middle Stage placed)								
4	White Birch	N	N	N	–			0	2.20
5	Guyana	N	+	N	N	Ⓡ	(Pass)	–	–
6	Rising Raja	N	N	N	–			0	2.60
7	Winter's Tale	N	N	N	–			2.80	2.40
8	Conquistador Cielo	N	+	N	O		(Pass)	–	–
9	Number	N	N	N	–			0	3.80

Totals: Four plays, win and place
One winner, returning $2.80 for $8.00
Four placed, returning $11.00 for $8.00
(Loss for day, $16 bet, returning $13.80)

Sunday, August 22

Race	Horse	Rating						Win	Place
								Result	
1	Zoom Googus	N	+	N	–			0	0
2	Red Brigade	N	+	N	–			0	3.80
3	Royal Hostage	+	+	+	O	Ⓜ	(Pass)	–	–
4	Spit Curl	N	N	N	–			0	0
5	Mystery Wiltness	N	N	N	N	Ⓦ	(Pass)	–	–
6	Muskoka Wyck	N	N	N	–			0	0
7	Nihoa	N	N	N	O		(Pass)	–	–
8	Star Gallant	N	N	N	N	Ⓦ	(Pass)	–	–
9	Disco Dad	N	N	N	–			0	0

Totals: Five plays, win and place
None won, returning 0 for $10
One placed, returning $3.80 for $10
(Loss for day, $20 bet, returning $3.80)

Monday, August 23

Race	Horse	Rating						Win	Place
								Result	
1	Salute to Mother	N	O	N	–		(Pass)	–	–
2	Current Pride	N	–	–	–			4.40	3.60
3	Chapter One	+	N	N	–			0	0
4	King of the Slopes	N	O	–	–		(Pass)	–	–
5	Tarantara	+	+	+	–			0	0
6	Lucky Luisa	+	N	N	O		(Pass)	–	–
7	Illuminate	N	N	N	N			0	0
8	Cassie's Birthday	N	N	N	+	Ⓦ		6.20	3.80
9	Dedelightful	N	N	N	–			7.00	4.20

Totals: Six plays, win and place
Three won, returning $17.60 for $12
Three placed, returning $11.60 for $12

Tuesday, August 24

Race	Horse	Rating						Win	Place
								Result	
1	Rapido's Repeat	N	N	N	–			5.00	3.00
2	Rainy Stranger	N	O	N	–		(Pass)	–	–
3	All About Eve	N	+	N	N	Ⓜ	(Pass)	–	–
4	Pearl Castle	N	O	N	–		(Pass)	–	–
5	Jousting	N	+	N	–			0	3.40
6	Phallocrat	N	+	N	–			4.80	3.80
7	Ambassador of Luck	U	–	–	–		(Pass)	–	–
8	Timely Writer	N	N	N	–			2.80	2.60
9	Well Organized	N	N	N	+			6.40	4.20

Totals: Five plays, win and place
Four won, returning $19.00 for $10.00
Five placed, returning $15.20 for $10.00

TOTAL PLAYS: 41 out of 63 races; 65% of all races carded

Of 41 plays, 19 won, a 46.3% return, for $92.40 for $82 bet
Of 41 plays, 29 placed, a 70.7% return for $91.00 for $82 bet

Flat Bet Win Profit: $10.40 off $82 bet — 12.7% return
Flat Bet Place Profit: $9.00 off $82 bet — 11% return

First of all, the percentage of plays was higher than in any previous study, since there were 41 out of 63, or 65%. But that is to be expected at tracks like Saratoga and Belmont and likewise at Santa Anita and Hollywood Park, where the highest grade animals perform. At tracks of lesser value, which were intermingled in the

1981 and early 1982 studies, you will find fewer plays than at the high-grade tracks.

In looking at these seven consecutive days, you will find two days where net losses were recorded. One day in particular, Sunday, August 22, 1982, when I was in the stands, was a disaster for favorite-players. Not one single favorite on the entire card was able to win.

The previous Saturday, on Travers Day, was almost as disastrous. If any of you had been there for those two days, and had used this method of playing favorites only, you would have surely had unprintable horseplayer language for this method. Two successive days of whopping losses would have dimmed anyone's enthusiasm for playing form factor favorites. But look at the overall results over a consecutive seven-day period. Some of the days were similar to the Golden Gate card in the last chapter.

But in recapitulation, where you have plays in 65% of all races and score with 46% winners and 70% for place, you are doing well indeed. The win percentage, on this limited basis, fell only slightly below the other studies, and the net profit was a little lower because of the numerous low priced horses. Horses like Winter's Tale and Timely Writer were not going to pay much on any card.

You may want to peek at the Travers, where Conquistador Cielo was the overwhelming favorite. He had the noticeable form defect of a stretch loss in his last race. I was almost certain he would lose that day, and I bet against him with the usual confidence with which I approach a bet against a favorite with a serious form defect. In case you are interested, my play was Aloma's Ruler, who ran a very fine race but could do no better than second.

On Disaster Day, Sunday, August 22, the feature race was the Forego Handicap at seven furlongs, with a field of five outstanding horses. Star Gallant, the favorite, was a no play because he was off a last-race win without the requisite + factors, and was up against an imposing array of formidable competition. I was not limiting my plan to favorites, as this is not my own method at all, as I will set forth shortly. Using my revised ability times, my top rated horse in that race was Engine One, who happened to be the longest priced horse in the field. Not even obeying my first three favorites only rule in *Investing at the Racetrack*, I could not refrain from betting Engine One with considerable enthusiasm. His lovely $17.60 payoff made it a rather nice day after all, especially since he was not my only winner on that most pleasant afternoon.

Of course, another important point about that particular day was that three favorites, Zoom Googus, Red Brigade, and Muskoka Wyck, all looked to be outstanding plays. None of them won, although my place ticket on Red Brigade was worth a return trip to the window for cashing. Thus, I must repeat again that even outstanding plays can lose, and do. You can have these bad days, as you will, even with the sound precepts that are in this book. My final response on that is, of course, the bottom line profit that turned up in these seven days.

But before we come to what I believe is the most remarkable and interesting observation about this seven-day period, we need to address once more the old "Graveyard of Favorites" bromide. There is no graveyard for properly selected favorites, at Saratoga or anywhere else. When you play only those without form defects and come back with 46% winners, there is not only no graveyard at all, but in fact a happy hunting ground.

Now, I want to emphasize with a blare of bugles the most important aspect of all about this seven-day period. Removing the 41 favorites that could be played under this method, this left 22 other favorites with form defects or last-race victories that removed them from consideration.

Of these 22 favorites, only two scored a victory! There were but six place returns in the 22 races for these non-qualifying favorites.

Thus, among all favorites there were 21 winners in 63 races, exactly 33%, the expected national return. Among these 63 favorites, there were 34 place returns for a 54% figure, which is slightly above the national expectancy.

But it was the qualified favorites that brought these figures up.

The fact that only two of the 22 unqualified favorites won is the most profound negative figure of all. While such a low number is not likely to occur over a period of time, the realities, as I have tried to show previously, are that favorites with form defects are very poor plays indeed. This can become a vital ingredient of any successful handicapping program. When you feel reasonably sure that the favorite will not win, you have a considerable amount supplemented in the win pool toward some other animal with a better price. This gives you a chance of playing a horse that will win with a better return to produce that most welcome and needed cushion.

But so much for playing favorites only. It is a sound method in itself, but I use it, as I think you should also do, as a base upon which to evaluate the whole race. Since I have learned that it does not pay to bet money on favorites with form defects, I will no longer do so, and that alone has been a magnificent advance in this challenging arena.

Method of Play Number Two: First and Second Favorites Off Form Only

This second method of play is a revision off the favorites-only version, and is precisely what we were attempting to set forth in the previous chapter on a day at the races at Golden Gate. The advantage of this method of play is that it widens your horizons and affords considerably more action. Under the favorites only method, you would pass any race where the favorite had a form defect and was washed out as a last race winner, and then go on to the next race. In this second method, you would then look at the second favorite to see if he qualified. If the second favorite had no form defects and was not an unqualified last race winner, he would then be our play.

In considering second betting choices, as previously indicated, when a third horse is very close in board odds to the technical second favorite, he will have to be considered also. If only one of those two horses escapes our elimination rules, that will be the play. If the favorite must be passed and both the second and near-second choices are fully qualified, you would have to use some handicapping method to separate them, which is a little beyond the narrow range of our method here.

This method is to be used, however, only when the favorite may not be played under the first version. If both the favorite and the second choice in the wagering are fully qualified on form, you would automatically stay with the favorite under this method because of the stabilized statistical probability of his winning.

The statistical advantage of this method is that first and second choices ordinarily win approximately 52% of all races run. When you look at only the two top betting choices in a race, you are already surveying a winner more than half the time. If you separate the two with some degree of successful regularity, your road to sound profits is assured.

The great disadvantage of this method of play, of course, is that you would have to pass up many good winners at good prices when your first two favorites falter. Under a limitation such as this, I would not have been allowed to play Engine One at Saratoga in the Forego Handicap where he was such a tempting selection with that $17.60 payoff that runs up your profits rather quickly.

But the play on first two favorites only is indeed most profitable, and like the concentration on favorites only, provides an excellent foundation for a wider ranging method of play. When you can confidently eliminate both the first and second choices in the betting and select some other horse as the winner, your returns will be moving toward the bountiful.

After my 1981 study revealed the basic strength of this method of play, I undertook to give it a more severe test in 1982, following up on 50 racing cards where there were exactly 450 races. This is slightly wider than the 1981 study. This time I separated profit and loss by racing days, playing one of the first two favorites only. Since no one likes to come home on any particular day as a loser, how you do on each individual day is also very important.

Out of these 50 racing days, there were 45 in which a net profit was scored! Some of the days were spectacular, like the June 17, 1982 afternoon from Golden Gate. On each of the five losing days, the setback was slight indeed (none as devastating as the Saratoga day presented here). Betting both win and place, there was never a single day when there was a total shutout. The worst day in the entire study turned up only three plays on the card and none of them managed to win. Two placed, however, and the place prices were very helpful in holding down the bottom line bad figures.

If these figures hold throughout a racing season, and I have no reason to believe otherwise, it means that this method of play would produce profits for you nine times out of every ten you go to the track.

If you are not interested in that, there are casinos both east and west where you compete against the house rather than your fellow player, and where you can be sure you will eventually be taken to the cleaners.

Method of Play Number Three: First and Second Favorites Off Form With Separation by Handicapping

The third successful method of play continues as a variation off the previous themes. This time we continue to consider the first two favorites (or even the third if you wish), and choose between them by other handicapping standards when both are fully qualified under our form rules. This would amount to exactly the same amount of action you would find in the second method of play, since you would always be on one of the two top rated choices unless both of them (or three if you extend it to the first three favorites) were loaded with form defects or last race winning deficiencies. The strength of this method, contrary to the first and second methods, is that you are not automatically wed to the favorite when that horse shows no form defects. Since by now you know that even the highest selectivity among favorites only will not produce, on the average, quite up to 50% winners, you have a partial opportunity to score on many of those occasions that exceed the 50% number.

If your separation method is sound, and would prevail at a higher percentage rate than the favorite would ordinarily prevail over the second choice, taking into account the higher prices on the second choice, you will be further ahead of the game by using this revised version of the second method.

I now use this method most of the time, relying on my revised ability times which I originally set forth in *Investing at the Racetrack*, to separate the two or three top contenders when they all have no form defects.

One of the best tests of this method came in the 1981 study at the Meadowlands. I focused on this track since it was the track among the four with the lowest percentage of winning favorites, and which would therefore provide the toughest challenge. Although favorites were taking a bad beating, this selection method scored profits on 11 of the 13 racing cards and turned in a healthy profit overall.

The real trick in making this method work better than any of the others is that you had better be right when you play one qualified horse against the other.

Method of Play Number Four: Using Form Requirements and Handicapping the Entire Card

This is the method of play most preferred by my youngest handicapping son, who has been lobbying with me so effectively for it that he is making considerable inroads into my more conservative play. This method brings you action, action, and more action. It also has some gorgeous ups-and-downs. But the beauty of it, as anyone can quickly see, is that it brings in some lovely prices. A $9 or $10 winner does a lot more for you than those struggling $4.20 favorites. And when you touch upon even higher levels, as I so happily did with Engine One at Saratoga, who was a product of this method, you are beginning to approach something to write home about. Here, you would take a hard look at every horse in the race. Those with form defects would be set aside. But every remaining horse with no form defects or no class level deficiencies would be considered for play, regardless of odds. In my case, using my own ability times, I would then go to that horse and stay with him up front and to place.

One of the best examples in this book is in the preceding chapter. Go back to the second race at Golden Gate and look again at Hasty Work. This horse paid $20.20 to win and qualified on every point. He had the additional strong factor of a five furlong workout. He also had the highest ability points in the race, and therefore was fully qualified for a play. He was an outstanding selection and with a win price of $20.20, you can forget about a few unhappy favorites.

Looking back over the 433 races that I studied so assiduously, there were numerous winners with no form defects and no other liabilities who were neither first nor second choices in the betting. A few of the prices turned out like this: $15.80, $20.80, $26.60, $30.80, all at Belmont; $34.00, $12.80, $21.60, $27.80, $17.20, $19.80, $18.80, $36.40, and so on at Meadowlands, leaving out some of the big balloons off the five furlong workouts. Many of these happy returns came in races where first and second favorites were saddled with form defects, which made these longer-priced horses exceptionally good plays. While I did not do ability points on these horses, I know from so many frequent situations of this kind that many of them had to be the highest rated animals in their races.

Some of those horses stood out in the form department, having two or more + form factors. At any time you see a double-plus form horse, regardless of odds, look out. Among the longer priced horses at Belmont in the 1981 study, there were seven winners with two or more + signs for form. At Meadowlands there were five, one of them being a $36.40 special. Three turned up at Keystone and five at Bowie.

But these were only the double-plus horses. There were many other strong plays with one + form factor that won and paid excellent prices. So there is indeed a lot of gold to be found in this area of play.

Yet I leave the method to you for the moment. It has its dangers if you miss the big boys—"shoulda, coulda, woulda." The argument for staying with the first two or three choices in the betting is that you know, without any handicapping at all, that you are striking within the 50/50 range of obtaining winners. And when I use these sound realities of play, combined with handicapping knowledge, experience, and sound selections, I cannot expect to do anything other than show a profit.

Conclusion

One could hardly end without the sermon for the day. It is an old refrain—you have heard it many times before. But it is not only the most important message of all, it is one that never seems to get totally accepted.

You can dress it up in a lot of old, over-worked words: Discipline. Patience. Determination. It all comes down to whether you really want to win or not. Most people seem to need to find a way to lose, even when they know better.

Most of you will say you want to win. But do you want to win with enough absolute, teeth-gritting resolution that you will not let anything stand in the way, as long as you really know how to do it?

The reality is that if you do not adhere strictly to the guidelines set forth in this book, what is revealed here will not work. It is very easy to lose. It is very easy to make a mistake and overlook an important factor—such as forgetting that a horse returning to the races off a layoff of 28 days or longer may have lost ground in the stretch in its last race and still not be handed a form defect of zero. It seems that every single time you make a mistake, it will cost you money. Often, one mistake on a racing card can turn a profitable day into a real loser, because one big error can take enough away from the winnings and add enough on to your losses that your whole day will be turned around. It happens again and again.

If you think passing a race is a sin, the sound methods of play here will be very difficult for you, with the possible exception of the last one, and then if you are undisciplined, you will blow that one, too. There are some races on the card where no horse can qualify on any count. You might even pick the winner—but so might the legendary old lady with the hat pin with a lucky stab.

Even the most brilliant handicappers can go to their destruction by the omnipresent habit of betting more on losers than on winners. I know an outstanding player who sends it in heavy, but who has the miserable trait of putting $100 on the nose of a winner and coming back with $500 up front on a loser. If he should ever overcome that single horrendous habit, he would earn a marvelous income at the racetrack. He tags some $20 and $30 horses with incredible acumen and then erratically gives it back on animals that do not measure up.

Again, that is why if you can keep away from the losers, the winners will take care of themselves. The form defects in this book, as you will find, are almost impossible to overcome. Maybe for a race here and there, horses with these burdens will win, but in the end, the statistics will bounce back just as they did at Saratoga, where in seven successive days, only two of 22 favorites with form defects were able to win with these handicaps.

It was not until early 1982 that I proudly sat one day and passed five races in a row. No matter that one of them represented a sad mistake, as I overlooked a salient point that might have caused me to play this passed winner. But the real achievement was in being able to calmly sit through five races in a row without marching to the windows. That exercise in itself taught me it could be done. Thus, I have finally learned to simply pass any race where there are no horses that I like, and sometimes this even applies to horses that have no form defects, because their ability may be suspect.

The form ratings in this book are not claimed to be perfect. Just as I continued to try to improve upon the methods of play set forth in *Investing at the Racetrack*, I will not stop searching for sounder applications of all the powerful form factors that are displayed here. In fact, even as this book is finished, I am beginning a new search and a new analysis into some occasional areas of at least two form factors, hoping to find even a slight percentage improvement. Whether I succeed or not may take a long period of time. But there is ever more to be learned.

But for now, I am going to turn to the *Daily Racing Form* to see how my horse will run today.

APPENDIX

Revised figures for energy adjustment in computing ability times as set forth in *Investing at the Racetrack* (Simon & Schuster, 1982).

For Fast Tracks		For Average Tracks		For Slow Tracks	
45:0	Add One Tick	45:4	Add One Tick	46:3	Add One Tick
45:1		46:0		46:4	
45:2		46:1		47:0	
45:3		46:2		47:1	
45:4	Add Two Ticks	46:3	Add Two Ticks	47:2	Add Two Ticks
46:0		46:4		47:3	
46:1		47:0		47:4	
46:2		47:1		48:0	
46:3	Add Three Ticks	47:2	Add Three Ticks	48:1	Add Three Ticks
46:4		47:3		48:2	
47:0		47:4		48:3	
47:1		48:0		48:4	
47:2	Add Four Ticks	48:1	Add Four Ticks	49:0	Add Four Ticks
47:3		48:2		49:1	
47:4		48:3		49:2	
48:0		48:4		49:3	
48:1	Add Five Ticks	49:0	Add Five Ticks	49:4	Add Five Ticks
48:2		49:1		50:0	
48:3		49:2		50:1	
48:4		49:3		50:1	

Examples of Fast Tracks: SA, Hol, Dmr, Lga, Sar
Examples of Normal Tracks: Aqu, Bel, AP, BM, GG, CD
Examples of Slow Tracks: Crc, Det, Lat